ACCOUNTING
The Language of Business

FIFTH EDITION

Sidney Davidson, Ph.D., CPA
University of Chicago

Clyde P. Stickney, D.B.A., CPA
Dartmouth College

Roman L. Weil, Ph.D., CPA, CMA
University of Chicago

THOMAS HORTON AND DAUGHTERS, INC. • 26662 S. New Town Drive
Sun Lakes, Arizona 85224

For Our Children

Copyright © 1974, 1975, 1977, 1979, 1982
Thomas Horton and Company

ISBN 0-913878-25-1

Library of Congress Cataloging in Publication Data

Davidson, Sidney 1919-
   Accounting: the language of business, fifth edition

1. Accounting—Terminology. 2. Accounting.

I. Stickney, Clyde P., 1944-   joint author.
II. Weil, Roman Lee, 1940-   joint author.
III. Title.
HF5621.D28   657.03   82-5974

Typography by York Graphic Services
York, Pennsylvania
Printed by R. R. Donnelley & Sons
Crawfordsville, Indiana U.S.A.

Preface

Business increases in importance. Accounting is the language of business. Understanding accounting, therefore, increases in importance. We hope this book will assist the student in becoming familiar with the language required to understand business communications. The first edition appeared in 1974. Since that time feedback from readers about the contents of the book has enabled us to refine the presentation—adding here, deleting there—to suit the wishes of teacher and students as well as those earning a living in business, generally. Although some of the material here will seem too advanced for the beginner, we think the book has something cost-effective for all interested in business.

WE ARE PROFIT-ORIENTED and are eager to learn from you how we can make the book more successful. We will pay the first person who makes a given suggestion incorporated in subsequent editions. Such suggestions might include typographical errors ($1), additional cross references ($1), errors of fact or substance ($2), and additional terms with their explanation ($2).

This edition contains the following sections.

Glossary. Accounting's vocabulary consists of many words that have other meanings in ordinary usage. Understanding the concepts and using accounting reports require that the reader know how to interpret the words used and their special meaning. The student of accounting and the reader of accounting reports will find the tasks easier the sooner he or she learns, for example, the difference between the meanings of *revenue* and *receipt*, between *fund* and *reserve*. The Glossary defines these and some 1,400 other terms. A glossary is not a dictionary, so that we have given definitions of terms only as they are, or should be, used in accounting.

Students and readers of financial reports will not encounter all the terms in the Glossary. We have tried to include, however, all the terms that are used in a wide range of textbooks, problems, financial reports, financial periodicals and newspapers. Textbook writers often include terms in problems that have not been carefully explained in the text preceding the problem. We suspect that students will find the Glossary particularly useful in understanding what the problems in a textbook are attempting to ask.

Many words and phrases in the Glossary are defined in terms of other entries in the Glossary. Terms in a given definition that are themselves explained elsewhere are *italicized*. Many of the entries in the Glossary are multiple-word phrases because much of the specialized terminology of accounting depends upon such phrases. We have tried to anticipate the most likely phrase that will occur to the reader and have used that phrase in the Glossary. Nevertheless, we probably have failed in some cases to put the explanation by the word or phrase that occurs to you. As Jim Schindler (our co-author before his death) used to say, "If you can't find what you're looking for under one listing, keep looking under others."

Words and phrases are alphabetized using the word-by-word principle. Thus, the following terms are defined in the order shown: *account, account form, account payable, accountancy, accounting, accounting standards, accounts receivable turnover*.

There are a few words in accounting, for example *cost* and *expense*, that mean different things to different people. We believe that the more precise the meaning of the words used, the easier is the understanding of accounting. Consequently, we give the restricted definition, for example, of *cost* that we think enhances the user's ability to understand but we also give the variants in meaning often used in practice. Further, certain terms used widely in the accounting profession, for example, *prepaid expenses* seem to us to be self-contradictory given our preference for restricted and unambiguoous definitions. We point ut these contradictions knowing that many people, nevertheless, use these terms.

General Electric Company's Annual Report.   GE's annual report is consistently amont the best published. We reproduce GE's annual report issued in 1982 along with our own comments and notes which should help in understanding it, and, we hope, other financial statements as well.

Accounting for Changing Prices.   The Financial Accounting Standards Board requires that excerpts from current cost constant dollar accounting statements be included in annual reports of companies of sufficient size. These rules attempt to have companies show the effects of changing prices on the conventional financial statements. We explain the nature of these items and illustrate them.

Accounting Magic.   This example shows how generally accepted accounting principles allow a range of accounting treatments so that two firms, exactly alike in all respects except for their accounting methods, can report drastically different incomes.

Penn Central Transportation Company's Balance Sheet Just Before Its Bankruptcy.   One of the most widely known bankruptcies, and one of the largest, was that of Penn Central. We reproduce the balance sheet so that the reader can see the limitations of analyzing the stockholders' equity section of the balance sheet in forecasting bankruptcy. The annual report shows retained earnings of almost half a billion dollars and stockholders' equity of almost $2 billion. Yet soon after the report was issued, the company petitioned for bankruptcy because it could not meet its obligations.

Pronouncements Governing Generally Accepted Accounting Principles.   We include a list of pronouncements governing generally accepted accounting principles and their dates of issuance.

We gratefully acknowledge the permission of the Dryden Press to reproduce material from our *Financial Accounting, Intermediate Accounting,* and *Managerial Accounting* texts published by them. Candice Harold and Eli Worman designed the book and planned the layout. Sandra Myers keyboarded the manuscript. We thank them for their help.

TABLE OF CONTENTS

Glossary

A

AAA. *American Accounting Association.*

Abacus. A scholarly journal containing articles on theoretical aspects of accounting. Published twice a year by the Sydney University Press, Sydney, Australia.

abatement. A complete or partial cancellation of a levy imposed by a government unit.

abnormal spoilage. Actual spoilage exceeding that expected to occur if operations are normally efficient. Usual practice treats this cost as an *expense* of the period rather than as a *product cost*. Contrast with *normal spoilage*.

aboriginal cost. In public utility accounting, the *acquisition cost* of an *asset* incurred by the first *entity* devoting that asset to public use. Most public utility regulation is based on aboriginal cost. If it were not, then public utilities could exchange assets among themselves at ever-increasing prices in order to raise the rate base and, then, prices based thereon.

absorption costing. The generally accepted method of *costing* that assigns all types of *manufacturing costs* (direct material and labor as well as fixed and variable overhead) to units produced. Sometimes called "full costing." Contrast with *direct costing*.

Accelerated Cost Recovery System. A form of *accelerated depreciation* enacted by the Congress in 1981. The system provides percentages of the asset's cost to be depreciated each year for tax purposes. *Salvage value* is ignored. These amounts are generally not used for *financial accounting*. See *3-5-10 rule*.

accelerated depreciation. Any method of calculating *depreciation* charges where the charges become progressively smaller each period. Examples are *double-declining-balance* and *sum-of-the-years'-digits* methods.

acceptance. A written promise to pay that is equivalent to a promissory *note*.

account. Any device for accumulating additions and subtractions relating to a single *asset, liability, owners' equity* item, including *revenues* and *expenses*.

account form. The form of *balance sheet* where *assets* are shown on the left and *equities* are shown on the right. Contrast with *report form*. See also *T-account*.

account payable. A *liability* representing an amount owed to a *creditor*, usually arising from purchase of *merchandise* or materials and supplies; not necessarily due or past due. Normally, a *current* liability.

account receivable. A claim against a *debtor* usually arising from sales or services rendered; not necessarily due or past due. Normally, a *current* asset.

accountability center. *Responsibility center.*

accountancy. The British word for *accounting*. In the United States, it means the theory and practice of accounting.

Accountants' Index. A publication of the *AICPA* that indexes, in detail, the accounting literature of the period.

accountant's opinion. *Auditor's report.*

accountant's report. *Auditor's report.*

accounting. An *information system* conveying information about a specific *entity*. The information is in financial terms and is restricted to information that can be made reasonably precise. The *AICPA* defines accounting as a service activity whose "function is to provide quantitative information, primarily financial in nature, about economic entities that is intended to be useful in making economic decisions."

accounting changes. As defined by *APB Opinion* No. 20, a change in (a) an *accounting principle* (such as a switch from *FIFO* to *LIFO* or from *sum-of-the-years'-digits* to *straight-line depreciation*), (b) an accounting estimate (such as estimated useful lives or salvage value of depreciable assets and estimates of *warranty* costs or *uncollectible accounts*), and (c) the reporting *entity*. Changes of type (a) should be disclosed. The cumulative effect of the change on *retained earnings* at the start of the period during which the change was made should be included in reported earnings for the period of change. Changes of type (b) should be treated as affecting only the period of change and, if necessary, future periods. The reasons for changes of type (c) should be disclosed and, in statements reporting on operations of the period of the change, the effect of the change on all other periods reported on for comparative purposes should also be, shown. In some cases (such as a change from *LIFO* to other inventory *flow assumptions* or in the method of accounting for long-term construction contracts), changes of type (a) are treated like changes of type (c). That is, for these changes all statements shown for prior periods must be restated to show the effect of adopting the change for those periods as well. See *all-inclusive concept* and *accounting errors*.

accounting conventions. Methods or procedures used in accounting. This term tends to be used when the method or procedure has not been given official authoritative sanction by a pronouncement of a group such as the *APB*, *FASB*, or *SEC*. Contrast with *accounting principles*.

accounting cycle. The sequence of accounting procedures starting with *journal entries* for various transactions and events and ending with the *financial statements* or, perhaps, the *post-closing trial balance*.

accounting entity. See *entity*.

accounting equation. *Assets = Equities. Assets = Liabilities + Owners' Equity.*

accounting errors. Arithmetic errors and misapplications of *accounting principles* in previously published financial statements that are corrected in the current period with direct *debits* or *credits* to *retained earnings*. In this regard, they are treated like *prior-period adjustments*, but, technically, they are not classified by *APB Opinion* No. 9 as prior-period adjustments. See *accounting changes* and contrast with changes in accounting estimates as described there.

accounting event. Any occurrence that is recorded in the accounting records.

accounting methods. *Accounting principles*. Procedures for carrying out accounting principles.

accounting period. The time period for which *financial statements* that measure *flows*, such as the *income statement* and the *statement of changes in financial position*, are prepared. Should be clearly identified on the financial statements. See *interim statements*.

accounting policies. *Accounting principles* adopted by a specific *entity*.

accounting principles. The methods or procedures used in accounting for events reported in the *financial statements*. This term tends to be used when the method or procedure has been given official authoritative sanction by a pronouncement of a group such as the *APB*, *FASB*, or *SEC*. Contrast with *accounting conventions* and *conceptual framework*.

Accounting Principles Board. See *APB*.

accounting procedures. See *accounting principles*, but usually this term refers to the methods for implementing accounting principles.

accounting rate of return. Income for a period divided by average investment during the period. Based on income, rather than discounted cash flows and, hence, is a poor decision-making aid or tool. See *ratio*.

Accounting Research Bulletin. ARB. The name of the official pronouncements of the former *Committee on Accounting Procedure* of the *AICPA*. Fifty-one bulletins were issued between 1939 and 1959. ARB No. 43 summarizes the first forty-two bulletins.

Accounting Research Study. ARS. One of a series of studies published by the Director of Accounting Research of the *AICPA* "designed to provide professional accountants and others interested in the development of accounting with a discussion and documentation of accounting problems." Fifteen such studies were published between 1961 and 1974.

The Accounting Review. Scholarly publication of the *American Accounting Association*.

Accounting Series Release. ASR. See *SEC*.

accounting standards. *Accounting principles*.

Accounting Standards Executive Committee. AcSEC. The senior technical committee of the *AICPA* authorized to speak for the AICPA in the areas of *financial accounting* and reporting as well as *cost accounting*.

Accounting Trends and Techniques. An annual publication of the *AICPA* that surveys the reporting practices of 600 large corporations. It presents tabulations of specific practices, terminology, and disclosures along with illustrations taken from individual annual reports.

accounts receivable turnover. *Net sales* on account for a period divided by the average balance of net accounts receivable. See *ratio*.

accretion. Increase in economic worth through physical change, usually said of a natural resource such as an orchard, caused by natural growth. Contrast with *appreciation*.

accrual. Recognition of an *expense (or revenue)* and the related *liability (or asset)* that is caused by an *accounting event*, frequently by the passage of time, and that is not signaled by an explicit cash transaction. For example, the recognition of interest expense or revenue (or wages, salaries, or rent) at the end of a period even though no explicit cash transaction is made at that time. Cash flow follows accounting recognition; contrast with *deferral*.

accrual basis of accounting. The method of recognizing *revenues* as goods are sold (or delivered) and as *services* are rendered, independent of the time when cash is received. *Expenses* are recognized in the period when the related revenue is recognized independent of the time when cash is paid out. *SFAC No. 1* says "accrual accounting attempts to record the financial effects on an enterprise of transactions and other events and circumstances that have cash consequences for the enterprise in the periods in which those transactions, events, and circumstances occur rather than only in the periods in which cash is received or paid by the enterprise." Contrast with the *cash basis of accounting*. See *accrual* and *deferral*. The basis would more correctly be called "accrual/deferral" accounting.

6

accrued. Said of a *revenue (expense)* that has been earned (recognized) even though the related *receivable (payable)* is not yet due. This adjective should not be used as part of an account title. Thus, we prefer to use Interest Receivable (Payable) as the account title, rather than Accrued Interest Receivable (Payable). See *matching convention.* See *accrual.*

accrued depreciation. An incorrect term for *accumulated depreciation.* Acquiring an asset with cash, capitalizing it, and then amortizing its cost over periods of use is a process of *deferral* and allocation, not of *accrual.*

accrued payable. A *payable* usually resulting from the passage of time. For example, *salaries* and *interest* accrue as time passes. See *accrued.*

accrued receivable. A *receivable* usually resulting from the passage of time. See *accrued.*

accumulated depreciation. A preferred title for the *contra-asset* account that shows the sum of *depreciation* charges on an asset since it was acquired. Other titles used are *allowance* for *depreciation* (acceptable term) and *reserve* for *depreciation* (unacceptable term).

accurate presentation. The qualitative accounting objective suggesting that information reported in financial statements should correspond as precisely as possible with the economic effects underlying transactions and events. See *fair presentation* and *full disclosure.*

acid test ratio. *Quick ratio.*

acquisition cost. Of an *asset,* the net *invoice* price plus all *expenditures* to place and ready the asset for its intended use. The other expenditures might include legal fees, transportation charges, and installation costs.

ACRS. Accelerated Cost Recovery System.

AcSEC. *Accounting Standards Executive Committee* of the *AICPA.*

activity accounting. *Responsibility accounting.*

activity-based depreciation. *Production method of depreciation.*

actual cost (basis). *Acquisition* or *historical cost.* Also contrast with *standard* cost.

actual costing. Method of allocating costs to products using actual *direct materials,* actual *direct labor,* and actual *factory overhead.* Contrast with *normal costing* and *standard cost system.*

actuarial. Usually said of computations or analyses that involve both *compound interest* and probabilities, such as the computation of the *present value* of a life-contingent *annuity.* Sometimes the term is used if only one of the two is involved.

actuarial accrued liability. A 1981 *report* of the Joint Committee on Pension Terminology (of various actuarial societies) stated that the terms ''supplemental actuarial value,'' ''past service cost,'' and ''prior service cost'' are no longer recommended and that this term be used instead. It will take a few years for this term to become standard in accounting. The Joint Committee defines this term as ''the portion . . . of the actuarial present value of pension plan benefits . . . not provided for by future normal costs.'' *Present value* at a given time of a *pension plan's* unrecognized benefits assigned to employees for their service before that given time. Called ''prior service cost'' in *APB Opinion* No. 8 and supplemental actuarial value is *SFAS No. 35*; includes *past service cost.*

Such obligations are not recognized as liabilities in the accounting records but must be disclosed in the notes to the financial statements; contrast with *normal cost.*

additional paid-in capital. An alternative acceptable title for the *capital contributed in excess of par (or state) value account.*

adequate disclosure. *Fair presentation* of *financial statements* requires *disclosure* of *material* items. This *auditing standard* does not, however, require publicizing all information detrimental to a company. For example, the company may be threatened with a lawsuit and disclosure might seem to require a *debit* to a *loss* account and a *credit* to an *estimated liability.* But the mere making of this entry might adversely affect the actual outcome of the suit. Such entries need not be made although impending suits should be disclosed.

adjunct account. An *account* that accumulates additions to another account. For example, Premium on Bonds Payable is adjunct to the liability Bonds Payable; the effective liability is the sum of the two account balances at a given date. Contrast with *contra account.*

adjusted acquisition (historical) cost. Cost adjusted to a *constant dollar amount* to reflect *general price level changes.* See also *book value.*

adjusted bank balance of cash. The *balance* shown on the statement from the bank plus or minus amounts, such as for unrecorded deposits or outstanding checks, to reconcile the bank's balance with the correct cash balance. See *adjusted book balance of cash.*

adjusted basis. The *basis* used to compute gain or loss on disposition of an *asset* for tax purposes. Also, see *book value.*

adjusted book balance of cash. The *balance* shown in the firm's account for cash in bank plus or minus amounts, such as for *notes* collected by the bank or bank service charges, to reconcile the account balance with the correct cash balance. See *adjusted book balance of cash.*

adjusted trial balance. *Trial balance* taken after *adjusting entries* but before *closing entries.* Contrast with *pre-* and *post-closing trial balances.* See *unadjusted trial balance* and *post-closing trial balance.* See also *work sheet.*

adjusting entry. An entry made at the end of an *accounting period* to record a *transaction* or other *accounting event,* which for some reason has not been recorded or has been improperly recorded during the accounting period. An entry to update the accounts. See *work sheet.*

adjustment. A change in an *account* produced by an *adjusting* entry. Sometimes the term is used to refer to the process of restating *financial statement* amounts to *constant dollars.*

administrative expense. An *expense* related to the enterprise as a whole as contrasted to expenses related to more specific functions such as manufacturing or selling.

admission of partner. Legally, when a new partner joins a *partnership,* the old partnership is dissolved and a new one comes into being. In practice, however, the old accounting records may be kept in use and the accounting entries reflect the manner in which the new partner joined the firm. If the new partner merely purchases the interest of another partner, the only accounting is to change the name for one capital account. If the new partner contributes *assets* and *liabilities* to the partnership, then the new assets must be recognized with debits and the liabilities and other source of capital, with credits. See *bonus method*.

ADR. See *asset depreciation range*.

advances from (by) customers. A preferred title for the *liability* account representing *receipts* of *cash* in advance of delivering the *goods* or rendering the *service* (that will cause *revenue* to be recognized). Sometimes called "deferred revenue" or "deferred income."

advances to affiliates. *Loans* by a parent company to a *subsidiary*. Frequently combined with "investment in subsidiary" as "investments and advances to subsidiary" and shown as a *noncurrent asset* on the parent's *balance sheet*. These advances are eliminated in *consolidated financial statements*.

advances to suppliers. A preferred term for *disbursements* of cash in advance of receiving *assets* or *services*.

adverse opinion. An *auditor's report* stating that the financial statements are not fair or are not in accord with *GAAP*.

affiliated company. Said of a company controlling or controlled by another company.

after closing. *Postclosing*; said of a *trial balance* at the end of the period.

after cost. Said of *expenditures* to be made subsequent to *revenue* recognition. For example, *expenditures* for *repairs* under warranty are after costs. Proper recognition of after costs involves a debit to expense at the time of the sale and a credit to an *estimated liability*. When the liability is discharged, the debit is to the estimated liability and the credit is to the assets consumed.

agency fund. An account for *assets* received by governmental units in the capacity of trustee or agent.

agency theory. A branch of economics relating the behavior of principals (such as owner non-managers or bosses) and their *agents* (such as nonowner managers or subordinates). The principal assigns responsibility and authority to the agent but the agent has his or her own risks and preferences different from those of the principal. The principal is unable to observe all activities of the agent. Thus the principal must be careful about the kinds of observations of or reports sought from the agent, perhaps through an independent *auditor*, and the sorts of incentive contracts that the principal makes with the agent.

agent. One authorized to transact business, including executing contracts, for another.

aging accounts receivable. The process of classifying *accounts receivable* by the time elapsed since the claim came into existence for the purpose of estimating the amount of uncollectible accounts receivable as of a given date. See *sales contra*, *estimated un-collectibles* and *allowance for uncollectibles*.

aging schedule. A listing of *accounts receivable*, classified by age, used in *aging accounts receivable*.

AICPA. American Institute of Certified Public Accountants. The national organization that represents *CPAs*. See *AcSEC*. It oversees the writing and grading of the Uniform CPA Examination. Each state, however, sets its own requirements for becoming a CPA in that state. See *certified public*

all capital earnings rate. *Rate of return on assets*.

all financial resources. All *assets* less all *liabilities*. Sometimes the *statement of changes in financial position* explains the changes in all financial resources rather than only the changes in *working capital*.

all-inclusive (income) concept. Under this concept, no distinction is drawn between *operating* and *nonoperating revenues* and *expenses*; thus the only entries to retained earnings are for *net income* and *dividends*. Under this concept all income, *gains*, and *losses* are reported in the *income statement*; thus, events usually reported as *prior-period adjustments* and as *corrections of errors* are included in net income. This concept in its pure form is not the basis of *GAAP*, but *APB Opinions* Nos. 9 and 30 move very far in this direction. They do permit retained earnings entries for prior-period adjustments and correction of errors.

allocate. To spread a *cost* from one *account* to several accounts, to several products, or activities, or to several periods.

allocation of income taxes. See *deferred income*.

allowance. A balance sheet *contra account* generally used for *receivables* and depreciable assets. See *sales (or purchase) allowance* for another use of this term.

allowance for funds used during construction. One principle of public utility regulation and rate setting is that customers should pay the full costs of producing the services (e.g., electricity) that they use—nothing more and nothing less. Thus an electric utility is even more careful than other businesses to capitalize into an *asset account* the full costs, but no more, of producing a new electric power generating plant. One of the costs of building a new plant is the *interest* cost on money tied up during construction. If *funds* are explicitly borrowed by an ordinary business, the journal entry for interest of $1,000 is typically:

```
Interest Expense ............1,000
    Interest Payable ...........          1,000
Interest expense for the period.
```

If the firm is constructing a new plant, then another entry would be made capitalizing interest into the plant-under-construction account:

```
Construction Work in Progress .......750
    Interest Expense.................          750
Capitalize relevant portion of interest
relating to construction work in prog-
ress into the asset account.
```

The cost of the *plant asset* is increased; when the plant is used, *depreciation* is charged; the interest will become an expense through the depreciation process in the later periods of use, not currently as the interest is paid. Thus the full cost of the electricity generated during a given period is reported as expense in that period.

But suppose, as is common, that the electric utility does not explicitly borrow the funds, but uses some of its own funds, including funds raised from equity shares as well as from debt. Even though there is not explicit interest expense, there is the *opportunity cost* of the funds. Put another way, the cost of the plant under construction is not less in an economic sense just because the firm used its own cash, rather than borrowing. The public utility using its own funds, on which $750 of interest would be payable if the funds had been explicitly borrowed, will make the following entry:

The allowance account is a form of *revenue*, to appear on the income statement, and will be closed to Retained Earnings, increasing it. On the *funds statement*, it is an income or revenue item not producing funds and so must be subtracted from net income in deriving *funds provided by operations*. *SFAS No. 34* specifically prohibits non-utility companies from capitalizing the opportunity cost (interest) on own funds used into plant under construction.

allowance for uncollectibles (accounts receivable). A *contra* to Accounts Receivable that shows the estimated amount of *accounts receivable* that will not be collected. When such an allowance is used, the actual *write-off* of specific accounts receivable (*debit* allowance, *credit* specific account) does not affect *revenue* or *expense* at the time of the write-off. The revenue reduction is recognized when the allowance is credited; the amount of the credit to the allowance may be based on a percentage of sales on account for a period of time or computed from *aging accounts receivable*. This contra account enables an estimate to be shown of the amount of receivables that will be collected without identifying specific uncollectible accounts. See *allowance method*.

allowance method. A method of attempting to *match* all *expenses* of a transaction with its associated *revenues*. Usually involves a debit to expense and a credit to an *estimated liability*, such as for estimated warranty expenditures, or a debit to a revenue (*contra*) account and a credit to an asset (*contra*) account, such as for uncollectible accounts. See *allowance for uncollectibles* for further explanation. When the allowance method is used for *sales discounts*, sales are recorded at *gross invoice* prices (not reduced by the amounts of discounts made available). An estimate of the amount of discounts to be taken is debited to a *revenue contra account* and *credited* to an allowance account, shown contra to *accounts receivable*.

American Accounting Association. AAA. An organization primarily for academic accountants, but open to all interested in accounting. It publishes *The Accounting Review*.

American Institute of Certified Public Accountants. See *AICPA*.

American Stock Exchange. AMEX. ASE. A public market where various corporate *securities* are traded.

AMEX. *American Stock Exchange.*

amortization. Strictly speaking, the process of liquidating or extinguishing ("bringing to death") a *debt* with a series of payments to the *creditor* (or to a *sinking fund*). From that usage has evolved a related use involving the accounting for the payments themselves: "amortization schedule" for a mortgage which is a table showing the allocation between *interest* and *principle*. The term has come to mean writing off ("liquidating") the cost of an asset. In this context it means the general process of *allocating acquisition cost* of an asset to either the periods of benefit as *expenses* or to *inventory* accounts as *product costs*. Called *depreciation* for *plant assets*, *depletion* for *wasting assets* (natural resources), and "amortization" for *intangibles*. *SFAC No. 3* refers to amortization as "the accounting process of reducing an amount by

periodic payments or write-downs." The expressions "unamortized debt discount or premium" and "to amortize debt discount or premium" relate to *accruals*, not to *deferrals*. The expressions "amortization of long-term assets" and "to amortize long-term assets" refer to deferrals, not accruals.

analysis of changes in working capital accounts. The *statement of changes in financial position* explains the causes of the changes in *working capital* during a period. This part of the statement, which may appear in footnotes, shows the net changes in the specific working capital accounts that have been explained in the main section of the statement.

analysis of variances. See *variance analysis*.

annual report. A report for shareholders and other interested parties prepared once a year, includes a *balance sheet*, an *income statement*, a *statement of changes in financial position*, a reconciliation of changes in *owners' equity* accounts, a *summary of significant accounting principles*, other explanatory *notes*, the *auditor's report*, and, comments from management about the year's events. See *10-K* and *financial statements*.

annuitant. One who receives an *annuity*.

annuity. A series of payments, usually made at equally spaced time intervals.

annuity certain. An *annuity* payable for a definite number of periods. Contrast with *contingent annuity*.

annuity due. An *annuity* whose first payment is made at the start of period 1 (or at the end of period 0). Contrast with *annuity in arrears*.

annuity in advance. An *annuity due*.

annuity in arrears. An *odinary annuity* whose first payment occurs at the end of the first period.

annuity method of depreciation. See *compound interest depreciation*.

antidilutive. Said of a *potentially dilutive security* that will increase *earnings per share* if it is *exercised* or *converted* into common stock. In computing *primary* and *fully diluted earnings per share*, antidilutive securities may not be assumed to be exercised or converted and hence do not affect reported earnings per share in a given period.

APB. Accounting Principles Board of the *AICPA*. It set *accounting principles* from 1959 through 1973, issuing 31 *APB Opinions*. It was superseded by the *FASB*.

APB Opinion. The name given to pronouncements of the APB that make up much of *generally accepted accounting principles*; there are 31 APB Opinions, issued from 1962 through 1973.

APB Statement. The *APB* issued four Statements between 1962 and 1970. The Statements were approved by at least two-thirds of the Board, but they are recommendations, not requirements. For example, Statement No. 3 (1969) suggested the publication of *constant dollar financial statements* but did not require them.

APBs. An abbreviation used for *APB Opinions*.

application of funds. Any transaction that reduces *funds* (however "funds" is defined). A *use of funds*.

applied cost. A *cost* that has been *allocated* to a department, product, or activity; need not be based on actual costs incurred.

applied overhead. *Overhead costs* charged to departments, products or activities.

appraisal. The process of obtaining a valuation for an *asset* or *liability* that involves expert opinion rather than evaluation of explicit market transactions.

appraisal method of depreciation. The periodic *depreciation* charge is the difference between the beginning and end-of-period appraised value of the *asset* if that difference is positive. If negative, there is no charge. Not generally accepted.

appreciation. An increase in economic worth caused by rising market prices for an *asset*. Contrast with *accretion*.

appropriated retained earnings. See *retained earnings, appropriated*.

appropriation. In governmental accounting, an *expenditure* authorized for a specified amount, purpose, and time.

appropriation account. In governmental accounting, an account set up to record specific authorizations to spend; it is credited with appropriation amounts. *Expenditures* during the period and *encumbrances* outstanding at the end of the period are closed (debited) to this account at the end of the period.

ARB. Accounting Research Bulletin.

arbitrage. Strictly speaking, the simultaneous purchase in one market and sale in another of a *security* or commodity in hope of making a *profit* on price differences in the different markets. Often this term is loosely used when the item sold is somewhat different from the item purchased; for example, the sale of shares of *common stock* and the simultaneous purchase of a *convertible bond* that is convertible into identical common shares.

arm's length. Said of a transaction negotiated by unrelated parties, each acting in his or her own self interest; the basis for a *fair market value* determination.

arrears. Said of *cumulative preferred stock dividends* that have not been declared up to the current date. See *annuity in arrears* for another context.

ARS. Accounting Research Study.

articles of incorporation. Document filed with state authorities by persons forming a corporation. When the document is returned with a certificate of incorporation, it becomes the corporation's *charter*.

articulate. Said of the relationship between any operating statement (for example, *income statement* or *statement of changes in financial position*) and *comparative balance sheets*, where the operating statement explains (or reconciles) the change in some major balance sheet category (for example, *retained earnings* or *working capital*).

ASE. *American Stock Exchange*.

ASR. *Accounting Series Release*.

assess. To value property for the purpose of property taxation; the assessment is computed by the taxing authority. To levy a charge on the owner of property for improvements thereto, such as for sewers or sidewalks.

assessed valuation. A dollar amount for real estate or other property used by a government as a basis for levying taxes. The amount may or may not bear some relation to *market value*.

asset. *SFAC No. 3* defines assets as "probable future economic benefits obtained or controlled by a particular entity as a result of past transactions. An asset has three essential characteristics: (a) it embodies a probable future benefit that involves a capacity, singly or in combination with other assets, to contribute directly or indirectly to future net cash inflows, (b) a particular enterprise can obtain the benefit and control others' access to it, and (c) the transaction or other event giving rise to the enterprise's right to or control of the benefit has already occurred." A footnote points out that "probable" means that which can be reasonably expected or believed but is neither certain nor proved. May be *tangible* or *intangible*, *short-term* (current) or *long-term* (noncurrent).

asset depreciation range. ADR. The range of *depreciable lives* allowed by the *Internal Revenue Service* for a specific depreciable *asset*.

asset turnover. Net sales divided by average assets. See *ratio*.

assignment of accounts receivable. Transfer of the legal ownership of an *account receivable* through its sale. Contrast with *pledging* accounts receivable where the receivables serve as *collateral* for a *loan*.

at par. Said of a *bond* or *preferred stock* issued or selling at its *face amount*.

attachment. The laying claim to the *assets* of a borrower or debtor by a lender or creditor when the borrower has failed to pay debts on time.

attest. Rendering of an *opinion* by an auditor that the *financial statements* are fair. This procedure is called the "attest function" of the CPA. See *fair presentation*.

attribute measured. When making physical measurements, such as of a person, one needs to decide the units with which to measure, such as inches or centimeters or pounds or grams. One chooses the attribute—height or weight—independently of the measuring unit—English or metric. In conventional accounting the attribute measured in *historical cost* and the measuring unit is *nominal dollars*. Some theorists argue that accounting is more useful when the attribute measured is *current cost*. Others argue that accounting is more useful when the measuring unit is *constant dollars*. Some, including us, think both changes from conventional accounting should be made. The attribute historical cost can be measured in nominal dollars or in constant dollars. The attribute current cost can also be measured in nominal dollars or constant dollars. Choosing between two attributes and two measuring units implies four different accounting systems. Each of these four has its uses.

audit. Systematic inspection of accounting records involving analyses, tests, and *confirmations*. See *internal audit*.

audit committee. A committee of the board of directors of a *corporation* usually consisting of outside directors who nominate the independent auditors and discuss the auditors' work with them. If the auditors believe certain matters should be brought to the attention of shareholders, the auditors first bring these matters to the attention of the audit committee.

Audit Guides. See *Industry Audit Guides*.

audit program. The procedures followed by the *auditor* in carrying out the *audit*.

audit trail. A reference accompanying an *entry*, or *posting*, to an underlying source record or document. A good audit trail is essential for efficiently checking the accuracy of accounting entries. See *cross-reference*.

auditing standards. A set of ten standards promulgated by the *AICPA*, including three general standards, three standards of field work, and four standards of reporting. According to the AICPA, these standards "deal with the measures of the quality of the performance and the objectives to be attained," rather than with specific auditing procedures.

Auditing Standards Advisory Council. An *AICPA* committee.

Auditing Standards Board. Operating committee of the *AICPA* promulgating auditing rules.

auditor. One who checks the accuracy, fairness, and general acceptability of accounting records and statements and then *attests* to them.

auditor's opinion. *Auditor's report.*

auditor's report. The auditor's statement of the work done and an opinion of the *financial statements*. Opinions are usually unqualified ("clean"), but may be *qualified*, or the auditor may disclaim an opinion in the report. Often called the "accountant's report." See *adverse opinion*.

AudSEC. The former Auditing Standards Executive Committee of the *AICPA*, now functioning as the *Auditing Standards Board*.

authorized capital stock. The number of *shares* of stock that can be issued by a corporation; specified by the *articles of incorporation*.

average. The arithmetic mean of a set of numbers; obtained by summing the items and dividing by the number of items.

average collection period of receivables. See *ratio*.

average-cost flow assumption. An *inventory flow assumption* where the cost of units is the *weighted average* cost of the *beginning inventory* and purchases. See *inventory equation*.

average tax rate. The rate found by dividing *income tax expense* by *net income* before taxes. Contrast with *marginal tax rate, statutory tax rate*.

avoidable cost. A *cost* that will cease if an activity is discontinued. An *incremental* or *variable cost*. See *programmed cost*.

B

bad debt. An *uncollectible account receivable*; see *sales contra, estimated uncollectibles*.

bad debt expense. See *sales contra, estimated uncollectibles*.

bad debt recovery. Collection, perhaps partial, of a specific account receivable previously written off as uncollectible. If the *allowance method* is used, the *credit* is usually to the *allowance* account. If the direct write-off method is used, the credit is to a *revenue account*.

bailout period. In a *capital budgeting* context, the total time that must elapse before net accumulated cash inflows from a project including potential *salvage value* of assets at various times equal or exceed the accumulated cash outflows. Contrast with *payback period*, which assumes completion of the project and uses terminal salvage value. Bailout is superior to payback because bailout takes into account, at least to

some degree, the *present value* of the cash flows after termination date being considered. The potential salvage value at any time includes some estimate of the flows that can occur after that time.

balance. The sum of *debit* entries minus the sum of *credit* entries in an *account*. If positive, the difference is called a debit balance; if negative, a credit balance.

balance sheet. Statement of financial position that shows *total assets = total liabilities + owners' equity*.

balance sheet account. An account that can appear on a balance sheet. A *permanent account*; contrast with *temporary account*.

bank balance. The amount of the balance in a checking account shown on the *bank statement*. Compare with *adjusted bank balance* and see *bank reconciliation schedule*.

bank prime rate. See *prime rate*.

bank reconciliation schedule. A schedule that shows how the difference between the book balance of the cash in bank account and the bank's statement can be explained. Takes into account the amount of such items as checks issued that have not cleared or deposits that have not been recorded by the bank as well as errors made by the bank or the firm.

bank statement. A statement sent by the bank to a checking account customer showing deposits, checks cleared, and service charges for a period, usually one month.

bankrupt. Said of a company whose *liabilities* exceed its *assets* where a legal petition has been filed and accepted under the bankruptcy law. A bankrupt firm is usually, but need not be, *insolvent*.

base stock method. A method of inventory valuation that assumes that there is a minimum normal or base stock of goods that must be kept on hand at all times for effective continuity of operations. This base quantity is valued at *acquisition cost* of the inventory on hand in the earliest period when inventory was on hand. The method is not allowable for income tax purposes and is no longer used, but is generally considered to be the forerunner of the *LIFO* method.

basis. *Acquisition cost*, or some substitute therefor, of an asset used in computing gain or loss on disposition or retirement. *Attribute measured*.

basket purchase. Purchase of a group of assets for a single price; *costs* must be assigned to each of the assets so that the individual items can be recorded in the *accounts*.

bear. One who believes that security prices will fall. A "bear market" refers to a time when stock prices are generally declining. Contrast with *bull*.

bearer bond. See *registered bond* for contrast and definition.

beginning inventory. Valuation of *inventory* on hand at the beginning of the accounting period.

betterment. An *improvement*, usually *capitalized*.

bid. An offer to purchase, or the amount of the offer.

big bath. A *write-off* of a substantial amount of costs previously treated as *assets*. Usually caused when a corporation drops a line of business that required a large investment but that proved to be unprofitable. Sometimes used to describe a situation where a corporation takes a large write-off in one period in order to free later periods of gradual write-offs of those amounts. In this sense it frequently occurs when there is a change in top management.

Big Eight. The eight largest U.S. *public accounting (CPA)* partnerships; in alphabetical order: Arthur Andersen & Co.; Coopers & Lybrand; Deloitte Haskins & Sells; Ernst & Whinney; Peat, Marwick, Mitchell & Co.; Price Waterhouse; Touche Ross & Co.; and Arthur Young & Company. A ninth firm, Klynveld Main Goerdeler, is actually larger than many of these when world-wide operations are measured.

Big Nine. See *Big Eight*.

bill. An *invoice* of charges and *terms of sale* for *goods and services*. Also, a piece of currency.

bill of materials. A specification of the quantities of *direct materials* expected to be used to produce a given job or quantity of output.

board of directors. The governing body of a corporation elected by the shareholders.

bond. A certificate to show evidence of debt. The *par value* is the *principal* or face amount of the bond payable at maturity. The *coupon rate* is the amount of interest payable in one year divided by the principal amount. Coupon bonds have attached to them coupons that can be redeemed at stated dates for interest payments. Normally, bonds carry semiannual coupons.

bond conversion. The act of exchanging *convertible bonds* for *preferred* or *common stock*.

bond discount. From the standpoint of the issuer of a *bond* at the issue date, the excess of the *par value* of a bond over its initial sales price; at later dates the excess of par over the sum of (initial issue price plus the portion of discount already amortized). From the standpoint of a bondholder, the difference between par value and selling price when the bond sells below par.

bond indenture. The contract between an issuer of *bonds* and the bondholders.

bond premium. Exactly parallel to *bond discount* except that the issue price (or current selling price) is higher than *par value*.

bond ratings. Ratings of corporate and *municipal bond* issues by Moody's Investors Service and by Standard & Poor's Corporation, based on the issuer's existing *debt* level, its previous record of payment, the *coupon rate* on the bonds, and the safety of the *assets* or *revenues* that are committed to paying off *principal* and *interest*. Moody's top rating is Aaa; Standard & Poor's is AAA.

bond redemption. Retirement of *bonds*.

bond refunding. To incur *debt*, usually through the issue of new *bonds*, intending to use the proceeds to retire an *outstanding* bond issue.

bond sinking fund. See *sinking fund*.

bond table. A table showing the current price of a *bond* as a function of the *coupon rate*, years to *maturity*, and effective *yield to maturity* (or *effective rate*).

bonus. Premium over normal *wage* or *salary*, paid usually for meritorious performance.

bonus method. When a new partner is admitted to a *partnership* and the new partner is to be credited with *capital* in

excess proportion to the amount of *tangible* assets he or she contributes, two methods may be used to recognize this excess, say $10,000. First, $10,000 may be transferred from the old partners to the new one. This is the bonus method. Second, goodwill in the amount of $10,000 may be recognized as an asset with the credit to the new partner's capital account. This is the *goodwill method*. (Notice that the new partner's percentage of total ownership is not the same under the two methods.) If the new partner is to be credited with capital in smaller proportion than the amount of contribution, then there will be bonus or goodwill for the old partners.

book. As a verb, to record a transaction. As a noun, usually plural, the *journals* and *ledgers*. As an adjective, see *book value*.

book inventory. An *inventory* amount that results, not from physical count, but from the amount of beginning inventory plus *invoice* amounts of net purchases less invoice amounts of *requisitions* or withdrawals; implies a *perpetual* method.

book of original entry. A *journal*.

book value. The amount shown in the books or in the *accounts* for an *asset*, *liability*, or *owners' equity* item. Generally used to refer to the net amount of an *asset* or group of assets shown in the account which records the asset and reductions, such as for *amortization*, in its cost. Of a firm, the excess of total assets over total liabilities. *Net assets*.

book value per share of common stock. Common *shareholders' equity* divided by the number of shares of *common stock outstanding*. See *ratio*.

bookkeeping. The process of analyzing and recording transactions in the accounting records.

boot. The additional money paid or received along with a used item in a trade-in or exchange transaction for another item. See *trade-in transaction*.

borrower. See *loan*.

branch. A sales office or other unit of an enterprise physically separated from the home office of the enterprise but not organized as a legally separate *subsidiary*. The term is rarely used to refer to manufacturing units.

branch accounting. An accounting procedure that enables the financial position and operations of each *branch* to be reported separately but later combined for published statements.

breakeven analysis. See *breakeven chart*.

breakeven chart. Two kinds of breakeven charts are shown here. The charts are based on the information for a month shown below. Revenue is $30 per unit.

Cost Classification	Variable Cost, Per Unit	Fixed Cost, Per Month
Manufacturing costs:		
Direct material	$ 4	—
Direct labor	9	—
Overhead	4	$3,060
Total manufacturing costs............	$17	$3,060
Selling, general and administrative costs............	5	1,740
Total costs	$22	$4,800

The cost-volume-profit graph presents the relationship of changes in volume to the amount of *profit*, or *income*. On such a graph, total *revenue* and total *costs* for each volume level are indicated and profit or loss at any volume can be read directly from the chart. The profit volume graph does not show revenues and costs but more readily indicates profit (or loss) at various output levels.

Two caveats should be kept in mind about these graphs. Although the curve depicting *variable cost* and total cost is shown as being a straight line for its entire length, it is likely that at very low or very high levels of output, variable cost would probably be different from $22 per unit. The variable-cost figure was probably established by studies of operations at some broad central area of production, called the *relevant range*. For very low (or very high) levels of activity, the chart may not be applicable. For this reason, the total-cost and profit-loss curves are sometimes shown as dotted lines at lower (or higher) volume levels. Second, this chart is simplified because it assumes a single-product firm. For a multiproduct firm, the horizontal axis would have to be stated in dollars rather than in physical units of output. Breakeven charts for multiproduct firms necessarily assume that constant proportions of the several products are sold and changes in this mixture as well as in costs or selling prices would invalidate such a chart.

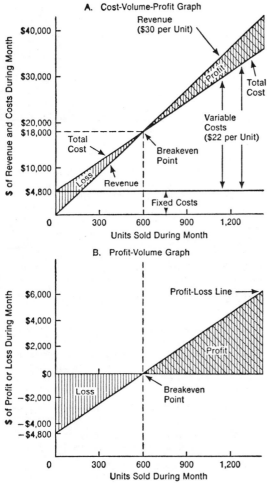

breakeven point. The volume of sales required so that total *revenues* and total *costs* are equal. May be expressed in units (*fixed costs/contribution per unit*) or in sales dollars [selling price per unit × (fixed costs/contribution per unit)].

budget. A financial plan that is used to estimate the results of future operations. Frequently used to help control future operations. In governmental operations, budgets often become the law.

budgetary accounts. In governmental accounting, the accounts that reflect estimated operations and financial condition, as affected by estimated *revenues, appropriations,* and *encumbrances.* In contrast to *proprietary accounts* that record the transactions.

budgetary control. Management of governmental (non-governmental) unit in accordance with an official (approved) *budget* in order to keep total expenditures within authorized (planned) limits.

budgeted cost. See *standard cost* for definition and contrast.

budgeted statements. *Pro forma* statements prepared before the event or period occurs.

bull. One who believes that security prices will rise. A "bull market" refers to a time when stock prices are generally rising. Contrast with *bear.*

burden. See *overhead costs.*

business combination. As defined in APB *Opinion* No. 16, the bringing together into a single accounting *entity* of two or more incorporated or unincorporated businesses. The *merger* will be accounted for either with the *purchase method* or the *pooling-of-interests method.* See *conglomerate.*

business entity. *Entity. Accounting entity.*

bylaws. The rules adopted by the shareholders of a corporation that specify the general methods for carrying out the functions of the corporation.

byproduct. A *joint product* whose sales value is so small relative to the sales value of the other joint product(s) that it does not receive normal accounting treatment. The costs assigned to byproducts reduce the costs of the main product(s). Byproducts are allocated a share of joint costs such that the expected gain or loss upon their sale is zero. Thus, byproducts are shown in the *accounts* at *net realizable value.*

C

CA. *Chartered accountant.*

call premium. See *callable bond.*

call price. See *callable bond.*

callable bond. A *bond* for which the issuer reserves the right to pay a specific amount, the call price, to retire the obligation before *maturity* date. If the issuer agrees to pay more than the *face amount* of the bond when called the excess of the payment over the face amount is the "call premium."

Canadian Institute of Chartered Accountants. The national organization that represents *chartered accountants* in Canada.

cancelable lease. See *lease.*

capacity. Stated in units of product, the amount that can be produced per unit of time. Stated in units of input, such as *direct labor* hours, the amount of input that can be used in production per unit of time. This measure of output or input is used in allocating *fixed costs* if the amounts producible are normal, rather than maximum, amounts.

capacity costs. A *fixed cost* incurred to provide a firm with the capacity to produce or to sell. Consists of *standby costs* and *enabling costs*. Contrast with *programmed costs*.

capacity variance. Standard fixed *overhead* rate per unit of normal *capacity* (or base activity) times (units of base activity budgeted or planned for a period minus actual units of base activity worked or assigned to product during the period). Often called a "volume variance."

capital. *Owners' equity* in a business. Often used, equally correctly, to mean the total assets of a business. Sometimes used to mean *capital assets*.

capital asset. Properly used, a designation for income tax purposes that describes property held by a taxpayer, except *cash*, inventoriable *assets*, goods held primarily for sale, most depreciable property, *real estate*, *receivables*, certain *intangibles*, and a few other items. Sometimes this term is imprecisely used to describe *plant* and *equipment*, which are clearly not capital assets under the income tax definition. Often the term is used to refer to an *investment* in *securities*.

capital budget. Plan of proposed outlays for acquiring long-term *assets* and the means of *financing* the acquisition.

capital budgeting. The process of choosing *investment* projects for an enterprise by considering the *present value* of cash flows and deciding how to raise the funds required by the investment.

capital consumption allowance. The term used for *depreciation expense* in national income accounting and the reporting of funds in the economy.

capital contributed in excess of par (or stated) value. A preferred title for the account that shows the amount received by the issuer for *capital stock* in excess of *par (or stated) value*.

capital expenditure (outlay). An *expenditure* to acquire long-term *assets*.

capital gain. The excess of proceeds over *cost*, or other *basis*, from the sale of a *capital asset* as defined by the Internal Revenue Code. If the capital asset has been held for a sufficiently long time before sale, then the tax on the gain is computed at a rate lower than is used for other gains and ordinary income.

capital lease. A *lease* treated by the *lessee* as both the borrowing of funds and the acquisition of an *asset* to be *amortized*. Both the *liability* and the asset are recognized on the balance sheet. Expenses consist of *interest* on the *debt* and *amortization* of the asset. The *lessor* treats the lease as the sale of the asset in return for a series of future cash receipts. Contrast with *operating lease*.

capital loss. A negative capital gain; see *capital gain*.

capital rationing. In a *capital budgeting* context, the imposing of constraints on the amounts of total capital expenditures in each period.

capital stock. The ownership shares of a corporation. Consists of all classes of *common* and *preferred stock*.

capital structure. The composition of a corporation's equities; the relative proportions of *short-term debt*, *long-term debt*, and *owners' equity*.

capital surplus. An inferior term for *capital contributed in excess of par (or stated) value*.

capitalization of a corporation. A term used by investment analysts to indicate *shareholders' equity* plus *bonds outstanding*.

capitalization of earnings. The process of estimating the economic worth of a firm by computing the *net present value* of the predicted *net income* (not *cash flows*) of the firm for the future.

capitalization rate. An *interest rate* used to convert a series of payments or receipts or earnings into a single *present value*.

capitalize. To record an *expenditure* that may benefit a future period as an *asset* rather than to treat the expenditure as an *expense* of the period of its occurrence. Whether or not expenditures for advertising or for research and development should be capitalized is controversial, but *SFAS No. 2* requires expensing of *R&D* costs. We believe expenditures should be capitalized if they lead to future benefits and thus meet the criterion to be an asset.

carryback, carryforward, carryover. The use of losses or tax credits in one period to reduce income taxes payable in other periods. There are three common kinds of carrybacks: for net operating losses, for *capital losses*, and for the *investment credit*. The first two are applied against taxable income and the third against the actual tax. In general, carrybacks are for three years with the earliest year first. Operating losses and the investment credit can be carried forward for seven years. Corporate capital loss carryforwards are for five years. The capital loss for individuals can be carried forward indefinitely.

carrying cost. Costs (such as property taxes and insurance) of holding, or storing, *inventory* from the time of purchase until the time of sale or use.

carrying value (amount). *Book value*.

CASB. Cost Accounting Standards Board. A board of five members authorized by the U.S. Congress to "promulgate cost-accounting standards designed to achieve uniformity and consistency in the cost-accounting principles followed by defense contractors and subcontractors under federal contracts." The *principles* promulgated by the CASB are likely to have considerable weight in practice where the *FASB* has not established a standard. Although the Congress allowed the CASB to go out of existence in 1980, its standards have the same force as before.

cash. Currency and coins, negotiable checks, and balances in bank accounts.

cash basis of accounting. In contrast to the *accrual basis of accounting*, a system of accounting in which *revenues* are recognized when *cash* is received and *expenses* are recognized as *disbursements* are made. No attempt is made to *match revenues* and *expenses* in determining *income*. See *modified cash basis*.

cash budget. A schedule of expected cash *receipts* and *disbursements*.

cash collection basis. The *installment method* for recognizing *revenue*. Not to be confused with the *cash basis of accounting*.

cash cycle. The period of time that elapses during which *cash* is converted into *inventories*, inventories are converted into *accounts receivable*, and receivables are converted back into cash. *Earnings cycle*.

cash disbursements journal. A specialized *journal* used to record *expenditures* by *cash* and by *check*. If a *check register* is also used, a cash disbursements journal records only expenditures of currency and coins.

cash discount. A reduction in sales or purchase price allowed for prompt payment.

cash dividend. See *dividend*.

cash equivalent value. A term used to describe the amount for which an *asset* could be sold. *Market value. Fair market price (value)*.

cash flow. Cash *receipts* minus *disbursements* from a given *asset*, or group of assets, for a given period.

cash flow statement. A statement similar to the typical *statement of changes in financial position* where the flows of cash, rather than of *working capital*, are explained.

cash receipts journal. A specialized *journal* used to record all *receipts of cash*.

cash (surrender) value of life insurance. An amount equal, not to the face value of the policy to be paid in event of death, but to the amount that could be realized if the policy were immediately canceled and traded with the insurance company for cash. If a firm owns a life insurance policy, the policy is reported as an asset at an amount equal to this value.

cash yield. See *yield*.

cashier's check. A bank's own *check* drawn on itself and signed by the cashier or other authorized official. It is a direct obligation of the bank. Compare with *certified check*.

CCA. *Current cost accounting; current-value accounting*.

central corporate expenses. General *overhead expenses* incurred in running the corporate headquarters and related supporting activities of a corporation. These expenses are treated as *period expenses*. Contrast with *manufacturing overhead*. A major problem in *line-of-business reporting* is the treatment of these expenses.

certificate. The document that is the physical embodiment of a *bond* or a *share of stock*. A term sometimes used for the *auditor's report*.

certificate of deposit. Federal law constrains the *rate of interest* that banks can pay. Under current law banks are allowed to pay a rate higher than the one allowed on a *time deposit* if the depositor promises to leave funds on deposit for several months or more. When the bank receives such funds, it issues a certificate of deposit. The depositor can withdraw the funds before maturity if a penalty is paid.

certified check. The *check* of a depositor drawn on a bank on the face of which the bank has inserted the words "accepted" or "certified" with the date and signature of a bank official. The check then becomes an obligation of the bank. Compare with *cashier's check*.

certified financial statement. A financial statement attested to by an independent *auditor* who is a *CPA*.

certified internal auditor. See *CIA*.

certified public accountant. CPA. An accountant who has satisfied the statutory and administrative requirements of

his or her jurisdiction to be registered or licensed as a public accountant. In addition to passing the Uniform CPA Examination administered by the *AICPA*, the CPA must meet certain educational, experience, and moral requirements that differ from jurisdiction to jurisdiction. The jurisdictions are the 50 states, the District of Columbia, Guam, Puerto Rico, and the Virgin Islands.

chain discount. A series of *discount* percentages; for example, if a chain discount of 10 and 5 percent is quoted, then the actual, or *invoice*, price is the nominal, or list, price times .90 times .95, or 85.5% of invoice price.

change fund. Coins and currency issued to cashiers, delivery drivers, and so on.

changes, accounting. See *accounting changes*.

changes in financial position. See *statement of changes in financial position*.

charge. As a noun, a *debit* to an account; as a verb, to debit.

charge off. To treat as a *loss* or *expense* an amount originally recorded as an *asset*; use of this term implies that the charge is not in accord with original expectations.

chart of accounts. A list of names and numbers of *accounts* systematically organized.

charter. Document issued by a state government authorizing the creation of a corporation.

chartered accountant. CA. The title used in Australia, Canada, and the United Kingdom for an accountant who has satisfied the requirements of the institute of his or her jurisdiction to be qualified to serve as a *public accountant*. In Canada, each provincial institute or order has the right to administer the examination and set the standards of performance and ethics for Chartered Accountants in its province. For a number of years, however, the provincial organizations have pooled their rights to qualify new members through the Interprovincial Education Committee and the result is that there are nationally-set and graded examinations given in English and French. The pass/fail grade awarded by the Board of Examiners (a subcommittee of the Inter-provincial Education Committee) is rarely deviated from.

check. You know what a check is. The Federal Reserve Board defines a check as "a *draft* or order upon a bank or banking house purporting to be drawn upon a deposit of funds for the payment at all events of a certain sum of money to a certain person therein named or to him or his order or to bearer and payable instantly on demand." It must contain the phrase "pay to the order of." The amount shown on the check's face must be clearly readable and it must have the signature of the drawer. Checks need not be dated, although they usually are. The *balance* in the *cash account* is usually reduced when a check is issued, not later when it clears the bank and reduces cash in bank.

check register. A *journal* to record *checks* issued.

CIA. Certified Internal Auditor. One who has satisfied certain requirements of the *Institute of Internal Auditors* including experience, ethics, education, and passing examinations.

CICA. *Canadian Institute of Chartered Accountants*.

CIF. Cost, insurance, and freight; a term used in contracts along with the name of a given port to indicate that the quoted price includes insurance, handling, and freight charges up to delivery by the seller at the given port.

circulating capital. *Working capital.*

clean opinion. See *auditor's report.*

clean surplus concept. The notion that the only entries to the *retained earnings* account are to record *net income* and dividends. See *comprehensive income.* Contrast with *current operating performance concept.* This concept, with minor exceptions, is now controlling in *GAAP.* (See *APB Opinions* Nos. 9 and 30.)

clearing account. An account containing amounts to be transferred to another account(s) before the end of the *accounting period.* Examples are the *income summary* account (whose balance is transferred to retained earnings) and the purchases account (whose balance is transferred to *inventory* or to *cost of goods sold*).

close. As a verb, to transfer the *balance* of a *temporary* or *contra* or *adjunct* account to the main account to which it relates; for example, to transfer *revenue* and *expense* accounts directly, or through the *income summary* account, to an *owner's equity* account, or to transfer *purchase discounts* to purchases.

closed account. An account with equal debits and credits, usually as a result of a closing entry. See *ruling an account.*

closing entries. The entries that accomplish the transfer of balances in temporary accounts to the related balance sheet accounts. See *work sheet.*

closing inventory. *Ending inventory.*

COLA. Cost of living adjustment. See *indexation.*

CMA. Certificate in Management Accounting. Awarded by the Institute of Management Accounting of the *National Association of Accountants* to those who pass a set of examinations and meet certain experience and continuing education requirements.

CoCoA. *Continuously contemporary accounting.*

coding of accounts. The numbering of *accounts,* as for a *chart of accounts,* which is particularly necessary for computerized accounting.

coinsurance. Insurance policies that protect against hazards such as fire or water damage often specify that the owner of the property may not collect the full amount of insurance for a loss unless the insurance policy covers at least some specified "coinsurance" percentage, usually about 80 percent, of the *replacement cost* of the property. Coinsurance clauses induce the owner to carry full, or nearly-full, coverage.

collateral. Assets pledged by a *borrower* that will be given up if the *loan* is not paid.

collectible. Capable of being converted into cash; now, if due; later, otherwise.

combination. See *business combination.*

commercial paper. *Short-term notes* issued by corporate borrowers.

commission. Remuneration, usually expressed as a percentage, to employees based upon an activity rate, such as sales.

Committee on Accounting Procedure. CAP. Predecessor of the *APB.* The *AICPA's* principles-promulgating body from 1939 through 1959. Its 51 pronouncements are called *Accounting Research Bulletins.*

committed costs. *Capacity costs.*

common cost. *Cost* resulting from use of *raw materials,* a facility (for example, plant or machines), or a service (for example, fire insurance) that benefits several products or departments and must be allocated to those products or departments. Common costs result when multiple products are produced together although they could be produced separately; joint costs occur when multiple products are of necessity produced together. Many writers use common costs and *joint costs* synonymously. See *joint costs, indirect costs, and overhead.* See *sterilized allocation.*

common dollar accounting. *Constant dollar accounting.*

common monetary measuring unit. For U.S. corporations, the dollar. See also *stable monetary unit assumption* and *constant dollar accounting.*

common shares. *Shares* representing the class of owners who have residual claims on the assets and earnings of a corporation after all debt and preferred shareolders' claims have been met.

common-size statement. A *percentage statement* usually based on total *assets* or *net sales* or *revenues.*

common stock equivalent. A *security* whose primary value arises from its ability to be exchanged for *common shares;* includes *stock options, warrants,* and also *convertible bonds* or *convertible preferred stock* whose cash yield for any year within five years of issue is less than two-thirds the *prime rate* at the time of issue.

company-wide control. See *control system.*

comparative (financial) statements. Financial statements showing information for the same company for different times, usually two successive years. Nearly all published financial statements are in this form. Contrast with *historical summary.*

compensating balance. When a bank lends funds to a customer, it often requires that the customer keep on deposit in his or her checking account an amount equal to some percentage, say 20 percent, of the loan. The amount required to be left on deposit is the compensating balance. Such amounts effectively increase the *interest rate.* The amounts of such balances must be disclosed in *notes* to the *financial statements.*

completed contract method. Recognizing *revenues* and *expenses* for a job or order only when it is finished, except that when a loss on the contract is expected, revenues and expenses are recognized in the period when the loss is first forecast. This term is generally used only for long-term contracts. It is otherwise equivalent to the *sales basis* of *revenue recognition.*

completed sales basis. See *sales basis of revenue recognition.*

composite depreciation. *Group depreciation* of dissimilar items.

composite life method. *Group depreciation,* which see, for items of unlike kind. The term may be used when a single item, such as a crane, which consists of separate units with differing service lives, such as the chassis, the motor, the lifting mechanism, and so on, is depreciated as a whole rather than treating each of the components separately.

compound entry. a *journal entry* with more than one *debit* or more than one *credit*, or both. See *trade-in transaction* for an example.

compound interest. *Interest* calculated on *principal* plus previously undistributed interest.

compound interest depreciation. A method designed to hold the *rate of return* on an asset constant. First find the *internal rate of return* on the cash inflows and outflows of the asset. The periodic depreciation charge is the cash flow for the period less the internal rate of return multiplied by the asset's book value at the beginning of the period. When the cash flows from the asset are constant over time, the method is sometimes called the "annuity method" of depreciation.

compounding period. The time period for which *interest* is calculated. At the end of the period, the interest may be paid to the lender or added (that is, converted) to principal for the next interest-earning period, which is usually a year or some portion of a year.

comprehensive budget. *Master budget.*

comprehensive income. Defined in *SFAS No. 3* as "the change in equity (net assets) of an entity during a period from transactions and other events and circumstances from non-owner sources. It includes all changes in equity during a period except those resulting from investments by owners and distributions to owners." In this definition, "equity" means *owners' equity.*

comptroller. Same meaning and pronunciation as *controller.*

conceptual framework. A coherent system of interrelated objectives and fundamentals, promulgated by the *FASB* primarily through its *SFAC* publications, expected to lead to consistent standards for *financial accounting* and reporting.

confirmation. A formal memorandum delivered by the customers or suppliers of a company to its independent *auditor* verifying the amounts shown as receivable or payable. The confirmation document is originally sent by the auditor to the customer. If the auditor asks that the document be returned whether the *balance* is correct or incorrect, then it is called a "positive confirmation." If the auditor asks that the document be returned only if there is an error, it is called a "negative confirmation."

conglomerate. *Holding company.* This term is used when the owned companies are in dissimilar lines of business.

conservatism. A *reporting objective* that calls for anticipation of all *losses* and *expenses* but defers recognition of *gains* or *profits* until they are *realized* in *arm's length* transactions. In the absence of certainty, events are to be reported in a way that tends to minimize cumulative income.

consignee. See *on consignment.*

consignment. See *on consignment.*

consignor. See *on consignment.*

consistency. Treatment of like *transactions* in the same way in consecutive periods so that financial statements will be more comparable than otherwise. The reporting policy implying that procedures, once adopted, should be followed from period to period by a reporting *entity.* See *accounting changes* for the treatment of inconsistencies.

consol. A *bond* that never matures; a *perpetuity* in the form of a bond. Originally issued by Great Britain after the Napoleonic wars to consolidate debt issues of that period. The term arose as an abbreviation for "consolidated annuities."

consolidated financial statements. Statements issued by legally separate companies that show financial position and income as they would appear if the companies were one economic *entity.*

constant dollar. A hypothetical unit of *general purchasing power,* denoted "C$" by the *FASB.*

constant dollar accounting. Accounting where items are measured in *constant dollars.* See *historical-cost/constant-dollar accounting* and *current-cost/constant-dollar accounting.*

constant dollar date. The time at which the *general purchasing power* of one *constant dollar* is exactly equal to the *general purchasing power* of one *nominal dollar*; that is, the date when C$1 = $1. When the constant dollar date is mid-period, then the nominal amounts of *revenues* and *expenses* spread evenly throughout the period are equal to their constant dollar amounts, but end-of-period *balance sheet* amounts measured in constant mid-period dollars differ from their nominal dollar amounts. When the constant dollar date is at the end of the period, then the constant dollar and nominal dollar amounts on a balance sheet for that date are identical.

constructive receipt. An item is included in taxable income when the taxpayer can control funds whether or not cash has been received. For example, *interest* added to *principal* in a savings account is deemed by the *IRS* to be constructively received.

Consumer Price Index. CPI. A *price index* computed and issued monthly by the Bureau of Labor Statistics of the U.S. Department of Labor. The index attempts to track the price level of a group of goods and services purchased by the average consumer. The *FASB* requires use of the CPI in *constant dollar accounting* Contrast with *GNP Implicit Price Deflator.*

contingency. A potential *liability*; if a specified event were to occur, such as losing a lawsuit, a liability would be recognized. The contingency is merely disclosed in notes, rather than shown in the balance sheet. *SFAS No. 5* requires treatment as a contingency until the outcome is "probable" and the amount of payment can be reasonably estimated, perhaps within a range. When the outcome becomes probable (the future event is "likely" to occur) and the amount can be reasonably estimated (using the lower end of a range if only a range can be estimated), then the liability is recognized in the accounts, rather than being disclosed in the notes. A *material* contingency may lead to a qualified, "*subject to,*" auditor's opinion. *Gain* contingencies are not recorded in the accounts, but are merely disclosed in notes.

contingent annuity. An *annuity* whose number of payments depends upon the outcome of an event whose timing is uncertain at the time the annuity is set up; for example, an annuity payable for the life of the *annuitant.* Contrast with *annuity certain.*

contingent issue (securities). Securities issuable to specific individuals upon the occurrence of some event, such as the firm's attaining a specified level of earnings.

17

continuing appropriation. A governmental *appropriation* automatically renewed without further legislative action until it is altered or revoked or expended.

continuing operations. See *income from continuing operations*.

continuity of operations. The assumption in accounting that the business *entity* will continue to operate long enough for current plans to be carried out. The *going-concern assumption*.

continuous budget. A *budget* that perpetually adds a month in the future as the month just ended is dropped.

continuous compounding. *Compound interest* where the *compounding period* is every instant of time. See *e* for the computation of the equivalent annual or periodic rate.

continuous inventory method. The *perpetual inventory* method.

Continuously Contemporary Accounting. CoCoA. A name coined by the Australian theorist, Raymond J. Chambers, to indicate a combination of *current value accounting* where amounts are measured in *constant dollars* and based on exit values.

contra account. An *account*, such as *accumulated depreciation*, that accumulates subtractions from another account, such as machinery. Contrast with *adjunct account*.

contributed capital. The sum of the balances in *capital stock* accounts plus *capital contributed in excess of par (or stated) value* accounts. Contrast with *donated capital*.

contributed surplus. An inferior term for *capital contributed in excess of par value*.

contribution approach. Method of preparing *income statements* that separates *variable costs* from *fixed costs* in order to emphasize the importance of cost behavior patterns for purposes of planning and control.

contribution margin. *Revenue* from *sales* less all variable *expenses*. See *gross margin*.

contribution per unit. Selling price less *variable costs* per unit.

contributory. Said of a *pension plan* where employees, as well as employers, make payments to a pension *fund*. Note that the provisions for *vesting* are applicable only to the employer's payments. Whatever the degree of vesting of the employer's payments, the employee typically gets back all of his or her payments, with interest, in case of death, or other cessation of employment, before retirement.

control (controlling) account. A summary *account* with totals equal to those of entries and balances that appear in individual accounts in a *subsidiary ledger*. Accounts Receivable is a control account backed up with an account for each customer. The balance in a control account should not be changed unless a corresponding change is made in the subsidiary accounts.

control system. A device for ensuring that actions are carried out according to plan or for safeguarding *assets*. A system for ensuring that actions are carried out according to plan can be designed for a single function within the firm, called "operational control," for autonomous segments within the firm that generally have responsibility for both revenues and costs, called "divisional control," or for activities of the firm as a whole, called "company-wide control." Systems designed for safeguarding *assets* are called "internal control" systems.

controllable cost. A *cost* whose amount can be influenced by the way in which operations are carried out, such as advertising costs. These costs can be *fixed* or *variable*. See *programmed costs* and *managed costs*.

controlled company. A company, a majority of whose voting stock is held by an individual or corporation. Effective control can sometimes be exercised when less than 50 percent of the stock is owned.

controller. The title often used for the chief accountant of an organization. Often spelled *comptroller*.

conversion. The act of exchanging a convertible security for another security.

conversion cost. *Direct labor* costs plus factory *overhead* costs incurred in producing a product. That is, the cost to convert raw materials to finished products. *Manufacturing cost*.

conversion period. *Compounding period*. Period during which a *convertible bond* or *convertible preferred stock* can be converted into *common stock*.

convertible bond. A *bond* that may be converted into a specified number of shares of *capital stock* during the *conversion period*.

convertible preferred stock. *Preferred stock* that may be converted into a specified number of shares of *common stock*.

co-product. A product sharing production facilities with another product. For example, if an apparel manufacturer produces shirts and jeans on the same line, these are co-products. Co-products are distinguished from *joint products* and *by-products* which, by their very nature must be produced together, such as the various grades of wood produced in a lumber factory.

copyright. Exclusive right granted by the government to an individual author, composer, playright, and the like for the life of the individual plus 50 years. If the copyright is granted to a firm, then the right extends 75 years after the original publication. The *economic life* of a copyright may be considerably less than the legal life as, for example, the copyright of this book.

corporation. A legal entity authorized by a state to operate under the rules of the entity's *charter*.

correction of errors. See *accounting errors*.

cost. The sacrifice, measured by the *price* paid or required to be paid, to acquire *goods* or *services*. See *acquisition cost* and *replacement cost*. The term "cost" is often used when referring to the valuation of a good or service acquired. When "cost" is used in this sense, a cost is an *asset*. When the benefits of the acquisition (the goods or services acquired) expire, the cost becomes an *expense* or *loss*. Some writers, however, use cost and expense as synonyms. Contrast with *expense*.

cost accounting. Classifying, summarizing, recording, reporting, and allocating current or predicted *costs*. A subset of *managerial accounting*.

Cost Accounting Standards Board. See *CASB*.

cost center. A unit of activity for which *expenditures* and *expenses* are accumulated.

cost effective. Among alternatives, the one whose benefit, or payoff, per unit of cost is highest. Sometimes said of an action whose expected benefits exceed expected costs whether or not there are other alternatives with larger benefit/cost ratios.

cost flow assumption. See *flow assumption*.

cost flows. Costs passing through various classifications within an entity. See *flow of costs* for a diagram.

cost method (for investments). Accounting for an investment in the *capital stock* or *bonds* of another company where the investment is shown at *acquisition cost*, and only *dividends* declared or *interest receivable* is treated as *revenue*.

cost method (for treasury stock). The method of showing *treasury stock* as a *contra* to all other items of *shareholders' equity* in an amount equal to that paid to reacquire the stock.

cost objective. Any activity for which a separate measurement of costs is desired. Examples include departments, products, and territories.

cost of capital. *Opportunity cost* of funds invested in a business. The rate of return required to be earned on an asset before the rational owner will devote that asset to a particular purpose. Sometimes measured as the average rate per year a company must pay for its *equities*. In efficient capital markets, the *discount rate* that equates the expected *present value* of all future cash flows to common shareholders with the market value of common stock at a given time.

cost of goods manufactured. The sum of all costs allocated to products completed during a period; includes materials, labor, and *overhead*.

cost of goods purchased. Net purchase price of goods acquired plus costs of storage and delivery to the place where the items can be productively used.

cost of goods sold. Inventoriable *costs* that are expensed because the units are sold; equals beginning inventory plus *cost of goods purchased* or *manufactured* minus *ending inventory*.

cost of sales. Generally refers to *cost of goods sold*; occasionally, to *selling expenses*.

cost or market, whichever is lower. See *lower of cost or market*.

cost percentage. One less *markup percentage*. *Cost* of *goods available for sale* divided by selling prices of goods available for sale (when *FIFO* is used). With LIFO, *cost of purchases* divided by selling price of purchases. See *markup* for further detail on inclusions in calculation of cost percentage.

cost pool. *indirect cost pool*.

cost principle. The *principle* that requires reporting *assets* at *historical* or *acquisition cost*, less accumulated *amortization*. This principle is based on the assumption that cost is equal to *fair market value* at the date of acquisition and subsequent changes are not likely to be significant.

cost recovery first method. A method of *revenue* recognition that *credits cost* as collections are received until all costs are recovered. Only after costs are completely recovered is *income* recognized. To be used in financial reporting only when the total amount of collections is highly uncertain. Can never be used in income tax reporting. Contrast with the *installment method* where *constant proportions* of each collection are credited both to cost and to income.

cost sheet. Statement that shows all the elements comprising the total cost of an item.

cost terminology. The word "cost" appears in many accounting terms. The accompanying exhibit classifies some of these by the distinctions the terms are used to make. Joel Dean was, to our knowledge, the first to attempt such distinctions; we have used some of his ideas here. Some terms have more detailed discussion under their own listings.

cost-to-cost. The *percentage of completion method* where the estimate of completion is the ratio of costs incurred to date divided by total costs expected to be incurred for the entire project.

cost-volume-profit graph (chart). A graph that shows the relation between *fixed costs, contribution per unit, breakeven point*, and *sales*. See *breakeven chart*.

costing. The process of calculating the cost of activities, products, or services. The British word for *cost accounting*.

coupon. That portion of a *bond* document redeemable at a specified date for *interest* payments. Its physical form is much like a ticket; each coupon is dated and is deposited at a bank, just like a check, for collection or is mailed to the issuer's agent for collection.

coupon rate. Of a *bond*, the amount of annual coupons divided by par value. Contrast with *effective rate*.

covenant. A promise with legal validity.

CPA. See *certified public accountant*. The *AICPA* suggests that no periods be shown in the abbreviation.

CPI. *Consummer price index*.

CPP. Current purchasing power; usually used as an adjective modifying the word "accounting" to mean the accounting that produces *constant dollar financial statements*.

Cr. Abbreviation for *credit*.

credit. As a noun, an entry on the right-hand side of an *account*. As a verb, to make an entry on the right-hand side of an account. Records increases in *liabilities, owner's equity, revenues* and *gains*; records decreases in *assets* and *expenses*. See *debit and credit conventions*. Also the ability or right to buy or borrow in return for a promise to pay later.

credit loss. The amount of *accounts receivable* that is, or is expected to become, *uncollectible*.

credit memorandum. A document used by a seller to inform a buyer that the buyer's *account receivable* is being credited (reduced) because of *errors, returns*, or *allowances*. Also, the document provided by a bank to a depositor to indicate that the depositor's balance is being increased because of some event other than a deposit, such as the collection by the bank of the depositor's *note receivable*.

creditor. One who lends.

cross-reference (index). A number placed by each *account* in a *journal entry* indicating the *ledger* account to which the entry is posted and placing in the ledger the page number of the journal where the entry was made. Used to link the *debit* and *credit* parts of an entry in the ledger accounts back to the original entry in the journal. See *audit trail*.

cross section analysis. Analysis of *financial statements* of various firms for a single period of time, as opposed to

Cost Terminology: Distinctions Among Terms Containing the Word "Cost"

Terms (Synonyms Given in Parentheses)			Distinctions and Comments
			1. The following pairs of terms distinguish the "attribute" or "basis" measured in accounting.
Historical Cost (Acquisition Cost)	vs.	Current Cost	A distinction used in financial accounting. Current cost can be used more specifically to mean replacement cost, net realizable value, or present value of cash flows. "Current cost" is often used narrowly to mean replacement cost.
Historical Cost (Actual Cost)	vs.	Standard Cost	The distinction between historical and standard costs arises in product costing for inventory valuation. Some systems record actual costs while others record the standard costs.
			2. The following pairs of terms denote various distinctions among historical costs. For each pair of terms, the sum of the two kinds of costs equals total historical cost used in financial reporting.
Variable Cost	vs.	Fixed Cost (Constant Cost)	Distinction used in breakeven analysis and in designing cost accounting systems, particularly for product costing. See (4), below, for a further subdivision of fixed costs and (5), below, for an economic distinction closely paralleling this one.
Traceable Cost	vs.	Common Cost (Joint Cost)	Distinction arises in allocating manufacturing costs to product. Common costs are allocated to product, but the allocations are more-or-less arbitrary. The distinction also arises in segment reporting and in separating manufacturing from nonmanufacturing costs.
Direct Cost	vs.	Indirect Cost	Distinction arises in designing cost accounting systems and in product costing. The distinction generally applies only to manufacturing costs.
Out-of-Pocket Cost (Outlay Cost; Cash Cost)	vs.	Book Cost	Virtually all costs recorded in financial statements require a cash outlay at one time or another. The distinction here separates expenditures to occur in the future from those already made and is used in making decisions. Book costs, such as for depreciation, reduce income without requiring a future outlay of cash. The cash has already been spent. See future vs. past costs in (5), below.
Incremental Cost (Marginal Cost)	vs.	Sunk Cost	Distinction used in making decisions. Incremental costs will be incurred (or saved) if a decision is made to go ahead (or to stop) some activity, but not otherwise. Sunk costs will be reported in financial statements whether the decision is made to go ahead or not, because cash has already been spent or committed. Not all sunk costs are book costs, as, for example, a salary promised but not yet earned, that will be paid even if a no-go decision is made.
Incremental Cost	vs.	Marginal Cost	The economist restricts the term marginal cost to the cost of producing one more unit. Thus the next unit has a marginal cost; the next week's output has an incremental cost. If a firm produces and sells a new product the related new costs would properly be called incremental, not marginal. If a factory is closed, the costs saved are incremental, not marginal.
Escapable Cost	vs.	Inescapable Cost (Unavoidable Cost)	Same distinction as incremental vs. sunk costs, but this pair is used only when the decision maker is considering stopping something—ceasing to produce a product, closing a factory, or the like. See next pair.
Avoidable Cost	vs.	Unavoidable Cost	A distinction sometimes used in discussing the merits of direct and absorption costing. Avoidable costs are treated as product cost and unavoidable costs are treated as period expenses under direct costing.
Controllable Cost	vs.	Uncontrollable Cost	The distinction here is used in allocating responsibility and in setting bonus or incentive plans. All costs can be affected by someone in the entity; those who design incentive schemes attempt to hold a person responsible for a cost only if that person can influence the amount of the cost.
			3. In each of the following pairs, used in historical cost accounting, the word "cost" appears in one of the terms where "expense" is meant.
Expired Cost	vs.	Unexpired Cost	The distinction is between *expense* and *asset*.

Cost Terminology: Distinctions Among Terms Containing the Word "Cost"

Terms (Synonyms Given in Parentheses)			Distinctions and Comments
Product Cost	vs.	Period Cost	The terms distinguish product cost from period expense. When a given asset is used, is its cost converted into work in process and then finished goods on the balance sheet until the goods are sold or is it an expense shown on this period's income statement? Product costs appear on the income statement as part of cost of goods sold in the period when the goods are sold. Period expenses appear on the income statement with an appropriate caption for the item in the period when the cost is incurred or recognized.

4. The following subdivisions of fixed (historical) costs are used in analyzing operations. The relation between the components of fixed costs is:

$$\text{Fixed Costs} = \text{Capacity Costs} + \text{Programmed Costs}$$

$\underbrace{\text{Semifixed} + \text{Fixed}}$	$\underbrace{\text{Standby} + \text{Enabling}}$
Costs Portions	Costs Costs
+ of	
"Pure" Semivariable	
Fixed Costs Costs	

Capacity Cost (Committed Cost)	vs.	Programmed Cost (Managed Cost; Discretionary Cost)	Capacity costs give a firm the capability to produce or to sell. Programmed costs, such as for advertising or research and development, may not be essential, but once a decision to incur them is made, they become fixed costs.
Standby Cost	vs.	Enabling Cost	Standby costs will be incurred whether capacity, once acquired, is used or not, such as property taxes and depreciation on a factory. Enabling costs, such as for security force, can be avoided if the capacity is unused.
Semifixed Cost	vs.	Semivariable Cost	A cost fixed over a wide range but that can change at various levels is a semifixed cost or "step cost." An example is the cost of rail lines from the factory to the main rail line where fixed cost depends on whether there are one or two parallel lines, but are independent of the number of trains run per day. Semivariable costs combine a strictly fixed component cost plus a variable component. Telephone charges usually have a fixed monthly component plus a charge related to usage.

5. The following pairs of terms distinguish among economic uses or decision making uses or regulatory uses of cost terms.

Opportunity Cost	vs.	Outlay Cost (Out-of-Pocket Cost)	Opportunity cost refers to the economic benefit foregone by using a resource for one purpose instead of for another. The outlay cost of the resource will be recorded in financial records. The distinction arises because a resource is already in the possession of the entity with a recorded historical cost. Its economic value to the firm, opportunity cost, generally differs from the historical cost; it can be either larger or smaller.
Future Costs	vs.	Past Cost	Effective decision making analyzes only the present and the future outlay costs, out-of-pocket costs, opportunity costs, are relevant for profit maximizing; past costs are used in financial reporting.
Short-Run Cost	vs.	Long-Run Cost	Short-run costs vary as output is varied for a given configuration of plant and equipment. Long-run costs can be incurred to change that configuration. This pair of terms is the economic analog of the accounting pair, see (2) above, variable and fixed costs. The analogy is not perfect because some short-run costs are fixed, such as property taxes on the factory, from the point of view of breakeven analysis.
Imputed Cost	vs.	Book Cost	In a regulatory setting some costs, for example the cost of owner's equity capital, are calculated and used for various purposes. Imputed costs are not recorded in the historical cost acounting records for financial reporting. Book costs are recorded.
Average Cost	vs.	Marginal Cost	The economic distinction equivalent to fully absorbed cost of product and direct cost of product. Average cost is total cost divided by number of units. Marginal cost is the cost to produce the next unit (or the last unit).

time series analysis where statements of a given firm are analyzed over several periods of time.

cumulative dividend. Preferred stock *dividends* that, if not paid, accrue as a commitment that must be paid before dividends to common shareholders can be declared.

cumulative preferred shares. *Preferred* shares with *cumulative dividend* rights.

current asset. *Cash* and other *assets* that are expected to be turned into cash, sold, or exchanged within the normal operating cycle of the firm, usually one year. Current assets include *cash, marketable securities, receivables, inventory,* and *current prepayments.*

current cost. *Cost* stated in terms of current values (of *productive capacity*) rather than in terms of *acquisition cost.* See *net realizable value, current selling price.*

current cost accounting. The *FASB*'s term for *financial statements* where the *attribute measured* is *current cost.*

current-cost/nominal-dollar accounting. Accounting based on *current cost* valuations measured in *nominal dollars.* Components of *income* include an *operating margin* and *holding gains and losses.*

current fund. In governmental accounting, a synonym for general fund.

current funds. *Cash* and other assets readily convertible into cash. In governmental accounting, funds spent for operating purposes during the current period. Includes *general, special revenue, debt service,* and *enterprise funds.*

current (gross) margin. See *operating margin (based on current costs).*

current liability. A debt or other obligation that must be discharged within a short time, usually the *earnings cycle* or one year, normally by expending *current assets.*

current operating performance concept. The notion tht or other obligation that must be discharged within a short time, usually the *earnings cycle* or one year, normally by expending *current assets.*

current operating performance concept. The notion that reported *income* for a period ought to reflect only ordinary, normal, and recurring operations of that period. A consequence is that *extraordinary* and nonrecurring items are entered directly in the Retained Earnings account. Contrast with *clean surplus concept.* This concept is no longer acceptable. (See *APB Opinions* Nos. 9 and 30.)

current ratio. Sum of *current assets* divided by sum of *current liabilities.* See *ratio.*

current replacement cost. Of an *asset,* the amount currently required to acquire an identical asset (in the same condition and with the same service potential) or an asset capable of rendering the same service at a current *fair market price.* If these two amounts differ, the lower is usually used. Contrast with *reproduction cost.*

current selling price. The amount for which an *asset* could be sold as of a given time in an *arm's length* transaction, rather than in a forced sale.

current value accounting. The form of accounting where all assets are shown at *current replacement cost (entry value)* or *current selling price* or *net realizable value (exit value)* and all *liabilities* are shown at *present value.* Entry and exit values may be quite different from each other so there is

no general agreement on the precise meaning of current value accounting.

current yield. Of a *bond,* the annual amount of *interest coupons* divided by current market price of the bond. Contrast with *yield to maturity.*

currently attainable standard cost. *Normal standard cost.*

customers' ledger. The *ledger* that shows accounts receivable of individual customers. It is the *subsidiary ledger* for the *controlling account,* Accounts Receivable.

D

days of average inventory on hand. See *ratio.*

DCF. *Discounted cash flow.*

DDB. *Double-declining-balance depreciation.*

debenture bond. A *bond* not secured with *collateral.*

debit. As a noun, an entry on the left-hand side of an *account.* As a verb, to make an entry on the left-hand side of an account. Records increases in *assets* and *expenses*; records decreases in *liabilities, owners' equity,* and *revenues.* See *debit and credit conventions.*

debit and credit conventions. The equality of the two sides of the *accounting equation* is maintained by recording equal amounts of *debits* and *credits* for each *transaction.* The conventional use of the *T-account* form and the rules for debit and credit in *balance sheet accounts* are summarized as follows.

Any Asset Account

Opening Balance Increase + Dr. Ending Balance	Decrease − Cr.

Any Liability Account

Decrease − Dr.	Opening Balance Increase + Cr. Ending Balance

Any Owners' Equity Account

Decrease − Dr.	Opening Balance Increase + Cr. Ending Balance

Revenue and expense accounts belong to the owner's equity group. The relationship and the rules for debit and credit in these accounts can be expressed as follows.

Owner's Equity

Decrease − Dr. Expenses		Increase + Cr. Revenues	
Dr.	Cr.	Dr.	Cr.
+ ☆	−	−	+ ☆

☆ Normal balance prior to closing.

debit memorandum. A document used by a seller to inform a buyer that the seller is debiting (increasing) the amount of the buyer's *account receivable*. Also, the document provided by a bank to a depositor to indicate that the depositor's *balance* is being decreased because of some event other than payment for a *check*, such as monthly service charges or the printing of checks.

debt. An amount owed. The general name for *notes, bonds, mortgages,* and the like that are evidence of amounts owed and have definite payment dates.

debt-equity ratio. Total *liabilities* divided by total equities. See *ratio*. Sometimes the denominator is merely total shareholders' equity. Sometimes the numerator is restricted to *long-term debt*.

debt financing. Raising *funds* by issuing *bonds, mortgages,* or *notes*. Contrast with *equity financing. Leverage*.

debt guarantee. See *guarantee*.

debt ratio. *Debt-equity ratio*.

debt service fund. In governmental accounting, a *fund* established to account for payment of *interest* and *principal* on all general obligation *debt* other than that payable from special *assessments*.

debt service requirement. The amount of cash required for payments of *interest*, current maturities of *principal* on outstanding *debt*, and payments to *sinking funds* (corporations) or to the *debt service fund* (governmental).

debtor. One who borrows.

declaration date. Time when a *dividend* is declared by the *board of directors*.

declining-balance depreciation. The method of calculating the periodic *depreciation* charge by multiplying the *book value* at the start of the period by a constant percentage. In pure declining balance depreciation the constant percentage is $1 - \sqrt[n]{s/c}$ where n is the *depreciable life*, s is *salvage value*, and c is *acquisition cost*. See *double-declining-balance depreciation*.

deep discount bonds. Said of *bonds* selling much below (exactly how much is not clear) *par value*.

defalcation. Embezzlement.

default. Failure to pay *interest* or *principal* on a *debt* when due.

defensive interval. A financial *ratio* equal to the number of days of normal cash *expenditures* covered by *quick assets*. It is defined as

$$\frac{\text{quick assets}}{\text{(all expenses except amortization and others not using funds/365)}}$$

The denominator of the ratio is the cash expenditure per day. This ratio has been found useful in predicting *bankruptcy*.

deferral. The accounting process concerned with past *cash receipts* and *payments*; in contrast to *accrual*. Recognizing a liability resulting from a current cash receipt (as for magazines to be delivered) or recognizing an asset from a current cash payment (or for prepaid insurance or a long-term depreciable asset).

deferral method. See *flow-through method* (of accounting for the *investment credit*) for definition and contrast.

deferred annuity. An *annuity* whose first payment is made sometime after the end of the first period.

deferred asset. *Deferred charge*.

deferred charge. *Expenditure* not recognized as an *expense* of the period when made but carried forward as an *asset* to be *written off* in future periods, such as for advance rent payments or insurance premiums. See *deferral*.

deferred cost. *Deferred charge*.

deferred credit. Sometimes used to indicate *advances from customers*. Also sometimes used to describe the *deferred income tax liability*.

deferred debit. *Deferred charge*.

deferred expense. *Deferred charge*.

deferred gross margin. *Unrealized gross margin*.

deferred income. *Advances from customers*.

deferred income tax (liability). An *indeterminate-term liability* that arises when the pretax income shown on the tax return is less than what it would have been had the same *accounting principles* been used in tax returns as used for financial reporting. *APB Opinion* No. 11 requires that the firm debit income tax *expense* and credit deferred income tax with the amount of the taxes delayed by using different accounting principles in tax returns from those used in financial reports. See *timing difference* and *permanent difference*. See *installment sales*. If, as a result of timing differences, cumulative taxable income exceeds cumulative reported income before taxes, the deferred income tax account will have a *debit* balance and will be reported as a *deferred charge*.

deferred revenue. Sometimes used to indicate *advances from customers*.

deferred tax. See *deferred income tax*.

deficit. A *debit balance* in the Retained Earnings account; presented on the balance sheet as a *contra* to shareholders' equity. Sometimes used to mean negative *net income* for a period.

defined-benefit plan. A *pension plan* where the employer promises specific dollar amounts to each eligible employee; the amounts usually depend on a formula which takes into account such things as the employee's earnings, years of employment, and age. The employer's cash contributions and pension expense are adjusted in relation to *actuarial* experience in the eligible employee group and investment performance of the pension *fund*. Sometimes called a "fixed-benefit" pension plan. Contrast with *money purchase plan*.

defined-contribution plan. A *money purchase (pension) plan* or other arrangement, based on formula or discretion, where the employer makes cash contributions to eligible individual employee *accounts* under the terms of a written plan document.

deflation. A period of declining *general price changes*.

demand deposit. *Funds* in a *checking account* at a bank.

demand loan. See *term loan* for definition and contrast.

denominator volume. Capacity measured in expected number of units to be produced this period; divided into *budgeted fixed costs* to obtain fixed costs applied per unit of product.

depletion. Exhaustion or *amortization* of a *wasting asset*, or natural resource. Also see *percentage depletion*.

depletion allowance. See *percentage depletion*.

deposit method (of revenue recognition). This method of *revenue* recognition is not distinct from the *completed sale* or *completed contract method*. In some contexts such as retail land sales, the customer must make substantial payments while still having the right to back out of the deal and receive a refund. When there is uncertainty about whether the deal will be completed but a cash collection is made by the seller, the seller must *credit* deposits, a *liability account*, rather than *revenue*. (In this regard, the accounting differs from the completed contract method where the account credited is offset against the *work in process inventory* account.) When the *sale* becomes complete, a revenue account is credited and the deposit account is *debited*.

deposit, sinking fund. Payments made to a *sinking fund*.

deposits in transit. Deposits made by a firm but not yet reflected on the *bank statement*.

depreciable cost. That part of the *cost* of an asset, usually *acquisition cost* less *salvage value*, that is to be charged off over the life of the asset through the process of *depreciation*.

depreciable life. For an *asset*, the time period or units of activity (such as miles driven for a truck) over which *depreciable cost* is to be allocated. For tax returns, depreciable life may be shorter than estimated *service life*.

depreciation. *Amortization of plant assets*; the process of allocating the cost of an asset to the periods of benefit—the *depreciable life*. Classified as a *production cost* or a *period expense*, depending upon the asset and whether *absorption* or *direct costing* is used. Depreciation methods described in this glossary include the *annuity method, appraisal method, composite method, compound interest method, declining-balance method, double-declining-balance method, production method, replacement method, retirement method, straight-line method, sinking fund method,* and *sum-of-the-years'-digits method*.

depreciation reserve. An inferior term for *accumulated depreciation*. See *reserve*. Do not confuse with a replacement fund.

Descartes' rule of signs. In a *capital-budgeting* context, the rule says that a series of cash flows will have a nonnegative number of *internal rates of return*. The number is equal to the number of variations in the sign of the cash flow series or is less than that number by an even integer. Consider the following series of cash flows, the first occurring now and the others at subsequent yearly intervals: $-100, -100, +50, +175, -50, +100$. The internal rates of return are the numbers for r that satisfy the equation

$$-100 - 100/(1 + r) + 50/(1 + r)^2 + 175/(1 + r)^3 \\ -50/(1 + r)^4 + 100/(1 + r)^5 = 0.$$

The series of cash flows has three variations in sign: a change from minus to plus, a change from plus to minus, and a change from minus to plus. The rule says that this series must have either one or three internal rates of return; in fact, it has only one, about 12 percent. But also see *reinvestment rate*.

determination. See *determine*.

determine. The verb "determine" and the noun "determination" are often used (in our opinion, overused) by accountants and those who describe the accounting process. A leading dictionary associates the following meanings with the verb "determine:" settle, decide, conclude, ascertain, cause, affect, control, impel, terminate, and decide upon. In addition, accounting writers can mean any one of the following: measure, allocate, report, calculate, compute, observe, choose, and legislate. In accounting, there are two distinct sets of meanings—those encompassed by the synonym "cause or legislate" and those encompassed by the synonym "measure." The first set of uses conveys the active notion of causing something to happen and the second set of uses conveys the more passive notion of observing something that someone else has caused to happen. An accountant who writes of cost or income "determination" generally means measurement or observation, not causation; management and economic conditions cause costs or income to be what they are. One who writes of accounting principles "determination" can mean choosing or applying (as in "determining depreciation charges" from an allowable set) or causing to be acceptable (as in the FASB "determining" the accounting for *leases*). In the long run, income is cash-in less cash-out, so management and economic conditions "determine" (cause) income to be what it is. In the short run, reported income is a function of accounting principles chosen and applied so the accountant "determines" (measures) income. A question such as "Who determines income?" has, therefore, no unambiguous answer. The meaning of "an accountant determining acceptable accounting principles" is also vague. Does the clause mean merely choosing one from the set of generally acceptable principles or does it mean using professional judgment to decide that some of the generally accepted principles are not correct under the current circumstances. We try never to use "determine" unless we mean "cause." Otherwise we use "measure," "report," "calculate," "compute," or whatever specific verb seems appropriate. We suggest that careful writers will always "determine" to use the most specific verb to convey meaning. "Determine" is seldom the best choice to convey specifity in describing a process where those who make decisions often differ from those who apply technique.

development-stage enterprise. As defined in *SFAS No. 7*, a firm whose planned principal *operations* have not commenced or having commenced, have not generated significant *revenue*. Such enterprises should be so identified, but no special *accounting principles* apply to them.

differential analysis. Analysis of *incremental costs*.

differential cost. *Incremental cost*. If a total cost curve is smooth (in mathematical terms, differentiable), then the curve graphing the derivative of the total cost curve is often said to show differential costs, the costs increments associated with infinitesimal changes in volume.

dilution. A potential reduction in *earnings per share* or *book value* per share by the potential *conversion* of securities or by the potential exercise of *warrants* or *options*.

dilutive. Said of a *security* that would reduce *earnings per share* if it were exchanged for *common stock*.

dipping into LIFO layers. See *LIFO inventory layer*.

direct cost. Cost of *direct material* and *direct labor* incurred in producing a product. See *prime cost*. In some accounting literature, this term is used to mean the same thing as *variable cost*.

direct costing. This method of allocating costs assigns only *variable manufacturing costs* to product and treats *fixed manufacturing costs* as *period* expenses. A better term for this concept is "variable costing."

direct labor (material) cost. Cost of labor (material) applied and assigned directly to a product; contrast with *indirect labor (material)*.

direct posting. A method of bookkeeping where *entries* are made directly in *ledger accounts*, without the use of a *journal*.

direct write-off method. See *write-off method*.

disbursement. Payment by *cash* or by *check*. See *expenditure*.

DISC. Domestic International Sales Corporation. A U.S. *corporation*, usually a *subsidiary*, whose *income* is primarily attributable to exports. *Income tax* on 50 percent of a DISC's income is usually deferred for a long period. Generally, this results in a lower overall corporate tax for the *parent* than would otherwise be incurred.

disclaimer of opinion. An *auditor's report* stating that an opinion cannot be given on the *financial statements*. Usually results from *material* restrictions on the scope of the audit or from material uncertainties about the accounts which cannot be resolved at the time of the audit.

disclosure. The showing of facts in *financial statements*, *notes* thereto, or the *auditor's report*.

discontinued operations. See *income from discontinued operations*.

discount. In the context of *compound interest*, *bonds* and *notes*, the difference between *face* or *future value* and *present value* of a payment. In the context of *sales* and *purchases*, a reduction in price granted for prompt payment. See also *chain discount*, *quantity discount*, and *trade discount*.

discount factor. The reciprocal of one plus the *discount rate*. If the discount rate is 10 percent per period, the discount factor for three periods is $(1.10)^{-3} = 0.75131$.

discount rate. *Interest rate* used to convert future payments to *present values*.

discounted bailout period. In a *capital budgeting* context, the total time that must elapse before discounted value of net accumulated cash flows from a project, including potential *salvage value* at various times of assets, equals or exceeds the *present value* of net accumulated cash outflows. Contrast with *discounted payback period*.

discounted cash flow. Using either the *net present value* or the *internal rate of return* in an analysis to measure the value of future expected cash *expenditures* and *receipts* at a common date.

discounted payback period. Amount of time over which the discounted present value of cash inflows from a project, excluding potential *salvage value* at various times if assets equals the discounted *present value* of the cash outflows.

discounting a note. See *note receivable discounted* and *factoring*.

discounts lapsed (lost). The sum of *discounts* offered for prompt payment that were not taken (or allowed) because of expiration of the discount period. See *terms of sale*.

discovery value accounting. See *reserve recognition accounting*.

Discussion Memorandum. A neutral discussion of all the issues concerning an accounting problem of current concern to the *FASB*. The publication of such a document usually implies that the FASB is considering issuing an *SFAS* or *SFAC* on this particular problem. The discussion memorandum brings together material about the particular problem to facilitate interaction and comment by those interested in the matter. It may lead to an *Exposure Draft*.

dishonored note. A *promissory note* whose maker does not repay the loan at *maturity* for a *term loan*, or on demand, for a *demand loan*.

disintermediation. Federal law regulates the maximum *interest rate* that both banks and savings and loan associations can pay for *time deposits*. When free-market interest rates exceed the regulated interest ceiling for such time deposits, some depositors withdraw their funds and invest them elsewhere at a higher interest rate. This process is known as "disintermediation."

distributable income. The portion of conventional accounting net income that can be distributed to owners (usually in the form of *dividends*) without impairing the physical capacity of the firm to continue operations at current levels. Pretax distributable income is conventional pretax income less the excess of *current cost* of goods sold and *depreciation* charges based on the replacement cost of *productive capacity* over cost of goods sold and depreciation on an *acquisition cost basis*. Contrast with *sustainable income*. See *inventory profit*.

distribution expense. *Expense* of selling, advertising, and delivery activities.

dividend. A distribution of assets generated from *earnings* to owners of a corporation; it may be paid in cash (cash dividend), with stock (stock dividend), with property, or with other securities (dividend in kind). Dividends, except stock dividends, become a legal liability of the corporation when they are declared. Hence, the owner of stock ordinarily recognizes *revenue* when a dividend, other than a stock dividend, is declared. See also *liquidating dividend* and *stock dividend*.

dividend yield. *Dividends* declared for the year divided by market price of the stock as of a given time of the year.

dividends in arrears. Dividends on *cumulative preferred stock* that have not been declared in accordance with the preferred stock contract. Such arrearages must usually be cleared before dividends on *common stock* can be declared.

dividends in kind. See *dividend*.

divisional control. See *control system*.

divisional reporting. *Line of business reporting*.

dollar sign rules. In presenting accounting statements or schedules, place a dollar sign beside the first figure in each column and beside any figure below a horizontal line drawn under the preceding figure.

dollar value LIFO method. A form of *LIFO* inventory accounting with inventory quantities (*layers*) measured in dollar, rather than physical, terms. Adjustments to account for changing prices are made by use of specific price indexes appropriate for the kinds of items in the inventory.

Domestic International Sales Corporation. See *DISC*.

donated capital. A *shareholders' equity* account credited when contributions, such as land or buildings, are freely given to the company. Do not confuse with *contributed capital*.

double-declining-balance depreciation. DDB. *Declining-balance depreciation*, which see, where the constant percentage used to multiply by book value in determining the depreciation charge for the year is $2/n$ and n is the *depreciable life* in periods. Maximum declining-balance rate permitted in the *income tax* laws. *Salvage value* is omitted from the depreciable amount. Thus if the asset cost \$100 and has a depreciable life of 5 years, the depreciation in the first year would be \$40 = 2/5 × \$100, in the second would be \$24 = 2/5 × (\$100 − \$40), and in the third year would be \$14.40 = 2/5 × (\$100 − \$40 − \$24). By the fourth year, the remaining undepreciated cost could be depreciated under the straight-line method at \$10.80 = 1/2 × (\$100 − \$40 − \$24 − \$14.40) per year for tax purposes.

double entry. The system of recording transactions that maintains the equality of the accounting equation; each entry results in recording equal amounts of *debits* and *credits*.

double T-account. *T-account* with an extra horizontal line showing a change in the account balance to be explained by the subsequent entries into the account, such as:

Plant

42,000

This account shows an increase in the asset account, plant, of \$42,000 to be explained. Such accounts are useful in preparing the *statement of changes in financial position*; they are not a part of the formal record keeping process.

double taxation. Corporate income is subject to the corporate income tax and the aftertax income, when distributed to owners, is subject to the personal income tax.

doubtful accounts. *Accounts receivable* estimated to be *uncollectible*.

Dr. The abbreviation for *debit*.

draft. A written order by the first party, called the drawer, instructing a second party, called the drawee (such as a bank) to pay a third party, called the payee. See also *check, cashier's check, certified check, NOW account, sight draft,* and *trade acceptance*.

drawee. See *draft*.

drawer. See *draft*.

drawing account. A *temporary account* used in *sole proprietorships* and *partnerships* to record payments to owners or partners during a period. At the end of the period, the drawing account is closed by crediting it and debiting the owner's or partner's share of income or, perhaps, his or her capital account.

drawings. Payments made to a *sole proprietor* or to a *partner* during a period. See *drawing account*.

dry-hole accounting. See *reserve recognition accounting* for definition and contrast.

dual transactions assumption (fiction). In presenting the *statement of changes in financial position*, some transactions not involving *working capital* accounts are reported as

though working capital was generated and then used. For example, the issue of *capital stock* in return for the *asset*, land, is reported in the statement of changes in financial position as though stock were issued for *cash* and cash were used to acquire land. Other examples of transactions that require the dual transaction fiction are the issue of the *mortgage* in return for a noncurrent asset and the issue of stock to bondholders on *conversion* of their *convertible bonds*.

duality. The axiom of *double-entry* record keeping that every *transaction* is broken down into equal *debit* and *credit* amounts.

E

e. The base of natural logarithms; 2.718281828459045.... If *interest* is compounded continuously during a period at stated rate of r per period, then the effective *interest rate* is equivalent to interest compounded once per period at rate i where $i = e^r - 1$. Tables of e^r are widely available. If 12 percent annual interest is compounded continuously, the effective rate is $e^{.12} - 1 = 12.75$ percent.

earned surplus. A term once used, but no longer considered proper, for *retained earnings*.

earnings. *Income*, or sometimes *profit*.

earnings cycle. The period of time that elapses for a given firm, or the series of transactions, during which *cash* is converted into *goods* and *services*, goods and services are sold to customers, and customers pay for their purchases with cash. *Cash cycle*.

earnings per share (of common stock). *Net income* to common shareholders (net income minus *preferred dividends*) divided by the average number of *common shares* outstanding; see also *primary earnings per share* and *fully diluted earnings per share*. See *ratio*.

earnings per share (of preferred stock). *Net income* divided by the average number of *preferred shares* outstanding during the period. This ratio indicates how well the preferred dividends are covered or protected; it does not indicate a legal share of *earnings*. See *ratio*.

earnings, retained. See *retained earnings*.

earn-out. An agreement between two merging firms under which the amount of payment by the acquiring firm to the acquired firm's shareholders depends on the future earnings of the *consolidated entity*.

easement. The acquired right or privilege of one person to use, or have access to, certain property of another. For example, a public utility's right to lay pipes or lines under property of another and to service those facilities.

economic entity. See *entity*.

economic life. The time span over which the benefits of an *asset* are expected to be received. The economic life of a *patent, copyright,* or *franchise* may be less than the legal life. *Service life*.

economic order quantity. In mathematical *inventory* analysis, the optimal amount of stock to order when inventory is reduced to a level called the "reorder point." If A represents the *incremental cost* of placing a single order, D represents the total demand for a period of time in units, and H represents the incremental holding cost during the period per unit of inventory, then the economic order quantity $Q = \sqrt{2\,AD/H}$. Q is sometimes called the "optimal lot size."

ED. *Exposure Draft.*

effective interest method. A systematic method for computing *interest expense* (or *revenue*) that makes the interest expense for each period divided by the amount of the net *liability (asset)* at the beginning of the period equal to the *yield rate* on the bond at the time of issue (acquisition). Interest for a period is yield rate (at time of issue) multiplied by the net liability (asset) at the start of the period. The *amortization* of discount or premium is the *plug* to give equal *debits* and *credits*. (Interest expense is a debit and the amount of coupon payments is a credit.)

effective (interest) rate. Of a bond, the *internal rate of return* or *yield to maturity* at the time of issue. Contrast with *coupon rate*. If the bond is issued for a price below *par*, the effective rate is higher than the coupon rate; if it is issued for a price greater than par, then the effective rate is lower than the coupon rate. In the context of *compound interest*, when the *compounding period* on a *loan* is different from one year, such as a nominal interest rate of 12 percent compounded monthly, then single payment that could be made at the end of a year that is economically equivalent to the series of interest payments exceeds the quoted nominal rate multiplied by the *principal*. If 12 percent per year is compounded monthly, the effective interest rate is 12.683 percent. In general, if the nominal rate is r percent per year and is compounded m times per year, then the effective rate is $(1 + r/m)^m - 1$.

efficiency variance. A term used for the *quantity variance* for labor or *variable overhead* in a *standard cost system*.

efficient market hypothesis. The supposition in finance that securities' prices reflect all available information and react nearly instantaneously and in an unbiased fashion to new information.

eliminations. *Work sheet* entries to prepare *consolidated* statements that are made to avoid duplicating the amounts of *assets, liabilities, owners' equity, revenues,* and *expenses* of the consolidated *entity* when the accounts of the *parent* and *subsidiaries* are summed.

employee stock option. See *stock option.*

Employee Stock Ownership Trust (or Plan). See *ESOT.*

employer, employee payroll taxes. See *payroll.*

enabling costs. A type of *capacity cost* that will stop being incurred if operations are shut down completely but must be incurred in full if operations are carried out at any level. Costs of a security force or of a quality control inspector for an assembly line might be examples. Contrast with *standby costs.*

encumbrance. In governmental accounting, an anticipated *expenditure*, or *funds* restricted for anticipated expenditure, such as for outstanding purchase orders. *Appropriations* less expenditures less outstanding encumbrances yields unencumbered balance.

ending inventory. The *cost of inventory* on hand at the end of the *accounting period*, often called ''closing inventory.'' The dollar amount of inventory to be carried to the subsequent period.

endorsee. See *endorser.*

endorsement. See *draft.* The *payee* signs the draft and transfers it to a fourth party, such as the payee's bank.

endorser. The *payee* of a *note* or *draft* signs it, after writing ''Pay to the order of X,'' transfers the note to person X, and presumably receives some benefit, such as cash, in return. The payee who signs over the note is called the endorser and person X is called the endorsee. The endorsee then has the rights of the payee and may in turn become an endorser by endorsing the note to another endorsee.

enterprise. Any business organization, usually defining the accounting *entity.*

enterprise fund. A *fund* established by a governmental unit to account for acquisition, operation, and maintenance of governmental services that are supposed to be self-supporting from user charges, such as for water or airports.

entity. A person, *partnership, corporation,* or other organization. The *accounting entity* for which accounting statements are prepared may not be the same as the entity defined by law. For example, a *sole proprietorship* is an accounting entity but the individual's combined business and personal assets are the legal entity in most jurisdictions. Several affiliated corporations may be separate legal entities while *consolidated financial statements* are prepared for the group of companies operating as a single economic entity.

entity theory. The view of the corporation that emphasizes the form of the *accounting equation* that says *assets = equities*. Contrast with *proprietorship theory.* The entity theory is less concerned with a distinct line between *liabilities* and *shareholders' equity* than is the proprietorship theory. Rather, all equities are provided to the corporation by outsiders who merely have claims of differing legal standings. The entity theory implies using a *multiple-step* income statement.

entry value. The *current cost* of acquiring an asset or service at a *fair-market price. Replacement cost.*

EOQ. *Economic order quantity.*

EPS. *Earnings per share.*

EPVI. *Excess present value index.*

equalization reserve. An inferior title for the allowance account when the *allowance method* is used for such things as maintenance expenses. Periodically, maintenance *expense* is debited and the allowance is credited. As maintenance *expenditures* are actually incurred, the allowance is debited and cash or the other asset expended is credited.

equities. *Liabilities* plus *owners' equity.* See, however, *equity.*

equity. A claim to *assets;* a source of assets. *SFAS No. 3* defines equity as ''the residual interest in the assets of an entity that remains after deducting its liabilities.'' Usage may be changing so that ''equity'' will exclude liabilities We prefer to keep the broader definition, including liabilities, because there is no other single word that serves this useful purpose.

equity financing. Raising *funds* by issuance of *capital stock.* Contrast with *debt financing.*

equity method. A method of accounting for an *investment* in the stock of another company in which the proportionate share of the earnings of the other company is debited to the investment account and credited to a *revenue* account as earned. When *dividends* are received, *cash* is debited and the investment account is credited. Used in reporting when the investor owns sufficient shares of stock of an unconsolidated company to exercise significant control over the actions of that company. One of the few instances where revenue is recognized without a change in *working capital*.

equity ratio. *Shareholders' equity* divided by total *assets*. See *ratio*.

equivalent production. *Equivalent units*.

equivalent units (of work). The number of units of completed output that would require the same costs as were actually incurred for production of completed and partially completed units during a period. Used primarily in *process costing* calculations to measure in uniform terms the output of a continuous process.

ERISA. Employee Retirement Income Security Act of 1974. The federal law that sets *pension plan* requirements.

error accounting. See *accounting errors*.

ESOP. Employee Stock Ownership Plan. See *ESOT*.

ESOT. Employee Stock Ownership Trust. A trust *fund* created by a corporate employer that can provide certain tax benefits to the corporation while providing for employee stock ownership. The corporate employer can contribute up to 25 percent of its payroll per year to the trust. The contributions are *deductions* from otherwise taxable income for federal *income tax* purposes. The assets of the trust must be used for the benefit of employees—for example, to fund death or retirement benefits. The assets of the trust are usually the *common stock*, sometimes nonvoting, of the corporate employer. As an example of the potential *tax shelter*, consider the case of a corporation with $1 million of *debt* outstanding, which it wishes to retire, and an annual payroll of $2 million. The corporation sells $1 million of common stock to the ESOT. The ESOT borrows $1 million with the loan guaranteed by, and therefore a *contingency* of, the corporation. The corporation uses the $1 million proceeds of the stock issue to retire its outstanding debt. (The debt of the corporation has been replaced with the debt of the ESOT.) The corporation can contribute $500,000 (= .25 × $2 million payroll) to the ESOT each year and treat the contribution as a deduction for tax purposes. After a little more than two years, the ESOT has received sufficient funds to retire its loan. The corporation has effectively repaid its original $1 million debt with pretax dollars. Assuming an income tax rate of 40 percent, it has saved $400,000 (= .40 × $1 million) of aftertax dollars *if* the $500,000 expense for the contribution to the ESOT for the pension benefits of employees would have been made, in one form or another, anyway. Observe that the corporation could use the proceeds ($1 million in the example) of the stock issue to the ESOT for any of several different purposes: financing expansion, replacing plant assets, or acquiring another company.

Basically this same form of pretax dollar financing through pensions is "almost" available with any corporate pension plan, but with one important exception. The trustees of an ordinary pension trust must invest the assets "prudently" and if they do not, they are personally liable to employees. Current judgment about "prudent" investment requires diversification—pension trust assets should be invested in a wide variety of investment opportunities. (Not more than 10 percent of a pension trust's assets can ordinarily be invested in the parent's common stock.) Thus the ordinary pension trust cannot, in practice, invest all, or even most, of its assets in the parent corporation's stock. This constraint does not apply to the investments of an ESOT. All ESOT assets may be invested in the parent company's stock.

The ESOT also provides a means for closely-held corporations to achieve wider ownership of shares without *going public*. The laws enabling ESOT's provide for independent professional appraisal of shares not traded in public markets and for transactions between the corporation and the ESOT or between the ESOT and the employees to be based on the appraised values of the shares.

estimated expenses. See *after cost*.

estimated liability. The preferred terminology for estimated costs to be incurred for such uncertain things as repairs under *warranty*. An estimated liability is shown in the *balance sheet*. Contrast with *contingency*.

estimated revenue. A term used in governmental accounting to designate revenue expected to accrue during a period whether or not it will be collected during the period. A *budgetary account* is usually established at the beginning of the budget period.

estimated salvage value. Synonymous with *salvage value* of an *asset* before its retirement.

estimates, changes in. See *accounting changes*.

except for. Qualification in *auditor's report*, usually caused by a change, approved by the auditor, from one acceptable accounting principle or procedure to another.

excess present value. In a *capital budgeting* context, *present value* of (anticipated net cash inflows minus cash outflows including initial cash outflow) for a project.

excess present value index. *Present value*, of future *cash* inflows divided by initial cash outlay.

exchange. The generic term for a transaction (or more technically, a reciprocal transfer) between one entity and another. In another context, the name for a market, such as the New York Stock Exchange.

exchange gain or loss. The phrase used by the *FASB* for *foreign exchange gain or loss*.

exchange rate. The *price* of one country's currency in terms of another country's currency. For example, the British pound might be worth $2.00 at a given time. The exchange rate would be stated as "one pound is worth two dollars" or "one dollar is worth .50 (= £1/$2.00) pounds."

excise tax. Tax on the manufacture, sale, or consumption of a commodity.

ex-dividend. Said of a stock at the time when the declared *dividend* becomes the property of the person who owned the stock on the *record date*. The payment date follows the ex-dividend date.

executory contract. An agreement providing for payment by a payor to a payee upon the performance of an act or service by the payee, such as a labor contract. Obligations under such contracts generally are not recognized as *liabilities*.

exemption. A term used for various amounts subtracted from gross income in computing taxable income. Not all such subtractions are called "exemptions." See *tax deduction*.

exercise. When the owner of an *option* or *warrant* purchases the security that the option entitles him or her to purchase, he or she has exercised the option or warrant.

exercise price. See *option*.

exit value. The proceeds that would be received if assets were disposed of in an *arm's-length transaction. Current selling price. Net realizable value.*

expected value. The mean or arithmetic *average* of a statistical distribution or series of numbers.

expendable fund. In governmental accounting, a *fund* whose resources, *principal*, and earnings may be distributed.

expenditure. Payment of *cash* for goods or services received. Payment may be made either at the time the goods or services are received or at a later time. Virtually synonymous with *disbursement* except that disbursement is a broader term and includes all payments for goods or services. Contrast with *expense*.

expense. As a noun, a decrease in *owners' equity* caused by the using up of *assets* in producing *revenue* or carrying out other activities that are part of the entity's *operations*. A "gone" asset; an expired cost. The amount is the *cost* of the assets used up. Do not confuse with *expenditure* or *disbursement*, which may occur before, when, or after the related expense is recognized. Use the word "cost" to refer to an item that still has service potential and is an asset. Use the word "expense" after the asset's service potential has been used. As a verb, to designate a past or current expenditure as a current expense.

expense account. An *account* to accumulate *expenses*; such accounts are closed at the end of the accounting period. A *temporary owners' equity* account. Also used to describe a listing of expenses by an employee submitted to the employer for reimbursement.

experience rating. A term used in insurance, particularly unemployment insurance, to denote changes from ordinary rates to reflect extraordinarily large or small amounts of claims over time by the insured.

expired cost. An *expense* or a *loss*.

Exposure Draft. ED. A preliminary statement of the *FASB* (or *APB* between 1962 and 1973) that shows the contents of a pronouncement the Board is considering making effective.

external reporting. Reporting to shareholders and the public, as opposed to internal reporting for management's benefit. See *financial accounting* and contrast with *managerial accounting*.

extraordinary item. A *material expense* or *revenue* item characterized both by its unusual nature and infrequency of occurrence that is shown along with its income tax effects separately from ordinary income and *income from discontinued operations* on the *income statement*. A *loss* from an earthquake would probably be classified as an extraordinary item. Gain (or loss) on retirement of *bonds* is treated as an extraordinary item under the terms of *SFAS No. 4*.

F

face amount (value). The nominal amount due at *maturity* from a *bond* or *note* not including contractual interest that may also be due on the same date. The corresponding amount of a stock certificate is best called the *par* or *stated value*, whichever is applicable.

factoring. The process of buying *notes* or *accounts receivable* at a *discount* from the holder to whom the debt is owed; from the holder's point of view, the selling of such notes or accounts. When a single note is involved, the process is called "discounting a note."

factory. Used synonymously with *manufacturing* as an adjective.

factory burden. Manufacturing *overhead*.

factory cost. *Manufacturing cost.*

factory expense. Manufacturing *overhead. Expense* is a poor term in this context because the item is a *product cost.*

factory overhead. Usually an item of *manufacturing cost* other than *direct labor* or *direct materials*.

fair-market price (value). Price (value) negotiated at *arm's length* between a willing buyer and a willing seller, each acting rationally in his or her own self-interest. May be estimated in the absence of a monetary transaction.

fair presentation (fairness). When the *auditor's report* says that the *financial statements* "present fairly . . . ," the auditor means that the accounting alternatives used by the entity are all in accordance with *GAAP*. In recent years, however, courts are finding that conformity with *generally accepted accounting principles* may be insufficient grounds for an opinion that the statements are fair. *SAS* No. 5 requires that the auditor judge the accounting principles used "appropriate in the circumstances" before attesting to fair presentation.

FASB. Financial Accounting Standards Board. An independent board responsible, since 1973, for establishing *generally accepted accounting principles*. Its official pronouncements are called "Statements of Financial Accounting Concepts" ("SFAC"), "Statements of Financial Accounting Standards" ("SFAS"), and "Interpretations of Financial Accounting Standards." See also *Discussion Memorandum* and *Technical Bulletin*.

FASB Interpretation. An official statement of the *FASB* interpreting the meaning of *Accounting Research Bulletins, APB Opinions,* and *Statements of Financial Accounting Standards*.

FASB Technical Bulletin. See *Technical Bulletin*.

favorable variance. An excess of actual *revenues* over expected revenues. An excess of *standard cost* over actual cost.

federal income tax. *Income tax* levied by the U.S. government on individuals and corporations.

Federal Unemployment Tax Act. See *FUTA*.

feedback. The process of informing employees about how their actual performance compares with the expected or desired level of performance in the hope that the information will reinforce desired behavior and reduce unproductive behavior.

FEI. *Financial Executives Institute.*

FICA. Federal Insurance Contributions Act. The law that sets "*Social Security*" *taxes* and benefits.

fiduciary. Someone responsible for the custody or administration of property belonging to another, such as an executor (of an estate), agent, receiver (in *bankruptcy*), or trustee (of a trust).

FIFO. First-in, first-out; the *inventory flow assumption* by which *ending inventory* cost is computed from most recent purchases and *cost of goods sold* is computed from oldest purchases including beginning inventory. See *LISH*. Contrast with *LIFO*.

finance. As a verb, to supply with *funds* through the *issue* of stocks, bonds, notes, or mortgages, or through the retention of earnings.

financial accounting. The accounting for *assets, equities, revenues,* and *expenses* of a business. Primarily concerned with the historical reporting of the *financial position* and operations of an *entity* to external users on a regular, periodic basis. Contrast with *managerial accounting*.

Financial Accounting Foundation. The independent foundation (committee) that raises funds to support the *FASB*.

Financial Accounting Standards Advisory Council. A committee giving advice to the *FASB* on matters of strategy and emerging issues.

Financial Accounting Standards Board. *FASB*.

Financial Executives Institute. An organization of financial executives, such as chief accountants, *controllers,* and treasurers, of large businesses.

financial expense. An *expense* incurred in raising or managing *funds*.

financial position (condition). Statement of the *assets* and *equities* of a firm displayed as a *balance sheet*.

financial ratio. See *ratio*.

financial statements. The *balance sheet, income statement, statement of retained earnings, statement of changes in financial position,* statement of changes in *owners' equity accounts,* and *notes* thereto.

financial structure. *Capital structure*.

financial reporting objectives. FASB *Statement of Financial Accounting Concepts No. 1* sets out the broad objectives of financial reporting that are intended to guide the development of specific *accounting standards*.

financing lease. *Capital lease*.

finished goods. Manufactured product ready for sale; a *current asset (inventory)* account.

firm. Informally, any business entity. (Strictly speaking, a firm is a *partnership*.)

first-in, first-out. See *FIFO*.

fiscal year. A period of 12 consecutive months chosen by a business as the *accounting period* for annual reports. May or may not be a *natural business year* or a calendar year.

FISH. An acronym, conceived by George H. Sorter, for *first-in, still-here*. FISH is the same cost flow assumption as *LIFO*. Many readers of accounting statements find it easier to think about inventory questions in terms of items still on hand. Think of LIFO in connection with *cost of goods sold* but of FISH in connection with *ending inventory*. See *LISH*.

fixed assets. *Plant assets*.

fixed assets turnover. *Sales* divided by average total *fixed assets*.

fixed benefit plan. A *defined-benefit (pension)* plan.

fixed budget. A plan that provides for specified amounts of *expenditures* and *receipts* that do not vary with activity levels. Sometimes called a "static budget." Contrast with *flexible budget*.

fixed cost (expense). An *expenditure* or *expense* that does not vary with volume of activity, at least in the short run. See *capacity costs,* which include *enabling costs* and *standby costs,* and *programmed costs* for various subdivisions of fixed costs. See *cost terminology*.

fixed liability. *Long-term* liability.

fixed manufacturing overhead applied. The portion of *fixed manufacturing overhead cost* allocated to units produced during a period.

flexible budget. *Budget* that projects receipts and expenditures as a function of activity levels. Contrast with *fixed budget*.

flexible budget allowance. With respect to manufacturing overhead, the total cost that should have been incurred at the level of activity actually experienced during the period.

float. *Checks* whose amounts have been *added* to the depositor's bank account, but not yet subtracted from the *drawer's* bank account.

flow. The change in the amount of an item over time. Contrast with *stock*.

flow assumption. When a *withdrawal* is made from *inventory,* the cost of the withdrawal must be computed by a flow assumption if *specific identification* of units is not used. The usual flow assumptions are *FIFO, LIFO,* and *weighted-average*.

flow of costs. *Costs* passing through various classifications within an *entity*. See the accompanying diagram for a summary of *product* and *period cost* flows.

flow-through method. Accounting for the *investment credit* to show all income statement benefits of the credit in the year of acquisition, rather than spreading them over the life of the asset acquired, called the "deferral method." The *APB* preferred the deferral-method in Opinion No. 2 (1962) but accepted the flow-through method in Opinion No. 4 (1964). The term is also used in connection with *depreciation* accounting where *straight-line method* is used for financial reporting and an *accelerated* method for tax reporting. Followers of the flow-through method would not recognize a *defered tax liability. APB Opinion* No. 11 prohibits the use of the flow-through approach in financial reporting although it has been used by some regulatory commissions.

FOB. Free on board some location (for example, FOB shipping point; FOB destination); the *invoice* price includes delivery at seller's expense to that location. Title to goods usually passes from seller to buyer at the FOB location.

footing. Adding a column of figures.

footnotes. More detailed information than that provided in the *income statement, balance sheet, statement of retained earnings,* and *statement of changes in financial position*; these are considered an integral part of the statements and are covered by the *auditor's report*. Sometimes called "notes."

forecast. An estimate or projection of costs or revenues or both.

foreign currency. For *financial statements* prepared in a given currency, any other currency.

foreign exchange gain or loss. Gain or loss from holding *net* foreign *monetary items* during a period when the *exchange rate* changes.

Flow of Costs (and Sales Revenue)

Assets, Goods and Services

[a] The credit in the entry to record these items is usually to a payable; for all others, the credit is usually to an asset, or to an asset contra account.

[b] When sales to customers are recorded, the Sales account is credited. The debit is usually to Cash or Accounts Receivable.

Form 10-K. See *10-K*.

forward exchange contract. An agreement to exchange at a specified future date currencies of different countries at a specified rate call the "forward rate".

franchise. A privilege granted or sold, such as to use a name or to sell products or services.

free on board. *FOB*.

freight-in. The *cost* of freight or shipping incurred in acquiring *inventory*, preferably treated as a part of the cost of *inventory*. Often shown temporarily in an *adjunct account* that is closed at the end of the period with other purchase accounts to the inventory account by the acquirer.

freight-out. The *cost* of freight or shipping incurred in selling *inventory*, treated by the seller as a selling *expense* in the period of sale.

full costing. *Absorption costing.* See *reserve recognition accounting* for another definition in the context of accounting for natural resources.

full disclosure. The reporting policy requiring that all significant or *material* information is to be presented in the financial statements. See *fair presentation*.

fully diluted earnings per share. Smallest *earnings per share* figure on *common stock* that can be obtained by computing an earnings per share for all possible combinations of assumed *exercise* or *conversion* of *potentially dilutive securities*. Must be reported on the *income statement* if it is less than 97 percent of earnings available to common shareholders divided by the average number of common shares outstanding during the period.

fully vested. Said of a *pension plan* when an employee (or his or her estate) has rights to all the benefits purchased with the employer's contributions to the plan even if the employee is not employed by this employer at the time of death or retirement.

function. In governmental accounting, said of a group of related activities for accomplishing a service or regulatory program for which the governmental unit is responsible. In mathematics, a rule for associating a number, called the dependent variable, with another number or numbers, called independent variable(s).

functional classification. *Income statement* reporting form in which *expenses* are reported by functions, that is, cost of goods sold, administrative expenses, financing expenses, selling expenses; contrast with *natural classification*.

fund. An *asset* or group of assets set aside for a specific purpose. See also *fund accounting*.

fund accounting. The accounting for resources, obligations, and *capital* balances, usually of a not-for-profit or governmental *entity*, which have been segregated into *accounts* representing logical groupings based on legal, donor, or administrative restrictions or requirements. The groupings are described as "funds." The accounts of each fund are *self-balancing* and from them a *balance sheet* and an operating statement for each fund can be prepared. See *fund* and *fund balance*.

fund balance. In governmental accounting, the excess of assets of a *fund* over its liabilities and reserves; the not-for-profit equivalent of *owners' equity*.

funded. Said of a *pension plan* or other obligation when *funds* have been set aside for meeting the obligation when it becomes due. The federal law for pension plans requires that all *normal costs* be funded as recognized. In addition, *actuarial actuarial liability* of pension plans must be funded over 30 or over 40 years, depending on the circumstances.

funding. Replacing *short-term* liabilities with *long-term* debt.

funds. Generally *working capital*; current assets less current liabilities. Sometimes used to refer to *cash* or to cash and *marketable securities*.

funds provided by operations. An important subtotal in the *statement of changes in financial position*. This amount is the total of revenues producing *funds* less *expenses* requiring funds. Often, the amount is shown as *net income* plus expenses not requiring funds (such as depreciation charges) minus revenues not producing funds (such as revenues recognized under the *equity method* of accounting for a long-term investment). The statement of changes in financial position maintains the same distinctions between *continuing operations*, *discontinued operations*, and *income* or *loss* from *extraordinary items* as does the *income statement*.

funds statement. An informal name often used for the *statement of changes in financial position*.

funny money. Said of securities such as *convertible preferred stock*, *convertible bonds*, *options*, and *warrants* that have aspects of *common stock* equity but that did not reduce reported *earnings per share* prior to the issuance of *APB Opinions* No. 9 in 1967 and No. 15 in 1969.

FUTA. Federal Unemployment Tax Act which provides for taxes to be collected at the federal level, to help subsidize the individual states' administration of their unemployment compensation programs.

future value. Value at a specified future date of a sum increased at a specified *interest rate*.

G

GAAP. *Generally accepted accounting principles.* A plural noun.

gain. Increase in *owners' equity* caused by a transaction not part of a firm's typical, day-to-day operations and not part of owners' *investment* or *withdrawals*. The term "gain" (or "*loss*") is distinguished in two separate ways from related terms. First, gains (and losses) are generally used for nonoperating, incidental, peripheral, or nonroutine transactions: gain on sale of land in contrast to *gross margin* on *sale* of *inventory*. Second, gains and losses are *net* concepts, not gross concepts: gain or loss results from subtracting some measure of *cost* from the measure of inflow. *Revenues* and *expenses*, on the other hand, are gross concepts; their difference is a net concept. Gain is nonroutine and net, *profit* or *margin* is routine and net; revenue is routine and gross. Loss is net but can be either routine ("loss on sale of inventory") or not ("loss on disposal of segment of business").

gain contingency. See *contingency*.

general debt. Debt of a governmental unit legally payable from general revenues and backed by the full faith and credit of the governmental unit.

general expenses. *Operating expenses* other than those specifically assigned to cost of goods sold, selling, and administration.

general fixed asset (group of accounts). Accounts showing those long-term assets of a governmental unit not accounted for in *enterprise, trust,* or intragovernmental service funds.

general fund. Assets and liabilities of a nonprofit entity not specifically earmarked for other purposes; the primary operating fund of a governmental unit.

general journal. The formal record where transactions, or summaries of similar transactions, are recorded in *journal entry* form as they occur. Use of the adjective "general" usually implies only two columns for cash amounts or that there are also various *special journals,* such as a *check register* or *sales journal,* in use.

general ledger. The name for the formal *ledger* containing all of the financial statement accounts. It has equal debits and credits as evidenced by the *trial balance.* Some of the accounts in the general ledger may be *controlling accounts,* supported by details contained in *subsidiary ledgers.*

general partner. Member of *partnership* personally liable for all debts of the partnership; contrast with *limited partner.*

general price index. A measure of the aggregate prices of a wide range of goods and services in the economy at one time relative to the prices during a base period. See *consumer price index* and *GNP Implicit Price Deflator.* Contrast with *specific price index.*

general price level adjusted statements. See *constant dollar accounting.*

general price level changes. Changes in the aggregate prices of a wide range of goods and services in the economy. These price changes are measured using a *general price index.* Contrast with *specific price changes.*

general purchasing power. The command of the dollar over a wide range of goods and services in the economy. The general purchasing power of the dollar is inversely related to changes in a general price index. See *general price index.*

general purchasing power accounting. See *constant dollar accounting.*

generally accepted accounting principles. GAAP. As previously defined by the *APB* and now by the *FASB,* the conventions, rules, and procedures necessary to define accepted accounting practice at a particular time; includes both broad guidelines and relatively detailed practices and procedures.

generally accepted auditing standards. The standards, as opposed to particular procedures, promulgated by the *AICPA* (in *Statements on Auditing Standards*) that concern "the auditor's professional quantities" and "the judgment exercised by him in the performance of his examination and in his report." Currently, there are ten such standards: three general ones (concerned with proficiency, independence, and degree of care to be exercised), three standards of field work, and four standards of reporting. The first standard of reporting requires that the *auditor's report* state whether or not the *financial statements* are prepared in accordance with *generally accepted accounting principles.* Thus the typical auditor's report says that the examination was conducted in accordance with generally accepted auditing standards and that the statements are prepared in accordance with generally accepted accounting principles. See *auditor's report.*

GNP Implicit Price Deflator (Index). A *price index* is-

sued quarterly by the Office of Business Economics of the U.S. Department of Commerce. This index attempts to trace the price level of all *goods and services* comprising the *gross national product.* Contrast with *consumer price index.*

going concern assumption. For accounting purposes a business is assumed to remain in operation long enough for all its current plans to be carried out. This assumption is part of the justification for the *acquisition cost* basis, rather than a *liquidation* or *exit value* basis of accounting.

going public. Said of a business when its *shares* become widely traded, rather than being closely held by relatively few shareholders. Issuing shares to the general investing public.

goods. Items of merchandise, supplies, raw materials, or finished goods. Sometimes the meaning of "goods" is extended to include all *tangible* items, as in the phrase "goods and services."

goods available for sale. The sum of *beginning inventory* plus all acquisitions of merchandise or finished goods during an *accounting period.*

goods in process. *Work in process.*

goodwill. The excess of cost of an acquired firm (or operating unit) over the current of *fair-market value* of the separately identifiable *net assets* of the acquired unit. Before goodwill is recognized, all identifiable assets, whether or not on the books of the acquired unit, must be given a *fair market value.* For example, a firm has developed a *patent* which is not recognized on its books because of *SFAS No. 2.* If another company acquires the firm, the acquirer will recognize the patent at an amount equal to its estimated fair market value. Informally the term is used to indicate the value of good customer relations, high employee morale, a well-respected business name, and so on, that are expected to result in greater than that normal earning power.

goodwill method. A method of accounting for the *admission* of a new partner to a *partnership* when the new partner is to be credited with a portion of capital different from the value of the *tangible* assets contributed as a fraction of tangible assets on the partnership. See *bonus method* for a description and contrast.

GPL. General price level; usually used as an adjective modifying the word "accounting" to mean *constant dollar accounting.*

GPLA. General price level adjusted accounting; *constant dollar accounting.*

GPP. General purchasing power; usually used as an adjective modifying the word "accounting" to mean *constant dollar accounting.*

graded vesting. Said of a *pension plan* where not all employee benefits are currently *vested.* By law, the benefits must become vested according to one of several formulas as time passes.

grandfather clause. An exemption in new accounting *pronouncements* exempting transactions that occurred before a given date from the new accounting treatment. For example, *APB Opinion* No. 17, adopted in 1970, exempted *goodwill* acquired before 1970 from required *amortization.* The term "grandfather" appears in the title to *SFAS No. 10.*

gross. Not adjusted or reduced by deductions or subtractions. Contrast with *net.*

gross margin. *Net sales* minus *cost of goods sold.*

gross margin percent. $100 \times (1 - cost\ of\ goods\ sold/net\ sales) = 100 \times (gross\ margin/net\ sales)$.

gross national product. GNP. The market value within a nation for a year of all goods and services produced as measured by final sales of goods and services to individuals, corporations, and governments plus the excess of exports over imports.

gross price method (of recording purchase or sales discounts). The *purchase* (or *sale*) is recorded at its *invoice price*, not deducting the amounts of *discounts* available. Discounts taken are recorded in a *contra* account to purchases (or sales). Information on discounts lapsed is not made available, and for this reason, most firms prefer the *net-price method* of recording purchase discounts.

gross profit. *Gross margin.*

gross profit method. A method of estimating *ending inventory* amounts. *Cost of goods sold* is measured as some fraction of sales; the *inventory equation* is then used to value *ending inventory.*

gross profit ratio. *Gross margin* divided by *net sales.*

gross sales. All *sales* at *invoice* prices, not reduced by *discounts, allowances, returns*, or other adjustments.

group depreciation. A method of calculating *depreciation* charges where similar assets are combined, rather than depreciated separately. No gain or loss is recognized on retirement of items from the group until the last item in the group is sold or retired. See *composite life method.*

guarantee. A promise to answer for payment of debt or performance of some obligation if the person liable for the debt or obligation fails to perform. A guarantee is *contingency* of the *entity* making the promise. Often, the words "guarantee" and "warranty" are used to mean the same thing. In precise usage, however, "guarantee" means promise to fulfill the promise of some person to perform a contractual obligation such as to pay a sum of money, whereas "warranty" is most often used to refer to promises about pieces of machinery or other products. See *warranty.*

H

hidden reserve. The term refers to an amount by which *owners' equity* has been understated, perhaps deliberately. The understatement arises from an undervaluation of *assets* or overvaluation of *liabilities.* By undervaluing assets on this period's *balance sheet, net income* in some future period can be made to look artificially high by disposing of the asset: actual *revenues* less artificially low cost of assets sold yields artificially high net income. There is no *account* that has this title.

historical cost. *Acquisition cost; original cost*; a *sunk cost.*

historical-cost/constant-dollar accounting. Accounting based on *historical cost* valuations measured in *constant dollars.* *Nonmonetary items* are restated to reflect changes in the *general purchasing power* of the dollar since the time the specific *assets* were acquired or *liabilities* were incurred. A *gain* or *loss* is recognized on *monetary items* as they are held over time periods when the general purchasing power of the dollar changes.

historical summary. A part of the *annual report* to shareholders that shows important items, such as *net income, revenues, expenses, asset* and *equity* totals, *earnings per share*, and the like, for five or ten periods including the current one. Usually not as much detail is shown in the historical summary as in *comparative statements*, which typically report as much detail for the two preceding years as for the current year. Annual reports may contain both comparative statements and a historical summary.

holding company. A company that confines its activities to owning *stock* in, and supervising management of, other companies. A holding company usually owns a controlling interest in, that is more than 50 percent of the voting stock of, the companies whose stock it holds. Contrast with *mutual fund.* See *conglomerate.* In British usage, the term refers to any company with controlling interest in another company.

holding gain or loss. Difference between end-of-period price and beginning-of-period price of an asset held during the period. Realized holding gains and losses are not ordinarily separately reported in financial statements. Unrealized gains are not usually reflected in income at all. Some unrealized losses, such as on inventory or marketable securities, are reflected in income or *owners' equity* as the losses occur; see *lower of cost or market.* See *inventory profit* for further refinement, including *gains* on *assets* sold during the period.

holding gain or loss net of inflation. Increase or decrease in the *current cost* of an asset while it is held measured in units of *constant dollars.*

horizontal analysis. *Time series analysis.*

human resource accounting. A term used to describe a variety of proposals that seek to report and emphasize the importance of human resources—knowledgeable, trained, and loyal employees—in a company's earning process and total assets.

hurdle rate. Required rate of return in a *discounted cash flow* analysis.

hybrid security. *Security*, such as a *convertible bond*, containing elements of both *debt* and *owners' equity.*

hypothecation. The *pledging* of property, without transfer of title or possession, to secure a loan.

I

I. *Identity matrix.*

IAA. *Interamerican Accounting Association.*

ideal standard costs. *Standard costs* set equal to those that would be incurred under the best possible conditions.

identity matrix. A square *matrix* with ones on the main diagonal and zeros elsewhere; a matrix I such that for any other matrix A, $IA = AI = A$. The matrix equivalent to the number one.

IIA. *Institute of Internal Auditors.*

IMA. Institute of Management Accounting. See *CMA* and *National Association of Accountants.*

imprest fund. *Petty cash fund.*

improvement. An *expenditure* to extend the useful life of an *asset* or to improve its performance (rate of output, cost) over that of the original asset. Such expenditures are *capitalized* as part of the asset's cost. Sometimes called "betterment." Contrast with *maintenance* and *repair.*

imputed cost. A cost that does not appear in accounting

records, such as the *interest* that could be earned on cash spent to acquire inventories rather than, say, government bonds. Or, consider a firm that owns the buildings it occupies. This firm has an imputed cost for rent in an amount equal to what it would have to pay to use similar buildings owned by another.

imputed interest. See *interest, imputed*.

income. *Excess of revenues* and *gains* over *expenses* and *losses* for a period; *net income*. Sometimes used with an appropriate modifier to refer to the various intermediate amounts shown in a *multiple-step income statement*. Sometimes used to refer to revenues, as in "rental income." See *comprehensive income*.

income accounts. *Revenue* and *expense accounts*.

income determination. See *determine*.

income distribution account. *Temporary account* sometimes debited when *dividends* are declared; closed to *retained earnings*.

income from continuing operations. As defined by *APB Opinion* No. 30, all *revenues* less all *expenses* except for the following: results of operations (including income tax effects) that have been or will be discontinued; *gains* or *losses*, including income tax effects, on disposal of segments of the business; gains or losses, including income tax effects, from *extraordinary items*; and the cumulative effect of *accounting changes*.

income from discontinued operations. *Income*, net of tax effects, from parts of the business that have been discontinued during the period or are to be discontinued in the near future. Such items are reported on separate line of the *income statement* after *income from continuing operations* but before *extraordinary items*.

income (revenue) bond. See *special revenue debt*.

income statement. The statement of *revenues, expenses, gains*, and *losses* for the period ending with *net income* for the period. The *earnings per share* amount is usually shown on the income statement; the *reconciliation* of beginning and ending balances of *retained earnings* may also be shown in a combined statement of income and retained earnings. See *income from continuing operations, income from discontinued operations, extraordinary items, multiple-step, single-step*.

income summary. An *account* used in problem solving that serves as a surrogate for the *income statement*. All *revenues* are closed to the Income Summary as *credits* and all *expenses*, as *debits*. The *balance* in the account, after all other *closing entries* are made, is then closed to the retained earnings or other *owners' equity* account and represents *net income* for the period.

income tax. An annual tax levied by the federal and other governments on the income of an entity.

income tax allocation. See *deferred tax liability* and *tax allocation: intrastatement*.

incremental. An adjective used to describe the change in *cost, expense, investment, cash flow, revenue, profit*, and the like if one or more units are produced or sold or if an activity is undertaken.

indenture. See *bond indenture*.

independence. The mental attitude required of the *CPA* in performing the *attest* function. It implies impartiality and that the members of the auditing CPA firm own no stock in the corporation being audited.

independent accountant. The *CPA* who performs the *attest* function for a firm.

indeterminate-term liability. A *liability* lacking the criterion of being due at a definite time. This term is our own coinage to encompass the *deferred income tax liability* and *minority interest*.

indexation. An attempt by lawmakers or parties to a contract to cope with the effects of *inflation*. Amounts fixed in law or contracts are "indexed" when these amounts change as a given measure of price changes. For example, a so-called escalator clause (*COLA*) in a labor contract might provide that hourly wages will be increased as the *consumer price index* increases. Many economists have suggested the indexation of numbers fixed in the *income tax* laws. If, for example, the personal *exemption* is $1,000 at the start of the period, prices rise by 10 percent during the period, and the personal exemption is indexed, then the personal exemption would automatically rise to $1,100 (= $1,000 + .10 × $1,000) at the end of the period.

indirect cost pool. Any grouping of individual costs that are not identified with a *cost objective*.

indirect costs. Costs of production not easily associated with the production of specific goods and services; *overhead costs*. May be *allocated* on some arbitrary basis to specific products or departments.

indirect labor (material) cost. An *indirect cost* for labor (material) such as for supervisors (supplies).

individual proprietorship. *Sole proprietorship*.

Industry Audit Guide. A series of publications by the *AICPA* providing specific *accounting* and *auditing principles* for specialized situations. Audit guides have been issued covering government contractors, state and local government units, investment companies, finance companies, brokers and dealers in securities, and many others.

inflation. A time of generally rising prices.

inflation accounting. Strictly speaking, *constant dollar accounting*. Some writers use the term, incorrectly, to mean *current cost accounting*.

information system. A system, sometimes formal and sometimes informal, for collecting, processing, and communicating data that are useful for the managerial functions of decision making, planning, and control, and for financial reporting under the *attest* requirement.

insolvent. Unable to pay debts when due. Said of a company even though *assets* exceed *liabilities*.

installment. Partial payment of a debt or collection of a receivable, usually according to a contract.

installment contracts receivable. The name used for *accounts receivable* when the *installment method* of recognizing revenue is used. Its *contra, unrealized gross margin*, is shown on the balance sheet as a subtraction from the amount receivable.

installment (sales) method. Recognizing *revenue* and *expense* (or *gross margin*) from a sales transaction in proportion to the fraction of the selling price collected during a period. Allowed by the *IRS* for income tax reporting, but acceptable in *GAAP* (*APB Opinion* No. 10) only when cash collections are reasonably uncertain. See *realized* (and *unrealized) gross margin*.

installment sales. Sales on account where the buyer promises to pay in several separate payments, called *installments*. Sometimes are, but need not be, accounted for on the *installment method*. If installment sales are accounted for with the sales *basis of revenue recognition* for financial reporting but with the installment method for income tax returns, then a *deferred income tax liability* arises.

Institute of Internal Auditors. IIA. The national association of accountants who are engaged in internal auditing and are employed by business firms. Administers a comprehensive professional examination; those who pass qualify to be designated CIA, certified internal auditor.

Institute of Management Accounting. See *CMA*.

insurance. A contract for reimbursement of specific losses; purchased with insurance premiums. Self-insurance is not insurance but merely the willingness to assume risk of incurring losses while saving the premium.

intangible asset. A nonphysical, *noncurrent* right that gives a firm an exclusive or preferred position in the marketplace. Examples are a *copyright, patent, trademark, goodwill, organization costs, capitalized* advertising cost, computer programs, licenses for any of the preceding, government licenses (e.g., broadcasting or the right to sell liquor), *leases*, franchises, mailing lists, exploration permits, import and export permits, construction permits, and marketing quotas.

Interamerican Accounting Association. An organization, headquartered in Mexico City, devoted to facilitating interaction between accounting practitioners in Central America, North America, and South America.

intercompany elimination. See *eliminations*.

intercompany profit. If one *affiliated company* sells to another, and the goods remain in the second company's *inventory* at the end of the period, then the first company's *profit* has not been realized by a sale to an outsider. That profit is called "intercompany profit" and is eliminated from net *income* in *consolidated income statements* or when the *equity method* is used.

interest. The charge or cost for using money; expressed as a rate per period, usually one year, called the interest rate. See *effective interest rate* and *nominal interest rate*.

interest, imputed. If a borrower merely promises to pay a single amount, sometime later than the present, then the present value (computed at a *fair market* interest rate, called the "imputed interest rate") of the promise is less than the *face amount* to be paid at *maturity*. The difference between the face amount and the present value of a promise is called imputed interest. See also *imputed cost*.

interest factor. One plus the *interest* rate.

interest method. See *effective interest method*.

interest rate. See *interest*.

interfund accounts. In governmental accounting, the accounts that show transactions between funds, especially interfund receivables and payables.

interim statements. Statements issued for periods less than the regular, annual *accounting period*. Most corporations are required to issue interim statements on a quarterly

basis. The basic issue in preparing interim reports is whether their purpose is to report on the interim period (1) as a self-contained accounting period, or (2) as an integral part of the year of which they are a part so that forecasts of annual performance can be made. *APB Opinion* No. 28 and the *SEC* require that interim reports be constructed largely to satisfy the second purpose.

internal audit. An *audit* conducted by employees to ascertain whether or not *internal control* procedures are working, as opposed to an external audit conducted by a *CPA*.

internal control. See *control system*.

internal rate of return. The discount rate that equates the net *present value* of a stream of cash outflows and inflows to zero.

internal reporting. Reporting for management's use in planning and control; contrast with *external reporting* for financial statement users.

Internal Revenue Service. IRS. Agency of the U.S. Treasury Department responsible for administering the Internal Revenue Code and collecting income, and certain other, taxes.

International Accounting Standards Committee. An organization that promotes the establishment of international accounting standards.

interperiod tax allocation. See *deferred income tax liability*.

interpolation. The estimation of an unknown number intermediate between two (or more) known numbers.

Interpretations of Statements of Financial Accounting Standards. See *FASB Interpretations*.

in the black (red). Operating at a profit (loss).

intrastatement tax allocation. See *tax allocation: intrastatement*.

inventoriable costs. *Costs* incurred that are added to the cost of manufactured products. *Product costs (assets)* as opposed to *period expenses*.

inventory. As a noun, the *balance* in an asset *account* such as raw materials, supplies, work in process, and finished goods. As a verb, to calculate the *cost* of goods on hand at a given time or to physically count items on hand.

inventory equation. *Beginning inventory + net additions − withdrawals = ending inventory*. Ordinarily, additions are net purchases and withdrawals are *cost of goods sold*. Notice that ending inventory, to be shown on the balance sheet, and cost of goods sold, to be shown on the income statement, are not independent of each other. The larger is one, the smaller must be the other. In valuing inventories, beginning inventory and net purchases are usually known. In some inventory methods (for example, some applications of the *retail inventory method*), costs of goods sold is measured and the equation is used to find the cost of ending inventory. In most methods, cost of ending inventory is measured and the equation is used to find the cost of goods sold (withdrawals). In *current cost* (in contrast to *historical cost*) accounting *additions* (in the equation) include holding gains, whether realized or not. Thus the current cost inventory equation is: Beginning Inventory (at Current Cost) + Purchases (where Current Cost is Historical Cost) + Holding Gains (whether Realized or Not) − Ending Inventory (at Current Cost) = Cost of Goods Sold (Current Cost).

inventory holding gains. See *inventory profit*.

inventory layer. See LIFO *inventory layer*.

inventory profit. This term has several possible meanings. Consider the data in the accompanying illustration. The *historical cost* data are derived in the conventional manner; the firm uses a *FIFO cost flow assumption*. The *current cost* data are assumed, but are of the kind that the *FASB* requires in *SFAS No. 33*.

The term *income from continuing operations* refers to revenues less expenses based on current, rather than historical, costs. To that subtotal add realized holding gains to arrive at realized (conventional) income. To that, add unrealized holding gains to arrive at *economic income*.

The term "inventory profit" often refers (for example in some *SEC* releases) to the realized holding gain, $110 in the illustration. The amount of inventory profit will usually be material when FIFO is used and prices are rising.

Others, including us, prefer to use the term "inventory profit" to refer to the total *holding gain*, $300 (= $110 + $190, both realized and unrealized), but this appears to be a lost cause.

In periods of rising prices and increasing inventories, the realized holding gains under a FIFO cost-flow assumption will be substantially larger than under LIFO. In the illustration, for example, assume under LIFO that the historical cost of goods sold is $4,800, that historical LIFO cost of beginning inventory is $600, and that historical LIFO cost of ending inventory is $800. Then income from continuing operations, based on current costs, remains $350 (= $5,200 − $4,850), realized holding gains are $50 (= $4,850 − $4,800), realized income is $400 (= $350 + $50), the unrealized holding gain for the year is $250 (= ($1,550 − $800)

− ($1,100 − $600)), and economic income is $650 (= $350 + $50 + $250). Because the only real effect of the cost flow assumption is to split the total holding gain into realized and unrealized portions, economic income is the same, independent of the cost flow assumption. The total of holding gains is $300 in the illustration. The choice of cost-flow assumption merely determines the portion reported as realized.

inventory turnover. Number of times the average *inventory* has been sold during a period; *cost of goods sold* for a period divided by average inventory for the period. See *ratio*.

invested capital. *Contributed capital.*

investee. A company whose *stock* is owned by another.

investment. An *expenditure* to acquire property or other assets in order to produce *revenue*; the *asset* so acquired; hence a *current* expenditure made in anticipation of future income. Said of *securities* of other companies held for the long term and shown in a separate section of the *balance sheet*; in this context, contrast with *marketable securities*.

investment credit. A reduction in income tax liability granted by the federal government to firms that buy new equipment. This item is a credit, in that it is deducted from the tax bill, not from pretax income. The tax credit has been a given percentage of the purchase price of certain assets purchased. The actual rules and rates have changed over the years. See *flow-through method* and *carryforward*.

investment tax credit. *Investment credit.*

invoice. A document showing the details of a sale or purchase transaction.

IRR. *Internal rate of return.*

IRS. *Internal Revenue Service.*

Inventory Profit Illustration

Assumed Data		(Historical) Acquisition Cost Assuming FIFO	Current Cost
Inventory, 1/1/82		$ 900	$1,100
Inventory, 12/31/82		1,160	1,550
Cost of Goods Sold for 1982		4,740	4,850
Sales for 1982	$5,200		
INCOME STATEMENT FOR 1982			
Sales		$5,200	$5,200
Cost of Goods Sold		4,740	4,850
(1) Income from Continuing Operations			$ 350
Realized Holding Gains			110[a]
(2) Realized Income = Conventional Net Income (under FIFO)		$ 460	$ 460
Unrealized Holding Gain			190[b]
(3) Economic income			$ 650

[a]Realized holding gain during a period is current cost of goods sold less historical cost of goods sold; for 1982 the realized holding gain under FIFO is $110 = $4,850 − $4,740. Some refer to this as "inventory profit."
[b]The total unrealized holding gain at any time is current cost of inventory on hand at that time less historical cost of that inventory. The unrealized holding gain during a period is unrealized holding gain at the end of the period less the unrealized holding gain at the beginning of the period. Unrealized holding gain prior to 1982 is $200 = $1,100 − $900. Unrealized holding gain during 1982 = ($1,550 − $1,160) − ($1,100 − $900) = $390 − $200 = $190.

issue. When a corporation exchanges its stock (or bonds) for cash or other assets, the corporation is said to issue, not sell, that stock (or bonds). Also used in the context of withdrawing supplies or materials from inventory for use in operations and drawing of a *check*.

issued shares. Those shares of *authorized capital stock* of a *corporation* that have been distributed to the shareholders. See *issue*. Shares of *treasury stock* are legally issued but are not considered to be *outstanding* for the purpose of voting, *dividend declarations* and *earnings per share* calculations.

J

job cost sheet. A schedule showing actual or budgeted inputs for a special order.

job development credit. The name used for the *investment credit* in the 1971 tax law on this subject.

job-order costing. Accumulation of *costs* for a particular identifiable batch of product, known as a job, as it moves through production.

joint cost. Cost of simultaneously producing or otherwise acquiring two or more products, called joint products, that must, by the nature of the process, be produced or acquired together, such as the cost of beef and hides of cattle. Generally, the joint costs of production are allocated to the individual products in proportion to their respective sales value at the *splitoff* point. Other examples include central *corporate expenses*, *overhead* of a department when several products are manufactured, and *basket purchases*. See *common cost*. See *sterilized allocation*.

joint product. One of two or more outputs with significant value produced by a process that must be produced or acquired simultaneously. See *by-product* and *joint cost*.

journal. The place where transactions are recorded as they occur. The book of original entry.

journal entry. A recording in a *journal*, of equal *debits* and *credits*, with an explanation of the *transaction*, if necessary.

journalize. To make an entry in a *journal*.

Journal of Accountancy. A monthly publication of the *AICPA*.

Journal of Accounting Research. Scholarly journal containing articles on theoretical and empirical aspects of accounting. Published three times a year by the Graduate School of Business of the University of Chicago.

journal voucher. A *voucher* documenting (and sometimes authorizing) a transaction, leading to an entry in the *journal*.

K

kiting. This term means slightly different things in banking and auditing contexts. In both, however, it refers to the wrongful practice of taking advantage of the *float*, the time that elapses between the deposit of a *check* in one bank and its collection at another. In the banking context, an individual deposits in Bank A a check written on Bank B. He (or she) then writes checks against the deposit created in Bank A. Several days later, he deposits in Bank B a check written on Bank A, to cover the original check written on Bank B. Still later, he deposits in Bank A a check written on Bank B. The process of covering the deposit in Bank A with a check written on Bank B and vice versa is continued until an actual deposit of cash can be arranged. In the auditing context, kiting refers to a form of *window dressing* where the amount of the account Cash in Bank is made to appear larger than it actually is by depositing in Bank A a check written on Bank B without recording the check written on Bank B in the *check register* until after the close of the *accounting period*.

know-how. Technical or business information of the type defined under *trade secret*, but that is not maintained as a secret. The rules of accounting for this asset are the same as for other *intangibles*.

L

labor variances. The *price* (or *rate*) and *quantity* (or *usage*) *variances* for *direct labor* inputs in a *standard cost system*.

land. An *asset shown at acquisition cost* plus the *cost* of any nondepreciable *improvements*. In accounting, implies use as a plant or office site, rather than as a *natural resource*, such as timberland or farm land.

lapping (accounts receivable). The theft, by an employee, of cash sent in by a customer to discharge the latter's *payable*. The theft from the first customer is concealed by using cash received from a second customer. The theft from the second customer is concealed by using the cash received from a third customer, and so on. The process is continued until the thief returns the funds or can make the theft permanent by creating a fictitious *expense* or receivable write off, or until the fraud is discovered.

lapse. To expire; said of, for example, an insurance policy or discounts made available for prompt payment that are not taken.

last-in, first-out. See *LIFO*.

layer. See *LIFO inventory layer*.

lead time. The time that elapses between placing an order and receipt of the *goods or services* ordered.

lease. A contract calling for the lessee (user) to pay the lessor (owner) for the use of an asset. A cancelable lease is one the lessee can cancel at any time. A noncancelable lease requires payments from the lessee for the life of the lease and usually has many of the economic characteristics of *debt financing*. Most long-term noncancelable leases meet the usual criteria to be classified as a *liability* but some leases entered into before 1977 need not be shown as a liability. *SFAS No. 13* and the *SEC* require disclosure in notes to the financial statements of the commitments for long-term noncancelable leases. See *capital lease* and *operating lease*.

leasehold. The *asset* representing the right of the *lessee* to use leased property. See *lease* and *leasehold improvement*.

leasehold improvement. An *improvement* to leased property. Should be *amortized* over *service life* or the life of the lease, whichever is shorter.

least and latest rule. Pay the least amount of taxes as late as possible within the law to minimize the *present value* of tax payments for a given set of operations.

ledger. A book of accounts. See *general ledger* and *subsidiary ledger*; contrast with *journal*. Book of final entry.

legal capital. The amount of *contributed capital* that, according to state law, must remain permanently in the firm as protection for creditors.

legal entity. See *entity*.

lender. See *loan*.

lessee. See *lease*.

lessor. See *lease*.

letter stock. Privately placed *common shares*; so called because the *SEC* requires the purchaser to sign a letter of intent not to resell the shares.

leverage. "Operating leverage" refers to the tendency of *net income* to rise at a faster rate than sales when there are *fixed costs*. A doubling of sales, for example, usually implies a more than doubling of net income. "Financial leverage" (or "capital leverage") refers to the increased rate of return on owners' equity (see *ratio*) when an investment earns a return larger than the *interest rate* paid for *debt* financing. Because the interest charges on debt are usually fixed, any *incremental* income benefits owners and none benefits debtors. When "leverage" is used without a qualifying adjective, it usually refers to financial leverage and means the use of *long-term* debt in securing *funds* for the *entity*.

leveraged lease. A special form of lease involving three parties-a *lender*, a *lessor*, and a *lessee*. The lender, such as a bank or insurance company, lends a portion, say 80 percent, of the cash required for acquiring the *asset*. The lessor puts up the remainder, 20 percent, of the cash required. The lessor acquires the asset with the cash, using the asset as security for the loan and leases it to the lessee on a *noncancelable* basis. The lessee makes periodic lease payments to the lessor, who in turn makes payments on the loan to the lender. Typically, the lessor has no obligation for the debt to the lender other than transferring a portion of the receipts from the lessee. If the lessee should default on required lease payments, then the lender can repossess the leased asset. The lessor is usually entitled to deductions for tax purposes for depreciation on the asset, for interest expense on the loan from the lender, and for any investment credit. The lease is leveraged in the sense that the lessor, who enjoys most of the risks and rewards of ownership, usually borrows most of the funds needed to acquire the asset. *See leverage*.

liability. A probable future sacrifice of economic benefits arising from present obligations of a particular *entity* to *transfer assets* or to provide services to other entities in the future as a result of past *transactions* or events. *SFAC No. 3* says that "probable" refers to that which can reasonably be expected or believed but is neither certain nor proved. A liability has three essential characteristics: (1) transfer of assets or services at a specified or determinable date, (2) the entity has little or no discretion to avoid the transfer, and (3) the event causing the obligation has already happened.

lien. The right of person A to satisfy a claim against person B by holding B's property as security or by seizing B's property.

life annuity. A *contingent annuity* in which payments cease at death of a specified person(s), usually the *annuitant(s)*.

LIFO. An *inventory* flow assumption where the *cost of goods sold* is the cost of the most recently acquired units and the *ending inventory cost* is computed from costs of the oldest units; contrast with *FIFO*. In periods of rising prices and increasing inventories, LIFO leads to higher reported expenses and therefore lower reported income and lower balance sheet inventories than does FIFO. See also *FISH* and *inventory profit*.

LIFO conformity rule. The *IRS* requires that companies which use a *LIFO cost flow assumption for income taxes* also use LIFO in computing *income* reported in *financial statements* and forbids disclosure of *pro forma* results from using any other cost flow assumption. During 1981, this rule was challenged by a federal court decision in the Insilco case.

LIFO, dollar value method. See *dollar value LIFO method*.

LIFO inventory layer. The *ending inventory* for a period is likely to be larger than the *beginning inventory*. Under a *LIFO cost flow assumption*, this increase in physical quantities is given a value computed by the prices of the earliest purchases during the year. The LIFO inventory then consists of layers, sometimes called "slices," which typically consist of relatively small amounts of physical quantities from each of the past several years. Each layer carries the prices from near the beginning of the period when it was acquired. The earliest layers will typically (in periods of rising prices) have prices very much less than current prices. If inventory quantities should decline in a subsequent period, the latest layers enter cost of goods sold first.

LIFO reserve. *Unrealized holding gain* in *ending inventory*: current or *FIFO historical* cost of ending inventory less LIFO *historical cost*. See *reserve*.

limited liability. Shareholders of corporations are not personally liable for debts of the company.

limited partner. Member of a *partnership* not personally liable for debts of the partnership; every partnership must have at least one *general partner* who is fully liable.

line of business reporting. See *segment reporting*.

line of credit. An agreement with the bank or set of banks for short-term borrowings on demand.

liquid. Said of a business with a substantial amount (the amount is unspecified) of *working capital*, especially *quick assets*.

liquid assets. *Cash, current marketable securities*, and, sometimes, *current receivables*.

liquidating dividend. *Dividend* declared in the winding up of a business to distribute the assets of the company to the shareholders. Usually treated by recipient as a return of *investment*, not as *revenue*.

liquidation. Payment of a debt. Sale of assets in closing down a business or a segment thereof.

liquidation value per share. The amount each *share* of stock will receive if the corporation is dissolved. For *preferred stock* with a *liquidation preference*, a stated amount per share.

liquidity. Refers to the availability of *cash*, or near cash resources, for meeting a firm's obligations.

LISH. An acronym, conceived by George H. Sorter, for *last-in, still here*. LISH is the same cost flow assumption as *FIFO*. Many readers of accounting statements find it easier to think about inventory questions in terms of items still on hand. Think of FIFO in connection with *cost of goods sold* but of LISH in connection with *ending inventory*. See *FISH*.

list price. The published or nominally quoted price for goods.

list price method. See *trade-in transaction*.

loan. An arrangement where the owner of property, called the lender, allows someone else, called the borrower, the use of the property for a period of time that is usually specified in the agreement setting up the loan. The borrower promises to return the property to the lender and, often, to make a payment for use of the property. Generally used when the property is *cash* and the payment for its use is *interest*.

long-lived (term) asset. An asset whose benefits are expected to be received over several years. A *noncurrent* asset, usually includes *investments, plant assets,* and *intangibles.*

long-term (construction) contract accounting. The *percentage of completion method* of *revenue* recognition. Sometimes used to mean the *completed contract method.*

loss. Excess of *cost* over net proceeds for a single transaction; negative *income* for a period. A cost expiration that produced no *revenue.* See *gain* for a discussion of related and contrasting terms.

loss contingency. See *contingency.*

lower of cost or market. A basis for valuation of *inventory* or *marketable equity securities.* The inventory value is set at the lower of *acquisition cost* or *current replacement cost* (market), subject to the following constraints: First, the market value of an item used in the computation cannot exceed its *net realizable value*—an amount equal to selling price less reasonable costs to complete production and to sell the item. Second, the market value of an item used in the computation cannot be less than the net realizable value minus the normal *profit* ordinarily realized on disposition of completed items of this type. The lower-of-cost-or-market valuation is chosen as the lower of acquisition *cost* or replacement cost *(market)* subject to the upper and lower bounds on replacement cost established in the first two steps. Thus,

Market Value = Midvalue of (Replacement Cost, Net Realizable Value, Net Realizable Value less Normal Profit Margin)

Lower-of-Cost-or-Market Valuation = Minimum (Acquisition Cost, Market Value).

The accompanying exhibit illustrates the calculation of the lower-of-cost-or-market valuation for four inventory items. Notice that each of the four possible outcomes occurs once in determining lower of cost or market. Item 1 uses acquisition cost; item 2 uses net realizable value; item 3 uses replacement cost; and item 4 uses net realizable value less normal profit.

		Item		
Calculation of Market Value	1	2	3	4
(a) Replacement Cost	$92	$96	$92	$85
(b) Net Realizable Value	95	95	95	95
(c) Net Realizable Value Less Normal Profit Margin [= (b) − $9]	86	86	86	86
(d) Market = Midvalue [(a), (b), (c)]	92	95	92	86
Calculation of Lower of Cost or Market				
(e) Acquisition Cost	90	97	96	90
(f) Market [= (d)]	92	95	92	86
(g) Lower of Cost or Market = Minimum [(e), (f)]	90	95	92	86

Lower of cost or market cannot be used for inventory on tax returns in a combination with a *LIFO* flow assumption.

In the context of inventory, once the asset is written down, a new "original cost" basis is established and subsequent increases in market value are ignored in the accounts.

In the context of *marketable equity securities* the method is applied separately to short-term and long-term portfolios of securities. Losses in market value on the short-term portfolio (and any subsequent recoveries in value up to original cost) are reported as part of *income from continuing operations* for the period. For the long-term portfolio, the losses (and subsequent recoveries, if any) are *debited* (or *credited*) directly to an *owners equity contra account.*

Note that hyphens are not used when the term is used as a noun but hyphens are used when the term is used as an adjectival phrase.

lump-sum acquisition. *Basket purchase.*

M

maintenance. *Expenditures* undertaken to preserve an *asset's* service potential for its originally-intended life; these expenditures are treated as *period expenses* or *product costs*; contrast with *improvement.* See *repair.*

make-or-buy decision. A managerial decision about whether the firm should produce a product internally or purchase it from others. Proper make-or-buy decisions in the short run result when *opportunity costs* are the only costs considered in decision making.

maker (of note) (of check). One who signs a *note* to borrow. One who signs a *check*; in this context synonymous with drawer; see *draft.*

management. Executive authority that operates a business.

Management Accounting. Monthly publication of the *NAA.*

management (managerial) accounting. Reporting designed to enhance the ability of management to do its job of decision making, planning, and control; contrast with *financial accounting.*

management audit. An audit conducted to ascertain whether the objectives, policies, and procedures for a firm or one of its operating units are properly carried out. Generally applies only to activities for which qualitative standards can be specified. See *audit* and *internal audit.*

management by exception. A principle of management where attention is focused only on performance that is significantly different from that expected.

managerial accounting. See *management accounting.*

manufacturing cost. Cost of producing goods, usually in a factory.

manufacturing expense. An imprecise, and generally incorrect, alternative title for *manufacturing overhead.*

manufacturing overhead. General manufacturing *costs* incurred in providing a capacity to carry on productive activities but that are not directly associated with identifiable units of product. *Fixed* manufacturing overhead costs are treated as a *product cost* under *absorption costing* but as an *expense* of the period under *direct costing.*

margin. *Revenue* less specified expenses. See *contribution margin, gross margin,* and *current margin.*

margin of safety. Excess of actual, or budgeted, sales over *breakeven* sales. Usually expressed in dollars; may be expressed in units of product.

marginal cost. The *incremental cost* or *differential cost* of the last unit added to production or the first unit subtracted from production. See *cost terminology*.

marginal costing. *Direct costing.*

marginal revenue. The increment in *revenue* from sale of one additional unit of product.

marginal tax rate. The tax imposed on the next dollar of taxable income generated; contrast with *average tax rate*.

markdown. See *markup* for definition and contrast.

markdown cancellation. See *markup* for definition and contrast.

market price. See *fair market price*.

market rate. The rate of *interest* a company must pay to borrow *funds* currently. See *effective rate*.

marketable equity securities. *Marketable securities* representing *owners' equity* interest in other companies, rather than *loans* to them.

marketable securities. *Stocks* and *bonds* of other companies held that can be readily sold on stock exchanges or over-the-counter markets and that the company plans to sell as cash is needed. Classified as *current assets* and as part of *working capital*. The same securities held for *long-term* purposes would be classified as *noncurrent assets*. *SFAS No. 12* requires the *lower-of-cost-or-market* valuation basis for all marketable equity securities but different accounting treatments (with differing effect on income) depending upon whether the security is a *current* or a *noncurrent asset*.

markon. See *markup* for definition and contrast.

markup. When a retailer acquires items for *inventory*, the items are given a selling price. The difference between the original selling price and cost is most precisely called "markon," although many business people use the term "markup," and because of confusion of this use of "markup" with its precise definition (see below), "original markup" is sometimes used. If the originally-established retail price is increased, the precise term for the amount of price increase is "markup," although "additional markup" is sometimes used. If a selling price is lowered, the terms "markdown" and "markup cancellation" are used. Markup cancellation" refers to reduction in price following "additional markups" and can, by definition, be no more than the amount of the additional markup; "cancellation of additional markup," although not used, is descriptive. "Markdown" refers to price reductions from the original retail price. A price increase after a markdown is a "markdown cancellation." If original cost is $12 and original selling price is $20, then markon (original markup) is $8; if the price is later increased to $24, the $4 increase is markup (additional markup); if the price is later lowered to $21, the $3 reduction is markup cancellation; if price is lowered further to $17, the $4 reduction is $1 markup cancellation and $3 markdown; if price is later increased to $22, the $5 increase is $3 of markdown cancellation and $2 of markup (additional markup). Markup cancellations and markdowns are separately counted because the former are deducted (while the latter are not) in computing the selling prices of goods available for sale for the denominator of the *cost percentage* used in the conventional *retail inventory method*.

markup cancellation. See *markup* for definition and contrast.

markup percentage. *Markup* divided by (acquisition cost plus *markup*).

master budget. A *budget* projecting all *financial statements* and their components.

matching convention. The concept of recognizing cost expirations *(expenses)* in the same accounting period when the related *revenues* are recognized. Combining or simultaneously recognizing the revenues and expenses that jointly result from the same *transactions* or other events.

material. As an adjective, it means relatively important. See *materiality*. Currently, no operational definition exists. As a noun, *raw material*.

material variances. *Price* and *quantity variances* for direct materials in *standard cost systems*. Sometimes used to mean variances that are significant; see *materiality*.

materiality. The concept that accounting should disclose separately only those events that are relatively important (no operable definition yet exists) for the business or for understanding its statements. *SFAC No. 2* suggests that accounting information is material if "the judgement of a reasonable person relying on the information would have been changed or influenced by the omission or misstatement."

matrix. A rectangular array of numbers or mathematical symbols.

matrix inverse. For a given square *matrix A*, the square matrix inverse is the matrix, A^{-1}, such that $AA^{-1} = A^{-1}A = I$, the *identity matrix*. Not all square matrices have inverses. Those that do not are called singular; those that do are nonsingular.

maturity. The date at which an obligation, such as the *principal* of a *bond* or a *note*, becomes due.

maturity value. The amount expected to be collected when a loan reaches *maturity*. Depending upon the context, the amount may be *principal* or principal and *interest*.

measuring unit. See *attribute measured* for definition and contrast.

merchandise. *Finished goods* bought by a retailer or wholesaler for resale; contrast with finished goods of a manufacturing business.

merchandise turnover. *Inventory turnover* for merchandise; see *ratio*.

merchandising business. As opposed to a manufacturing or service business, one that purchases (rather than manufactures) *finished goods* for resale.

merger. The joining of two or more businesses into a single *economic entity*. See *holding company*.

minority interest. A *balance sheet account* on *consolidated statements* showing the *equity* in a less-than-100-percent-owned *subsidiary* company allocable to those who are not part of the controlling (majority) interest. May be classified either as shareholders' equity or as a liability of *indeterminate term* on the consolidated balance sheet. On the *income statement*, the minority's interest in current period's income of the less-than-100-percent-owned subsidiary must be subtracted to arrive at consolidated *net income* for the period.

minority investment. A holding of less than 50 percent of the *voting stock* in another corporation. Accounted for with the *equity method* when sufficient shares are owned so that the investor can exercise "significant influence," and with the *lower-of-cost-or-market* otherwise. See *mutual fund*.

minutes book. A record of all actions authorized at corporate *board of director's* or shareholders' meetings.

mixed cost. A *semifixed* or a *semivariable* cost.

modified cash basis. The *cash basis of accounting* with long-term assets accounted for with the *accrual basis of accounting*. Most uses of the term "cash basis of accounting" actually mean "modified cash basis."

monetary assets, liabilities. See *monetary items*.

monetary gain or loss. The *gain* or loss *in general purchasing power* as a result of holding *monetary assets* or liabilities during a period when the *general purchasing power of the dollar* changes. During periods of *inflation*, holders of net monetary assets lose, and holders of net monetary liabilities gain, general purchasing power. During periods of *deflation*, holders of net monetary assets gain, and holders of net monetary liabilities lose, general purchasing power. Explicitly reported in *constant dollar accounting*.

monetary items. Amounts fixed in terms of dollars by statute or contract. *Cash, accounts receivable, accounts payable*, and *debt*. The distinction between monetary and nonmonetary items is important for *constant dollar accounting* and for *foreign exchange gain* or *loss* computations. In the foreign exchange context, account amounts denominated in dollars are not monetary items, whereas amounts denominated in any other currency are monetary.

money. A word seldom used with precision in accounting, at least in part because economists have not yet agreed on its definition. Economists use the term to refer to both a medium of exchange and a unit of value. See *cash* and *monetary items*.

money-purchase plan. A *pension plan* where the employer contributes a specified amount of cash each year to each employee's pension fund. Benefits ultimately received by the employee are not specifically defined but depend on the rate of return on the cash invested. Sometimes called a "defined-contribution" pension plan; contrast with *defined-benefit plan*. As of the mid-1970's most corporate pension plans were defined-benefit plans because both the law and *generally accepted accounting principles* for pensions made defined-benefit plans more attractive than money-purchase plans. *ERISA* makes money purchase plans relatively more attractive than they had been. We expect the relative number of money-purchase plans to increase.

mortality table. Data of life expectancies or probabilities of death for persons of specified ages and sex.

mortgage. A claim given by the borrower (mortgagor) to the lender (mortgagee) against the borrower's property in return for a loan.

moving average. An *average* computed on observations over time. As a new observation becomes available, the oldest one is dropped so that the average is always computed for the same number of observations and only the most recent ones. Sometimes, however, this term is used synonymously with *weighted average*.

moving average method. *Weighted-average method*.

multiple-step. Said of an *income statement* where various classes of *expenses* and *losses* are subtracted from *revenues* to show intermediate items such as *operating income*, income of the enterprise (operating income plus *interest* income), income to investors (income of the enterprise less *income taxes*), net income to shareholders (income to investors less interest charges), and income retained (income to shareholders less dividends). See *entity theory*.

municipal bond. A *bond* issued by a village, town, or city. *Interest* on such bonds is generally exempt from federal *income taxes* and from some state income taxes. Because bonds issued by state and county governments often have these characteristics, such bonds are often called "municipals" as well. Sometimes referred to as "tax exempts."

mutual fund. An investment company that issues its own stock to the public and uses the proceeds to invest in securities of other companies. A mutual fund usually owns less than five or ten percent of the stock of any one company and accounts for its investments using current *market values*; contrast with *holding company*.

mutually exclusive projects. Competing investment projects, where accepting one project eliminates the possibility of undertaking the remaining projects.

N

NAARS. *National Automated Accounting Research System.*

National Association of Accountants. NAA. A national society generally open to all engaged in activities closely associated with *managerial accounting*. Oversees the administration of the *CMA* Examinations through the Institute of Management Accounting.

National Automated Accounting Research System. NAARS. A computer-based information retrieval system containing, among other things, the complete text of most public corporate annual reports and *Forms 10-K*. The system is available to users through the *AICPA*.

natural business year. A 12-month period chosen as the reporting period so that the end of the period coincides with a low point in activity or inventories. See *ratio* for a discussion of analyses of financial statements of companies using a natural business year.

natural classification. *Income statement* reporting form in which *expenses* are classified by nature of items as acquired, that is, materials, wages, salaries, insurance, and taxes, as well as depreciation; contrast with *functional classification*.

natural resources. Timberland, oil and gas wells, ore deposits, and other products of nature that have economic value. The cost of natural resources is subject to *depletion*. Natural resources are "nonrenewable" (for example, oil, coal, gas, ore deposits) or "renewable" (timberland, sod fields); the former are often called "wasting assets." See also *reserve recognition accounting* and *percentage depletion*.

negative confirmation. See *confirmation*.

negative goodwill. Refer to *goodwill*. When the purchase price of the company acquired is less than the sum of the *fair market value* of the *net assets* acquired, *APB Opinion* No. 16 requires that the valuation of noncurrent assets (except *investments* in *marketable securities*) acquired be reduced until the purchase price equals the adjusted valuation of the fair market value of net assets acquired. If after the adjusted valuation of noncurrent assets is reduced to zero and the purchase price is still less than the net assets acquired, then the difference is shown as a credit balance in the balance sheet as negative goodwill and is amortized to income over a period not to exceed forty years. For negative goodwill to exist, someone must be willing to sell a company for less than the fair market value of net current assets and marketable securities. Because such a bargain purchase is rare, negative goodwill is rarely found in the financial statements; when it does appear, it generally signals unrecorded obligations, such as for *pensions*.

negotiable. Legally capable of being transferred by endorsement. Usually said of *checks* and *notes* and sometimes of *stocks* and *bearer bonds*.

net. Reduced by all relevant deductions.

net assets. *Owners' equity*; total *assets* minus total *liabilities*.

net bank position. From a firm's point of view, *cash* in a specific bank less *loans* payable to that bank.

net current assets. *Working capital = current assets − current liabilities.*

net current asset value (per share). *Working capital* divided by the number of common shares outstanding. Many security analysts think that when a common share trades in the market for an amount less than net current asset value, then the shares are undervalued and should be purchased. We find this view naive because it ignores the efficiency of capital markets generally and, specifically, unrecorded obligations such as for *pension plans*, not currently reported as liabilities in the *balance sheet* under *GAAP*.

net income. The excess of all *revenues* and *gains* for a period over all *expenses* and *losses* of the period. See *comprehensive income*.

net loss. The excess of all *expenses* and *losses* for a period over all *revenues* and *gains* of the period. Negative *net income*.

net markup. In the context of *retail inventory methods*, *markups* less markup cancellations; a figure that usually ignores *markdowns* and markdown cancellations.

net of tax method. A nonsanctioned method for dealing with the problem of income tax allocation; described in *APB Opinion* No 11. Deferred tax credit items are subtracted from specific asset amounts rather than being shown as a deferred credit or liability.

net of tax reporting. Reporting, such as for *income from discontinued operations, extraordinary items,* and *prior-period adjustments,* where the amounts presented in *financial statements* have been adjusted for all income tax effects. For example, if an extraordinary loss amounted to $10,000 and the marginal tax rate were 40 percent, then the extraordinary item would be reported "net of taxes" as a $6,000 loss. Hence, all income taxes may not be reported on one line of the income statement. The taxes will be allocated to *income from continuing operations, income from discontinued operations, extraordinary items,* cumulative effects of *accounting changes,* and *prior-period adjustments*.

net present value. Discounted or *present value* of all cash inflows and outflows of a project or from an *investment* at a given *discount rate*.

net price method (of recording purchase or sales discounts). The *purchase* (or *sale*) is recorded at its in-voice price less all *discounts* made available under the assumption that nearly all discounts will be taken. Discounts lapsed through failure to pay promptly are recorded in an *adjunct account* to purchases (or sales) or in the purchasing context, to an *expense* account. For purchases, management usually prefers to know about the amount of discounts lost because of inefficient operations, not the amounts taken, so that most managers prefer the net price method to the *gross price method*.

net realizable value. Selling price of an item less reasonable further costs to make the item ready for sale and to sell it. See *lower of cost or market*.

net sales. Sales (at gross invoice amount) less *returns, allowances*, freight paid for customers, and *discounts* taken.

net working capital. *Working capital*; the "net" is redundant in accounting. Financial analysts sometimes mean *current* assets when they speak of working capital, so for them the "net" is not redundant.

net worth. A misleading term, to be avoided, that means the same as *owners' equity*.

New York Stock Exchange. NYSE. A public market where various corporate *securities* are traded.

next-in, first-out. See *NIFO*.

NIFO. Next-in, first-out. In making decisions, many managers consider *replacement costs* (rather than *historical costs*) and refer to them as NIFO costs.

no par. Said of *stock* without a *par value*.

nominal accounts. *Temporary accounts* as opposed to *balance sheet accounts*. All nominal accounts are *closed* at the end of each *accounting period*.

nominal dollars. The measuring unit giving no consideration to differences in the *general purchasing power of the dollar* over time. The face amount of currency or coin, a *bond*, an *invoice*, a *receivable* is a nominal dollar amount. When that amount is adjusted for changes in *general purchasing power*, it is converted into a *constant dollar* amount.

nominal interest rate. A rate specified on a *debt* instrument, which usually differs from the market or *effective rate*. Also, a rate of *interest* quoted for a year. If the interest is compounded more often than annually, then the *effective interest rate* is higher than the nominal rate.

noncancelable. See *lease*.

noncontributory. Said of a *pension plan* where only the employer makes payments to a pension *fund*; contrast with *contributory*.

noncurrent. Due more than one year (or more than one *operating cycle*) hence.

nonexpendable fund. A governmental fund, whose *principal*, and sometimes earnings, may not be spent.

non-interest-bearing note. A *note* that bears no explicit interest. The *present value* of such a note at any time before *maturity* is less than the *face value* so long as *interest rates* are positive. *APB Opinion* No. 21 requires that the present value, not face value, of long-term non-interest-bearing notes be reported as the *asset* or *liability* amount in financial statements. See *interest, imputed*.

nonmonetary items. All items that are not monetary; see *monetary items*.

nonoperating. In the *income statement* context, said of revenues and expenses arising from transactions incidental to the company's main line(s) of business. In the *statement of changes in financial position* context, said of all sources or uses of *working capital* other than working capital provided by operations. See *operations*.

nonprofit corporation. An incorporated *entity*, such as a hospital, with owners who do not share in the earnings. It usually emphasizes providing services rather than maximizing income.

nonrecurring. Said of an event that is not expected to happen often for a given firm. Under *APB Opinion* No. 30, the effects of such events should be disclosed separately, but as part of *ordinary* items unless the event is also unusual. See *extraordinary* item.

normal cost. *Pension plan expenses* incurred during an *accounting period* for employment services performed during that period; contrast with *actuarial accrued liability* and see *funded*.

normal costing. Method of charging costs to products using actual *direct materials*, actual *direct labor*, and predetermined *factory-overheard* rates.

normal spoilage. Costs incurred because of ordinary amounts of spoilage; such costs should be prorated to units produced as *product costs*; contrast with *abnormal spoilage*.

normal standard cost. The *cost* expected to be incurred under reasonably efficient operating conditions with adequate provision for an average amount of rework, spoilage, and the like.

normal volume. The level of production over a time span, usually 1 year, that will satisfy demand by purchasers.

note. An unconditional written promise by the maker (borrower) to pay a certain amount on demand or at a certain future time. See *footnotes* for another context.

note receivable discounted. A *note* assigned by the holder to another. If the note is assigned with recourse, it is the *contingent liability* of the assignor until the debt is paid. See *factoring*.

NOW account. Negotiable order of withdrawal. A *savings account* on which orders to pay, much like *checks* but technically not checks, can be drawn and given to others who can redeem the order at the savings institution.

number of days sales in inventory (or receivables). Days of average inventory on hand (or average collection period for receivables). See *ratio*.

NYSE. *New York Stock Exchange*.

O

OASD(H)I. *Old Age, Survivors, Disability, and (Hospital) Insurance*.

objective. See *reporting objective* and *objectivity*.

objectivity. The reporting policy implying that formal recognition will not be given to an event in financial statements until the magnitude of the events can be measured with reasonable accuracy and is subject to independent verification.

obsolescence. A decline in *market value* of an *asset* caused by improved alternatives becoming available that will be more *cost-effective*; the decline in market value is unrelated to physical changes in the asset itself. See *partial obsolescence*.

Occupational Safety and Health Act. *OSHA*.

off balance sheet financing. A description often used for a *long-term, noncancelable lease* accounted for as an *operating lease*.

Old Age, Survivors, Disability, and (Hospital) Insurance. The technical name for Social Security under the Federal Insurance Contribution Act (FICA).

on (open) account. Said of a *purchase* or *sale* when payment is expected sometime after delivery and no *note* evidencing the *debt* is given or received. The purchaser has generally signed an agreement sometime in the past promising to pay for such purchases according to an agreed time schedule. When a sale (purchase) is made on open account, *Accounts Receivable (Payable)* is *debited* (*credited*).

on consignment. Said of goods delivered by the owner (the consignor) to another (the consignee) to be sold by the consignee; the owner is entitled to the return of the property or payment of an amount agreed upon in advance. The goods are assets of the consignor.

open account. Any *account* with a nonzero *debit* or *credit* balance. See *on (open) account*.

operating. An adjective used to refer to *revenue* and *expense* items relating to the company's main line(s) of business. See *operations*.

operating accounts. *Revenue, expense*, and *production cost accounts*; contrast with *balance sheet accounts*.

operating cycle. *Earnings cycle*.

operating expenses. *Expenses* incurred in the course of *ordinary* activities of an *entity*. Frequently, a classification including only *selling, general*, and *administrative expenses*, thereby excluding *cost of goods sold, interest*, and *income tax* expenses. See *operations*.

operating lease. A *lease* accounted for by the *lessee* without showing an *asset* for the lease rights (*leasehold*) or a *liability* for the lease payment obligations. Rental payments of the lessee are merely shown as *expenses* of the period. The asset remains on the *lessor's books* where rental collections appear as *revenues*; contrast with *capital lease*.

operating margin (based on current costs). *Revenues* from *sales* minus *current cost* of goods sold. A measure of operating efficiency that is independent of the *cost flow assumption* for *inventory*. Sometimes called "current (gross) margin." See *inventory profit* for illustrative computations.

operating ratio. See *ratio*.

operational control. See *control system*.

operations. A word not precisely defined in *accounting*. Generally, operating activities (producing and selling *goods* or *services*) are distinguished from financing activities (raising funds). Acquiring goods on account and then paying for them in one month, though generally classified as an operating activity, has the characteristics of a financing activity. Or consider the transaction of selling plant assets for a price in excess of book value. On the *income statement*, the gain is part of income from operations (continuing operations or discontinued operations, depending on the circumstances) but on the *statement of changes in financial position*, all of the funds received on disposition are reported below the "funds from operations'' section, as a nonoperating source of funds, disposition of noncurrent assets. In income tax accounting an ''operating loss'' results whenever deductions are greater than taxable revenues.

opinion. The *auditor's report* containing an attestation or lack thereof. Also, *APB Opinion*.

opportunity cost. The *present value* of the *income* (or *costs)* that could be earned (or saved) from using an *asset* in its best alternative use to the one being considered.

option. The legal right to buy something during a specified period at a specified price, called the *exercise* price. Employee stock options should not be confused with put and call options traded in various public markets.

ordinary annuity. An *annuity in arrears*.

ordinary income. For income tax purposes, reportable *income* not qualifying as *capital gains*.

organization costs. The *costs* incurred in planning and establishing an *entity*; example of an *intangible* asset. Often, since the amounts are not *material*, the costs are treated as *expenses* in the period incurred even though the *expenditures* clearly provide future benefits and should be treated as *assets*.

original cost. *Acquisition cost*. In public utility accounting, the acquisition cost of the *entity* first devoting the asset to public use.

original entry. Entry in a *journal*.

OSHA. Occupational Safety and Health Act. The federal law that governs working conditions in commerce and industry.

outlay. The amount of an *expenditure*.

out-of-pocket. Said of an *expenditure* usually paid for with cash. An *incremental* cost.

out-of-stock cost. The estimated decrease in future *profit* as a result of losing customers because insufficient quantities of *inventory* are currently on hand to meet customers' demands.

output. Physical quantity or monetary measurement of *goods* and *services* produced.

outside director. A member of a corporate board of directors who is not a company officer and does not participate in the corporation's day-to-day management.

outstanding. Unpaid or uncollected. When said of *stock*, the shares issued less *treasury stock*. When said of checks, it means a check issued that did not clear the *drawer's* bank prior to the *bank statement* date.

over-and-short. Title for an *expense account* used to account for small differences between book balances of cash and actual cash and vouchers or receipts in *petty cash* or *change funds*.

overapplied (overabsorbed) overhead. An excess of costs applied, or *charged*, to product for a period over actual *overhead* costs during the period. A *credit balance* in an overhead account after overhead is assigned to product.

overdraft. A check written on a checking account that contains funds less than the amount of the check.

overhead costs. Any *cost* not directly associated with the production or sale of identifiable goods and services. Sometimes called ''burden'' or ''indirect costs'' and, in Britain,

''oncosts.'' Frequently limited to manufacturing overhead. See *central corporate expenses* and *manufacturing overhead*.

overhead rate. Standard, or other predetermined rate at which *overhead costs* are applied to products or to services.

over-the-counter. Said of a *security* traded in a negotiated transaction, rather than in an auctioned one on an organized stock exchange, such as the *New York Stock Exchange*.

owners' equity. *Proprietorship*; assets minus *liabilities*; *paid-in capital* plus *retained earnings* of a corporation; partners' capital accounts in a *partnership*; owner's capital account in a *sole proprietorship*.

P

P & L. Profit and loss statement; *income statement*.

paid-in capital. Sum of balances in *capital stock* and *capital contributed in excess of par (or stated) value* accounts. Same as *contributed capital* (minus *donated capital*). Some use the term to mean only *capital contributed in excess of par (or stated value)*.

paid-in surplus. See *surplus*.

paper profit. A *gain* not yet realized through a *transaction*. An *unrealized holding gain*.

par. See *at par* and *face amount*.

par value. *Face amount* of a *security*.

par value method. The method of accounting for *treasury stock* that *debits* a common stock account with the *par value* of the shares required and allocates the remaining debits between the *additional paid-in capital* and *retained earnings* accounts; contrast with *cost method*.

parent company. Company owning more than 50 percent of the voting shares of another company, called the *subsidiary*.

partial obsolescence. As technology improves, the economic value of existing *assets* declines. In many cases, however, it will not pay a firm to replace the existing asset with a new one even though the new type, rather than the old, would be acquired if the acquisition were to be made currently. In these cases, the accountant should theoretically recognize a loss from partial obsolescence from the firm's owning an old, out-of-date asset, but *GAAP* does not permit recognition of partial obsolescence. The old asset will be carried at *cost* less *accumulated depreciation* until it is retired from service. See *obsolescence*.

partially funded. Said of a *pension plan* where not all earned benefits have been funded. See *funded* for funding requirements.

partially vested. Said of a *pension plan* where not all employee benefits are *vested*. See *graded vesting*.

participating dividend. *Dividend* paid to preferred shareholders in addition to the minimum preferred dividends when the *preferred stock* contract allows such sharing in earnings. Usually applied after dividends on *common stock* have reached a certain level.

participating preferred stock. *Preferred stock* with rights to *participating dividends*.

partner's drawing. A payment to a partner to be charged against his or her share of income or capital. The name of a *temporary account* to record such payments.

partnership. Contractual arrangement between individuals to share resources and operations in a jointly run business. See *general* and *limited partner* and *Uniform Partnership Act.*

past service cost. *Present value* at a given time of a *pension plan's* unrecognized, and usually unfunded, benefits assigned to employees for their service before the inception of the plan. A part of *actuarial accrued liability.* See *funded;* contrast with *normal cost.*

patent. A right granted for up to 17 years by the federal government to exclude others from manufacturing, using or selling a claimed design, product or plant (e.g., a new breed of rose) or from using a claimed process or method of manufacture. An asset if acquired by purchase. If developed internally, the development costs are *expensed* when incurred under current *GAAP.*

payable. Unpaid but not necessarily due or past due.

pay as you go. Said of an *income tax* scheme where periodic payments of income taxes are made during the period when the income to be taxed is being earned; in contrast to a scheme where no payments are due until the end of, or after, the period whose income is being taxed. (Called PAYE—pay as you earn—in Britain.) Sometimes used to describe an *unfunded pension plan,* where payments to pension plan beneficiaries are made from general corporate funds, not from cash previously contributed to a pension fund. Not acceptable as a method of accounting for pension plans.

payback period. Amount of time that must elapse before the cash inflows from a project equal the cash outflows.

payback reciprocal. One divided by the *payback period.* This number approximates the *internal rate of return* on a project when the project life is more than twice the payback period and the cash inflows are identical in every period after the initial period.

PAYE. See *pay as you go.*

payee. The person or entity to whom a cash payment is made or who will receive the stated amount of money on a check. See *draft.*

payout ratio. *Common stock dividends* declared for a year divided by net *income* to common stock for the year. A term used by financial analysts; contrast with *dividend yield.*

payroll taxes. Taxes levied because salaries or wages are paid; for example, *FICA* and unemployment compensation insurance taxes. Typically, the employer pays a portion and withholds part of the employee's wage fund.

P/E ratio. *Price-earnings ratio.*

Pension Benefit Guarantee Corporation. PBGC. A federal corporation established under *ERISA* to administer terminated pension plans and impose *liens* on corporate assets for certain unfunded pension liabilities.

pension fund. *Fund,* the assets of which are to be paid to retired ex-employees, usually as a *life annuity.* Usually held by an independent trustee and thus is not an *asset* of the employer.

pension plan. Details or provisions of employer's contract with employees for paying retirement *annuities* or other benefits. See *funded, vested, normal cost, past service cost, prior service cost, actuarial accrued liability, money-purchase plan,* and *defined-benefit plan.*

per books. An expression used to refer to the *book value* of an item at a specific time.

percent. Any number, expressed as a decimal, multiplied by 100.

percentage depletion (allowance). Deductible *expense* allowed in some cases by the federal *income tax* regulations; computed as a percentage of gross income from a *natural resource* independent of the unamortized cost of the asset. Because the amount of the total deductions for tax purposes is usually greater than the cost of the asset being *depleted,* many people think the deduction is an unfair tax advantage or "loophole."

percentage-of-completion method. Recognizing *revenues* and *expenses* on a job, order, or contract (a) in proportion to the *costs* incurred for the period divided by total costs expected to be incurred for the job or order ("cost-to-cost"), or (b) in proportion to engineers' or architects' estimates of the incremental degree of completion of the job, order, or contract during the period. Contrast with *completed-contract method.*

percentage statement. A statement containing, in addition to (or instead of) dollar amounts, ratios of dollar amounts to some base. In a percentage *income statement,* the base is usually either *net sales* or total *revenues* and in a percentage *balance sheet,* the base is usually total *assets.*

period. *Accounting period.*

period cost. An inferior term for *period expense.*

period expense (charge). *Expenditure,* usually based upon the passage of time, charged to operations of the accounting period rather than *capitalized* as an asset; contrast with *product cost.*

periodic inventory. A method of recording *inventory* that uses data on beginning inventory, additions to inventories, and ending inventory to find the cost of withdrawals from inventory.

periodic procedures. The process of making *adjusting entries, closing entries,* and preparing the *financial statements,* usually by use of *trial balances* and *work sheets.*

permanent account. An account which appears on the *balance sheet;* contrast with *temporary account.*

permanent difference. Difference between reported income and taxable income that will never be reversed and, hence, requires no entry in the *deferred income tax (liability)* account. An example is the difference between taxable and reportable income from interest earned on state and municipal bonds; contrast with *timing difference* and see *deferred income tax liability.*

perpetual annuity. *Perpetuity.*

perpetual inventory. Records on quantities and amounts of *inventory* that are changed or made current with each physical addition to or withdrawal from the stock of goods; an inventory so recorded. The records will show the physical quantities and, frequently, the dollar valuations that should be on hand at any time. Because *cost of goods sold* is explicitly computed, the *inventory equation* can be used to compute *ending inventory.* The computed amount of ending inventory can be compared to the actual amount of ending inventory as a *control* device. Contrast with *periodic inventory.*

perpetuity. An *annuity* whose payments continue forever.

The *present value* of a perpetuity in *arrears* is p/r where p is the periodic payment and r is the *interest rate* per period. If $100 is promised each year, in arrears, forever and the interest rate is 20 percent per year, then the value of the perpetuity is $500 = $100/.20.

personal account. *Drawing account.*

petty cash fund. Currency and coins maintained for expenditures that are made with cash on hand.

physical verification. *Verification*, by an *auditor*, performed by actually inspecting items in *inventory, plant assets*, and the like; may be based on statistical sampling procedures; in contrast to mere checking of written records.

plant. *Plant asset.*

plant assets. Buildings, machinery, equipment, land, and natural resources. The phrase "property, plant and equipment" is, therefore, a redundancy. In this context, "plant" means buildings.

plant asset turnover. Number of dollars of *sales* generated per dollar of *plant assets*. Equal to sales divided by average *plant assets*.

pledging. The borrower assigns *assets* as security or *collateral* for repayment of a loan.

pledging of receivables. The process of using expected collections on accounts receivable as *collateral* for a loan. The borrower remains responsible for collecting the receivable but promises to use the proceeds for repaying the debt.

plow back. To retain assets generated by earnings for continued investment in the business.

plug. For any *account*, beginning balance + additions − deductions = ending balance; if any three of the four items are known, the fourth can be found by plugging. In making a *journal entry*, often all *debits* are known, as are all but one of the *credits* (or vice versa). Because *double-entry* bookkeeping requires equal debits and credits, the unknown quantity can be computed by subtracting the sum of the known credits from the sum of all the debits (or vice versa). This process is also known as plugging. The unknown found is called the plug. For example, if a *discount* on *bonds payable* is being *amortized* with the *straight-line method*, then *interest expense* is a plug: interest expense = interest payable + discount amortization. See *trade-in transaction* for an example.

pooling of interests method. Accounting for a *business combination* by merely adding together the *book value* of the *assets* and *equities* of the combined firms. Contrast with *purchase method*. Generally leads to a higher reported *net income* for the combined firms than would be reported had the business combination been accounted for as a purchase because the *market values* of the merged assets are generally larger than their book values. See *APB Opinion* No. 16 for the conditions that must be met before the pooling of interests treatment is acceptable.

positive confirmation. See *confirmation*.

post. To record entries in an *account* in a *ledger*; usually the entries are transferred from a *journal*.

post-closing trial balance. *Trial balance* taken after all *temporary accounts* have been closed.

post-statement events. Events with *material* impact that occur between the end of the *accounting period* and the formal publication of the *financial statements*. Such events must be disclosed in notes for the auditor to give a *clean opinion*, even though the events are subsequent to the period being reported on.

potentially dilutive. A *security* that may be converted into, or exchanged for, common stock and thereby reduce reported *earnings per share: options, warrants, convertible bonds*, and *convertible preferred stock*.

PPB. *Program budgeting*; the second "P" means "plan".

practical capacity. Maximum level at which the plant or department can operate efficiently.

preclosing trial balance. *Trial balance* taken at the end of the period before *closing entries*. In this sense an *adjusted trial balance*. Sometimes taken before *adjusting entries* and then is synonymous with *unadjusted trial balance..*

predetermined (factory) overhead rate. Rate used in applying *overhead* to products or departments developed at the start of a period by dividing estimated overhead cost by the estimated number of units of the overhead allocation base (or *denominator volume*) activity.

preemptive right. The privilege of a shareholder to maintain a proportionate share of ownership by purchasing a proportionate share of any new stock issues.

preference as to assets. The rights of *preferred shareholders* to receive certain payments in case of dissolution before common shareholders receive payments.

preferred shares. *Capital stock* with a claim to *income* or *assets* after *bondholders* but before *common shares*. Dividends on preferred shares are *income distributions*, not *expenses*. See *cumulative preferred stock*.

premium. The excess of issue (or market) price over *par value*. For a different context, see *insurance*.

premium on capital stock. Alternative but inferior title for *capital contributed in excess of (par) or stated value*.

prepaid expense. An *expenditure* that leads to a *deferred charge* or *prepayment*; strictly speaking, a contradiction in terms for an *expense* is a gone asset and this title refers to past *expenditures*, such as for rent or insurance premiums, that still have future benefits and thus are *assets*.

prepaid income. An inferior alternative title for *advances from customers*. An item should not be called *revenue* or *income* until earned, when goods are delivered or services are rendered.

prepayments. *Deferred charges. Assets* representing *expenditures* for future benefits. Rent and insurance premiums paid in advance are usually classified as *current* prepayments.

present value. Value today of an amount or amounts to be paid or received later, discounted at some *interest* or *discount rate*.

price. The quantity of one *good* or *service*, usually *cash*, asked in return for a unit of another good or service. See *fair market price*.

price-earnings ratio. At a given time, the market value of a company's *common stock*, per share, divided by the *earnings per* common *share* for the past year. See *ratio*.

price index. A series of numbers, one for each period that purports to represent some *average* of prices for a series of periods, relative to a base period.

price level. The number from a *price index* series for a given period or date.

price level adjusted statements. *Financial statements* expressed in terms of dollars of uniform purchasing power. *Nonmonetary* items are restated to reflect changes in general *price levels* since the time specific *assets* were acquired and *liabilities* were incurred. A *gain* or *loss* is recognized on *monetary items* as they are held over time periods when the general *price level changes*. Conventional financial statements show *historical costs* and ignore differences in purchasing power in different periods.

price variance. In accounting for *standard costs*, (actual cost per unit − standard cost per unit) times quantity purchased.

primary earnings per share. Net *income* to *common shareholders* plus *interest (net of tax* effects) or *dividends* paid on *common stock equivalents* divided by (weighted-average of common share outstanding plus the net increase in the number of common shares that would become *outstanding* if all common stock equivalents were exchanged for common shares with cash proceeds, if any, used to retire common shares).

prime cost. Sum of *direct materials* plus *direct labor* costs assigned to product.

prime rate. The rate for loans charged by commercial banks to their most preferred risks. For the purpose of deciding whether a security is or is not a *common stock equivalent* in calculating *earnings per share*, the corporation should use the rate in effect at the bank at which it does business or an average of such rates if the corporation does business with more than one bank. The *Federal Reserve Bulletin* is considered the authoritative source of information about historical prime rates.

principal. An amount in which *interest* is charged or earned.

principle. See *generally accepted accounting principles*.

prior-period adjustment. A *debit* or *credit* made directly to *retained earnings* (that does not affect *income* for the period) to adjust earnings as calculated for prior periods. Such adjustments are now extremely rare. Theory might suggest that corrections of errors in accounting estimates (such as the *depreciable life* or *salvage value* of an asset) should be treated as adjustments to retained earnings. But *GAAP* require that corrections of such estimates flow through current, and perhaps future, *income statements*. See *accounting changes* and *accounting errors*.

prior service cost. *Actuarial accrued liability*.

pro forma statements. Hypothetical statements. Financial statements as they would appear if some event, such as a *merger* or increased production and sales had occurred or were to occur. Pro forma is often spelled as one word.

proceeds. The *funds* received from disposition of assets or from the issue of securities.

process costing. A method of *cost accounting* based on average costs (total cost divided by the *equivalent units* of work done in a period). Typically used for assembly lines or for products that are produced in a series of steps that are more continuous than discrete.

product. *Goods* or *services* produced.

product cost. Any *manufacturing cost* that can be inventoried. See *flow of costs* for example and contrast with *period expenses*.

production cost. *Manufacturing cost*.

production cost account. A *temporary account* for collecting *manufacturing costs* during a period.

production department. A department producing salable *goods* or *services*; contrast with *service department*.

production method (depreciation). The depreciable asset is given a *depreciable life* measured, not in elapsed time, but in units of output or perhaps in units of time of expected use. Then the *depreciation* charge for a period is a portion of depreciable cost equal to a fraction computed by dividing the actual output produced during the period by the expected total output to be produced over the life of the asset. Sometimes called the "units of production (or output) method."

production method (revenue recognition). *Percentage of completion method* for recognizing *revenue*.

productive capacity. In computing *current cost* of *long-term assets*, we are interested in the cost of reproducing the productive capacity (for example, the ability to manufacture one million units a year), not the cost of reproducing the actual physical assets currently used (see *reproduction cost*). Replacement cost of productive capacity will be the same as reproduction cost of assets only in the unusual case when there has been no technological improvement in production processes and the relative prices of goods and services used in production have remained approximately the same as when the currently used ones were acquired.

profit. Excess of *revenues* over *expenses* for a *transaction*; sometimes used synonymously with *net income* for the period.

profit and loss sharing ratio. The fraction of *net income* or loss allocable to a partner in a *partnership*. Need not be the same fraction as the partner's share of capital.

profit and loss statement. *Income statement*.

profit center. A unit of activity for which both *revenue* and *expenses* are accumulated; contrast with *cost center*.

profit margin. Sales minus all expenses as a single amount. Frequently used to mean ratio of sales minus all *operating* expenses divided by sales.

profit maximization. The doctrine that a given set of operations should be accounted for so as to make reported *net income* as large as possible; contrast with *conservatism*. This concept in accounting is slightly different from the profit maximizing concept in economics where the doctrine states that operations should be managed to maximize the present value of the firm's wealth, generally by equating *marginal costs* and *marginal revenues*.

profit-volume graph. See *breakeven chart*.

profit-volume ratio. *Net income* divided by net sales in dollars.

profitability accounting. *Responsibility accounting*.

program budgeting. Specification and analysis of inputs, outputs, costs, and alternatives that link plans to *budgets*.

programmed costs. A *fixed cost* not essential for carrying out operations. Research and development and advertising designed to generate new business are controllable, but once a commitment is made to incur them, they become fixed costs. Sometimes called *managed costs* or *discretionary costs*; contrast with *capacity costs*.

progressive tax. Tax for which the rate increases as the taxed base, such as income, increases; contrast with *regressive tax*.

project financing arrangement. As defined by *SFAS No. 47*, The financing of an investment project in which the lender looks principally to the *cash flows* and *earnings* of the project as the source of funds for repayment and to the *assets* of the project as *collateral* for the loan. The general *credit* of the project entity is usually not a significant factor, either because the entity is a *corporation* without other assets or because the financing is without direct *recourse* to the entity's owners.

projected financial statement. *Pro forma* financial statement.

promissory note. An unconditional written promise to pay a specified sum of money on demand or at a specified date.

proof of journal. The process of checking arithmetic accuracy of *journal entries* by testing for the equality of all *debits* with all *credits* since the last previous proof.

property dividend. A *dividend in kind*.

proprietary accounts. See *budgetary accounts* for contrast in context of governmental accounting.

proprietorship. *Assets* minus *liabilities* of an *entity*; equals *contributed capital* plus *retained earnings*.

proprietorship theory. The view of the corporation that emphasizes the form of the *accounting equation* that says *assets − liabilities = owners' equity*; contrast with *entity theory*. The major implication of a choice between these theories deals with the treatment of *subsidiaries*. For example, the view that *minority interest* is an *indeterminate-term liability* is based on the proprietorship theory. The proprietorship theory implies using a *single-step income statement*.

prorate. To *allocate* in proportion to some base; for example, allocate *service department* costs in proportion to hours of service used by the benefited department.

prospectus. Formal written document describing *securities* to be issued. See *proxy*.

protest fee. Fee charged by banks or other financial agencies when items (such as checks) presented for collection cannot be collected.

provision. Often the exact amount of an *expense* is uncertain, but must be recognized currently anyway. The entry for the estimated expense, such as for *income taxes* or expected costs under *warranty*, is:

Expense (Estimated) X
    Liability (Estimated) X

In American usage, the term "provision" is often used in the expense account title of the above entry. Thus, Provision for Income Taxes is used to mean the estimate of income tax expense. (In British usage, the term "provision" is used in the title for the estimated liability of the above entry, so that Provision for Income Taxes is a balance sheet account.)

proxy. Written authorization given by one person to another so that the second person can act for the first, such as to vote shares of stock. Of particular significance to accountants because the *SEC* presumes that financial information is distributed by management along with its proxy solicitations.

public accountant. Generally, this term is synonymous with *certified public accountant*. In some jurisdictions individuals have been licensed as public accountants without being CPAs.

public accounting. That portion of accounting primarily involving the *attest* function, culminating in the *auditor's report*.

PuPU. An acronym for *p*urchasing *p*ower *u*nit conceived by John C. Burton, former Chief Accountant of the *SEC*. Those who think *constant dollar accounting* is not particularly useful poke fun at it by calling it "PuPU accounting."

purchase allowance. A reduction in sales *invoice price* usually granted because the *goods* received by the purchaser were not exactly as ordered. The goods are not returned to the seller, but are purchased at a price lower than originally agreed upon.

purchase discount. A reduction in purchase *invoice price* granted for prompt payment. See *sales discount* and *terms of sale*.

purchase method. Accounting for a *business combination* by adding the acquired company's assets at the price paid for them to the acquiring company's assets. Contrast with *pooling of interests method*. The acquired assets are put on the books at current values, rather than original costs, the *amortization expenses* are usually larger (and reported income, smaller) than for the same business combination accounted for as a pooling of interests. The purchase method is required unless all criteria to be a pooling are met.

purchase order. Document authorizing a seller to deliver goods with payment to be made later.

Q

qualified report (opinion). *Auditor's report* containing a statement that the auditor was unable to complete a satisfactory examination of all things considered relevant or that the auditor has doubts about the financial impact of some material item reported in the financial statements. See *except for* and *subject to*.

quantity discount. A reduction in purchase price as quantity purchased increases; amount of the discount is constrained by law (Robinson-Patman Act). Not to be confused with *purchase discount*.

quantity variance. In *standard cost* systems, the standard price per unit times (actual quantity used minus standard quantity that should be used).

quasi-reorganization. A *reorganization* where no new company is formed or no court has intervened, as would happen in *bankruptcy*. The primary purpose is to absorb a *deficit* and get a "fresh start."

quick assets. *Assets* readily convertible into *cash*; includes cash, *current marketable securities* and *current receivables*.

quick ratio. Sum of (*cash, current marketable securities, and receivables*) divided by *current liabilities*. Some nonliquid receivables may be excluded from the numerator. Often called the "acid test ratio." See *ratio*.

R

Railroad Accounting Principles Board. RAPB. A board brought into existence by the Staggers Rail Act of 1980 to advise the Interstate Commerce Commission on matters of accounting affecting railroads. The RAPB had not started work by the time this book went to press.

RAPB. Railroad Accounting Principles Board.

R & D. See *research* and *development*.

rate of return on assets. *Net income* plus aftertax *interest charges* plus *minority interest* in income divided by average total *assets*. Perhaps the single most useful ratio for assessing management's overall operating performance. See *ratio*.

rate of return on common stock equity. See *ratio*.

rate of return on shareholders' (owners') equity. See *ratio*.

rate of return (on total capital). See *ratio* and *rate of return on assets*.

rate variance. *Price variance*, usually for *direct labor* costs.

ratio. The number resulting when one number is divided by another. Ratios are generally used to assess aspects of profitability, solvency, and liquidity. The commonly used financial ratios are of three kinds:

(1) those that summarize some aspect of *operations* for a period, usually a year, and

(2) those that summarize some aspect of *financial position* at a given moment—the moment for which a balance sheet has been prepared.

(3) those that relate some aspect of operations to some aspect of financial position.

The accompanying exhibit lists the most common financial ratios and shows separately both the numerator and denominator used to calculate the ratio.

For all ratios that require an average balance during the period, the average is most often derived as one-half the sum of the beginning and ending balances. Sophisticated analysts recognize, however, that when companies use a fiscal year different from the calendar year, this averaging of beginning and ending balances may be misleading. Consider, for example, the *rate of return on assets* of Sears, Roebuck & Company whose fiscal year ends on January 31. Sears chooses a January 31 closing date at least in part because inventories are at a low level and are therefore easy to count—the Christmas merchandise has been sold and the Easter merchandise has not yet all been received. Furthermore, by January 31, most Christmas sales have been collected or returned, so receivable amounts are not unusually large. Thus at January 31, the amount of total assets is lower than at many other times during the year. Consequently, the denominator of the rate of return on assets, total assets, for Sears is more likely to represent a smaller amount of total assets on hand during the year than the average amount. The return on assets rate for Sears and other companies who choose a fiscal year-end to coincide with low points in the inventory cycle is likely to be larger than if a more accurate estimate of the average amounts of total assets were used.

raw material. Goods purchased for use in manufacturing a product.

reacquired stock. *Treasury stock.*

real accounts. *Balance sheet accounts*; as opposed to *nominal accounts*. See *permanent accounts*.

real estate. *Land* and its *improvements*, such as landscaping and roads but not buildings.

realizable value. *Market value* or, sometimes, *net realizable value*.

realization convention. The accounting practice of delaying the recognition of *gains* and *losses* from changes in the market price of *assets* until the assets are sold. However, unrealized losses on *inventory* and *marketable securities* classified as *current assets* are recognized prior to sale when the *lower-of-cost-or-market* valuation basis is used.

realize. To convert into *funds*. When applied to a *gain* or *loss*, implies that an *arm's length transaction* has taken place. Contrast with *recognize*; a loss (as for example on *marketable equity securities*) may be recognized in the financial statements even though it has not yet been realized in a transaction.

realized gain (or loss) on marketable equity securities. An income statement account title for the difference between the proceeds of disposition and the *original cost* of *marketable equity securities*.

realized holding gain. See *inventory profit* for definition and an example.

rearrangement costs. Costs of re-installing assets perhaps in a different location. May be *capitalized* as part of the assets cost, just as is original installation cost.

recapitalization. *Reorganization.*

recapture. Various provisions of the *income tax* rules require refund by the taxpayer (recapture by the government) of various tax advantages under certain conditions. For example, the tax savings provided by the *investment credit* or by *accelerated depreciation* must be repaid if the item providing the tax savings is retired prematurely.

receipt. Acquisition of *cash*.

receivable. Any *collectible* whether or not it is currently due.

receivable turnover. See *ratio*.

reciprocal holdings. Company A owns stock of Company B and Company B owns stock of Company A.

recognize. To enter a transaction in the accounts. Not synonymous with *realize*.

reconciliation. A calculation that shows how one balance or figure is derived systematically from another, such as a *reconciliation of retained earnings* or a *bank reconciliation schedule*. See *articulate*.

record date. *Dividends* are paid on payment date to those who own the stock on the record date.

recourse. See *note receivable discounted*.

recovery of unrealized loss on marketable securities. An *income statement account title* for the *gain* during the current period on the current asset portfolio of *marketable equity securities*. This gain will be *recognized* only to the extent that net losses have been recognized in preceding periods in amounts no smaller than the current gain. (The Allowance for Declines in Marketable Equity Securities account can never have a *debit balance*.)

redemption. Retirement by the issuer, usually by a purchase or *call*, of *stocks* or *bonds*.

redemption premium. *Call premium.*

redemption value. The price to be paid by a corporation to retire *bonds* or *preferred stock* if called before *maturity*.

Financial Ratios Defined

Ratio	Numerator	Denominator
Rate of Return on Assets	Net Income + Interest Expense (net of tax effects)[a]	Average Total Assets During the Period
Profit Margin Ratio (before interest effects)	Net Income + Interest Expense (net of tax effects)[a]	Sales
Various Expense Ratios	Various Expenses	Sales
Total Assets Turnover Ratio	Sales	Average Total Assets During the Period
Accounts Receivable Turnover Ratio	Net Sales on Accounts	Average Accounts Receivable During the Period
Inventory Turnover Ratio	Cost of Goods Sold	Average Inventory During the Period
Plant Asset Turnover Ratio	Sales	Average Plant Assets During the Period
Rate of Return on Common Stock Equity	Net Income − Preferred Stock Dividends	Average Common Shareholders' Equity During the Period
Earnings per Share of Stock[b]	Net Income − Preferred Stock Dividends	Weighted Average Number of Common Shares Outstanding During the Period
Current Ratio	Current Assets	Current Liabilities
Quick or Acid-Test Ratio	Highly Liquid Assets (ordinarily, cash, marketable securities, and receivables)[c]	Current Liabilities
Long-Term Debt Ratio	Total Noncurrent Liabilities	Total Noncurrent Liabilities Plus Shareholders' Equity
Debt-Equity Ratio	Total Liabilities	Total Equities (liabilities plus shareholders' equity)
Times Interest Charges Earned	Net Income Before Interest and Income Taxes	Interest Expense

[a] If a consolidated subsidiary is not owned entirely by the parent corporation, the minority interest share of earnings must also be added back to net income.
[b] This calculation can be more complicated when there are convertible securities, options, or warrants outstanding.
[c] Receivables could conceivably be excluded for some firms and inventories included for others. Such refinements are seldom employed in practice.

refunding bond issue. Said of a *bond* issue whose proceeds are used to retire bonds already *outstanding*.

register. Collection of consecutive entries, or other information, in chronological order, such as a check register or an insurance register, which lists all insurance policies owned. If entries are recorded, it may serve as a *journal*.

registered bond. *Principal* of such a *bond* and *interest*, if registered as to interest, is paid to the owner listed on the books of the issuer. As opposed to a bearer bond where the possessor of the bond is entitled to interest and principal.

registrar. An *agent*, usually a bank or trust company, appointed by a corporation to keep track of the names of shareholders and distributions of earnings.

registration statement. Statement required by the Securities Act of 1933 of most companies wishing to have its securities traded in public markets. The statement discloses financial data and other items of interest to potential investors.

regressive tax. Tax for which the rate decreases as the taxed base, such as income, increases. Contrast with *progressive tax*.

Regulation S-X. The *SEC*'s regulation specifying the form and content of financial reports to the SEC.

rehabilitation. The improving of a used *asset* via an extensive repair. Ordinary *repairs* and *maintenance* restore or maintain expected *service potential* of an asset and are treated as *expenses*. A rehabilitation improves the asset beyond its current service potential, restoring the service potential to significantly higher level than before the rehabilitation. Once rehabilitated, the asset may be better, but need not be, than it was when new. *Expenditures* for rehabilitation, like those for *betterments* and *improvements*, are *capitalized*.

reinvestment rate. In a *capital budgeting* context, the rate at which cash inflows from a project occurring before the project's completion are invested. Once such a rate is assumed, there will never be multiple *internal rates of return*. See *Descartes' rule of signs*.

relative sales value method. A method for *allocating joint costs* in proportion to *realizable values* of the joint products. For example, joint products A and B together cost $100 and A sells for $60 whereas B sells for $90. Then A would be allocated ($60/$150) × $100 = .40 × $100 = $40 of cost while B would be allocated ($90/$150) × $100 = $60 of cost.

relevant cost. *Incremental cost. Opportunity cost.*

relevant range. Activity levels over which costs are linear or for which *flexible budget* estimates and *breakeven charts* will remain valid.

remittance advice. Information on a *check stub*, or on a document attached to a check by the *drawer*, which tells the *payee* why a payment is being made.

rent. A charge for use of land, buildings, or other assets.

reorganization. A major change in the *capital structure* of a corporation that leads to changes in the rights, interests, and implied ownership of the various security owners. Usually results from a *merger* or agreement by senior security holders to take action to forestall *bankruptcy*.

repair. An *expenditure* to restore an *asset's* service potential after damage or after prolonged use. In the second sense, after prolonged use, the difference between repairs and maintenance is one of degree and not of kind. Treated as an *expense* of the period when incurred. Because repairs and maintenance are treated similarly in this regard, the distinction is not important. A repair helps to maintain capacity intact at levels planned when the *asset* was acquired; contrast with *improvement*.

replacement cost. For an asset, the current fair market price to purchase another, similar asset (with the same future benefit or service potential). *Current cost.* See *reproduction cost* and *productive capacity.* See also *distributable income* and *inventory profit.*

replacement cost method of depreciation. The original-cost *depreciation* charge is augmented by an amount based upon a portion of the difference between the *current replacement cost* of the asset and its *original-cost.*

replacement system of depreciation. See *retirement method of depreciation* for definition and contrast.

report. *Financial statement; auditor's report.*

report form. This form of *balance sheet* typically shows *assets* minus *liabilities* as one total. Then below that it shows the components of *owners' equity* summing to the same total. Often, the top section shows *current* assets less current liabilities before *noncurrent assets* less noncurrent liabilities. Contrast with *account form.*

reporting objectives (policies). The general purposes for which financial statements are prepared. The FASB has discussed these in *SFAC No. 1.*

reproduction cost. The *cost* necessary to acquire an *asset* similar in all physical respects to another asset for which a *current value* is wanted. See *replacement cost* and *productive capacity* for further contrast.

required rate of return. The opportunity *cost of capital.*

requisition. A formal written order or request, such as for withdrawal of supplies from the storeroom.

resale value. *Exit value. Net realizable value.*

research and development. Research is activity aimed at discovering new knowledge in hopes that such activity will be useful in creating a new product, process, or service or improving a present product, process, or service. Development is the translation of research findings or other knowl-edge into a new or improved product, process, or service. *SFAS No.2* requires that costs of such activities be *expensed* as incurred on the grounds that the future benefits are too uncertain to warrant *capitalization* as an asset. This treatment seems questionable to us because we wonder why firms would continue to undertake R&D if there were no expectation of future benefit; if future benefits exist, then the *costs* should be assets.

reserve. When properly used in accounting, the term refers to an account that appropriates *retained earnings* and restricts dividend declarations. Appropriating retained earnings is it-self a poor and vanishing practice, so the word should seldom be used in accounting. In addition, used in the past to indicate an asset *contra* (for example, "reserve for depreciation") or an *estimated liability* for example, *reserve for warranty costs"*). In any case, reserve accounts have credit balances *and are not pools of funds* as the unwary reader might infer. If a company has set aside a pool of *cash (or marketable securities)* then that cash will be called a *fund.*

No other word in accounting is so misunderstood and mis-used by laymen and "experts" who should know better. A leading unabridged dictionary defines *reserve* as "Cash, or assets readily convertible into cash, held aside, as by a corpo-ration, bank, state or national government, etc. to meet ex-pected or unexpected demands." This definition is absolutely wrong in accounting. Reserves are not funds. For example, a contingency fund of $10,000 is created by depositing cash in a fund and this entry is made:

Dr. Contingency Fund 10,000
    Cr. Cash   10,000

The following entry may accompany this entry, if retained earnings are to be appropriated:

Dr. Retained Earnings. 10,000
    Cr. Reserve for Contingencies   10,000

The transaction leading to the first entry is an event of eco-nomic significance. The second entry has little economic impact for most firms. The problem with the word "reserve" arises because the second entry can be made without the first—a company can create a reserve, that is appropriate re-tained earnings, without creating a fund. The problem is at least in part caused by the fact that in common usage, "re-serve" means a pool of assets, as in the phrase "oil re-serves." The *Internal Revenue Service* does not help in dis-pelling confusion about the term *reserves.* The federal *income tax* return for corporations uses the title "Reserve for Bad Debts" to mean the "Allowance for Uncollectible Accounts" and speaks of the "Reserve Method" in referring to the *al-lowance method* for estimating *revenue* or *income* reductions from estimated *uncollectibles.*

reserve recognition accounting. In exploration for nat-ural resources, there is the problem of what to do with the expenditures for exploration. Suppose that $10 million is spent to drill 10 holes ($1 million each) and that nine of them are dry whereas one is a gusher containing oil with a *net realizable value* of $40 million. Dry-hole, or successful-efforts, accounting would *expense* $9 million and *capitalize* $1 million to be *depleted* as the oil was lifted from the ground. *SFAS No. 19*, now suspended, requires successful-efforts accounting. Full costing would expense nothing but capitalize the $10 million of drilling costs to be depleted as the oil is lifted from the single productive well. Reserve-recognition accounting would capitalize $40 million to be depleted as the oil is lifted, with a $30 million *credit* to *income* or *contributed capital*. The *balance sheet* shows the *net realizable value* of proven oil and gas reserves. The *income statement* has three sorts of items: (1) current income resulting from production or "lifting profit," which is the *revenue* from sales of oil and gas less the expense based on the current valuation amount at which these items had been carried on the balance sheet, (2) profit or loss from exploration efforts where the current value of new discoveries is revenue and all the exploration cost is expense, and (3) gain or loss on changes in current value during the year, which is in other contexts called a *holding gain or loss*.

residual income. In an external reporting context, this term refers to net income to common stock (net income less *preferred stock dividends*). In *managerial accounting*, this term refers to the excess of income for a division or *segment* of a company over the product of the *cost of capital* for the company multiplied by the average amount of capital invested in the division during the period over which the income was earned.

residual security. A *potentially dilutive security*. *Options*, *warrants*, *convertible bonds*, and *convertible preferred stock*.

residual value. At any time, the estimated or actual, *net realizable value* (that is, proceeds less removal costs) of an *asset*, usually a depreciable *plant asset*. In the context of depreciation accounting, this term is equivalent to *salvage value* and is preferable to *scrap value*, because the asset need not be scrapped. Sometimes used to mean net *book value*. In the context of a *noncancelable* lease, the estimated value of the leased asset at the end of the lease period. See *lease*.

responsibility accounting. Accounting for a business by considering various units as separate entities, or *profit centers*, giving management of each unit responsibility for the unit's *revenues* and *expenses*. Sometimes called "activity accounting." See *transfer price*.

responsibility center. Part or *segment* of an organization that is accountable for a specified set of activities. Also called "*accountability center*."

restricted assets. Governmental resources restricted by legal or contractual requirements for specific purpose.

restricted retained earnings. That part of *retained earnings* not legally available for *dividends*. See *retained earnings, appropriated*. Bond indentures and other loan contracts can curtail the legal ability of the corporation to declare dividends without formally requiring a retained earnings appropriation, but disclosure is required.

retail inventory method. Ascertaining cost amounts of *ending inventory* as follows (assuming FIFO): cost of ending inventory = (selling price of *goods available for sale* − sales) × *cost percentage*. Cost of goods sold is then computed from the inventory equation; costs of beginning inventory, purchases and ending inventory are all known. (When *LIFO* is used, the method is similar to the *dollar-value LIFO method*). See *markup*.

retail terminology. See *markup*.

retained earnings. Net *income* over the life of a corporation less all dividends (including capitalization through stock dividends); *owners' equity* less *contributed capital*.

retained earnings, appropriated. An *account* set up by

crediting it and debiting *retained earnings*. Used to indicate that a portion of retained earnings is not available for dividends. The practice of appropriating retained earnings is misleading unless all capital is earmarked with its use, which is not practicable. Use of formal retained earnings appropriations is declining.

retained earnings statement. *Generally accepted accounting principles* require that whenever *comparative balance sheets* and an *income statement* are presented, there must also be presented a *reconciliation* of the beginning and ending balances in the *retained earnings account*. This reconciliation can appear in a separate statement, in a combined statement of income and retained earnings or in the balance sheet.

retirement method of depreciation. No entry is recorded for *depreciation expense* until an *asset* is retired from service. Then, an entry is made *debiting* depreciation expense and *crediting* the asset account for the cost of the asset retired. If the retired asset has a *salvage value*, the amount of the debit to depreciation expense is reduced by the amount of salvage value with a corresponding debit to cash, receivables, or salvaged materials. The "replacement system of depreciation" is similar, except that the debit to depreciation expense equals the cost of the new asset less the salvage value, if any, of the old asset. These methods were used by some public utilities. For example, if ten telephone poles are acquired in year one for $60 each and are replaced in year ten for $100 each when the salvage value of the old poles is $5 each, then the accounting would be as follows:

Retirement Method.

Plant Assets......................	600	
Cash		600
To acquire assets in year one.		
Depreciation Expense	550	
Salvage Receivable	50	
Plant Assets....................		600
To record retirement and depreciation in year ten.		
Plant Assets......................	1,000	
Cash		1,000
To record acquisition of new assets in year ten.		

Replacement Method.

Plant Assets......................	600	
Cash		600
To acquire assets in year one.		
Depreciation Expense	950	
Salvage Receivable	50	
Cash		1,000
To record depreciation on old asset in amount quantified by net cost of replacement asset in year ten.		

The retirement method is like *FIFO*, in that the cost of the first assets is recorded as depreciation and the cost of the second assets is put on the balance sheet. The replacement method is like *LIFO* in that the cost of the second assets determines the depreciation expense and the cost of the first assets remains on the balance sheet.

retirement plan. *Pension plan*.

return. A schedule of information required by governmental bodies, such as the tax return required by the *Internal Revenue Service*. Also the physical return of merchandise. See also *return on investment*.

return of investment. return on capital. *Income* (before distributions to suppliers of capital) for a period. As a rate, this amount divided by average total assets. *Interest*, net of tax effects, should be added back to *net income* for the numerator. See *ratio*.

revenue. The increase in *owners' equity* caused by a service rendered on the sale of goods. The monetary measure of a service rendered. *Sales* of products, merchandise, and services, and earnings from *interest*, *dividends*, rents, and the like. The amount of revenue is the expected *net present value* of the *net assets* received. Do not confuse with *receipt of funds*, which may occur before, when, or after revenue is , recognized. Contrast with *gain* and *income*. See also *holding gain*. Some writers use the term *gross income* synonymously with *revenue*; such usage is to be avoided.

revenue center. A *responsibility center* within a firm that has control only over revenues generated; contrast with *cost center*. See *profit center*.

revenue expenditure. A phrase sometimes used to mean an *expense* in contrast to a capital *expenditure* to acquire an *asset* or to discharge a *liability*. Avoid using this phrase; use *period expense* instead.

revenue received in advance. An inferior term for *advances from customers*.

reversal (reversing) entry. An *entry* in which all *debits* and *credits* are the credits and debits, respectively, of another entry, and in the same amounts. It is usually made on the first day of an *accounting period* to reverse a previous *adjusting entry*, usually an *accrual*. The purpose of such entries is to make the bookkeeper's tasks easier. Suppose that salaries are paid every other Friday, with paychecks compensating employees for the 2 weeks just ended. Total salaries accrue at the rate of $5,000 per 5-day work week. The bookkeeper is accustomed to making the following entry every other Friday:

(1) Salary Expense.................. 10,000
    Cash 10,000
    To record salary expense and salary payments.

If paychecks are delivered to employees on Friday, June 25, 1982, then the *adjusting entry* made on June 30 (or, perhaps, later) to record accrued salaries for June 28, 29, and 30 would be

(2) Salary Expense.................. 3,000
    Salaries Payable.............. 3,000
    To charge second quarter operations with all salaries earned in second quarter.

The Salary Expense account would be closed as part of the June 30 *closing entries*. On the next pay-day, July 9, the salary entry would have to be

(3) Salary Expense.................. 7,000
    Salaries Payable.............. 3,000
    Cash 10,000
    To record salary payments split between expense for the third quarter (7 days) and liability carried over from the second quarter.

To make entry (3), the bookkeeper must look back into the records to see how much of the debit is to Salaries Payable accrued from the previous year so that total debits are properly split between third quarter expense and the liability carried over from the second quarter. Notice that this entry forces the bookkeeper both (a) to refer to balances in old accounts and (b) to make an entry different from the one customarily made, entry (1).

The reversing entry, made just after the books have been closed for the second quarter, makes the salary entry for July 9, 1982, the same as that made on all other Friday pay-days. The reversing entry merely *reverses* the adjusting entry (2):

(4) Salaries Payable................ 3,000
    Salary Expense.............. 3,000
    To reverse the adjusting entry.

This entry results in a zero balance in the Salaries Payable account and a *credit* balance in the Salary Expense account. If entry (4) is made just after the books are closed for the second quarter, then the entry on July 9 will be the customary entry (1). Entries (4) and (1) together have exactly the same effect as entry (3).

The procedure for using reversal entries is as follows: The required adjustment to record an accrual (*payable* or *receivable*) is made at the end of an *accounting period*; the closing entry is made as usual; as of the first day of the following period, an entry is made reversing the adjusting entry; when a payment is made (or received), the entry is recorded as though no adjusting entry had been recorded. Whether or not reversal entries are used affects the record-keeping procedures, but not the financial statements.

Also used to describe the entry reversing an incorrect entry before recording the correct entry.

reverse stock split. A stock split in which the number of shares *outstanding* is decreased. See *stock split*.

revolving fund. A *fund* whose amounts are continually expended and then replenished; for example, a *petty cash fund*.

revolving loan. A *loan* that is expected to be renewed at *maturity*.

right. The privilege to subscribe to new *stock* issues or to purchase stock. Usually, rights are contained in securities called *warrants* and the warrants may be sold to others. See also *preemptive right*.

risk. A measure of the variability of the *return on investment*. For a given expected amount of return, most people prefer less risk to more risk. Therefore, in rational markets, investments with more risk usually promise, or are expected to yield, a higher rate of return than investments with lower risk. Most people use "risk" and "uncertainty" as synonyms. In technical language, however, these terms have different meanings. "Risk" is used when the probabilities attached to the various outcomes are known, such as the probabilities of heads or tails in the flip of a fair coin. "Uncertainty" refers to an event where the probabilities of the outcomes, such as winning or losing a lawsuit, can only be estimated.

risk-adjusted discount rate. In a *capital budgeting* context, a decision maker compares projects by comparing their *net present values* for a given *interest* rate, usually the *cost of capital*. If a given project's outcome is considered to be much more or much less risky than the normal undertakings of the company, then the interest rate will be increased (if the project is more risky) or decreased (if less risky) and the rate used is said to be risk-adjusted.

risk premium. Extra compensation paid to an employee or extra interest paid to a lender, over amounts usually considered normal, in return for their undertaking to engage in activities more risky than normal.

ROI. *Return on investment,* but usually used to refer to a single project and expressed as a ratio: *income* divided by average *cost* of *assets* devoted to the project.

royalty. Compensation for the use of property, usually a patent, copyrighted material, or natural resources. The amount is often expressed as a percentage of receipts from using the property or as an amount per unit produced.

RRA. See *Reserve recognition accounting.*

RRR. Required rate of return.

Rule of 69. An amount of money invested at r percent per period will double in 69/r + .35 periods. This approximation is accurate to one-tenth of a period for interest rates between 1/4 and 100 percent per period. For example, at 10 percent per period, the rule says that a given sum will double in 69/10 + .35 = 7.25 periods. At 10 percent per period, a given sum doubles in 7.27+ periods.

rule of 72. An amount of money invested at r percent per period will double in 72/r periods. A reasonable approximation but not nearly as accurate as the *rule of 69.* For example, at 10 percent per period, the rule says that a given sum will double in 72/10 = 7.2 periods.

rule of 78. The rule followed by many finance companies for allocating earnings on *loans* among the months of a year on the sum-of-the-months'-digits basis when equal monthly payments from the borrower are to be received. The sum of the digits from 1 through 12 is 78, so 12/78 of the year's earnings are allocated to the first month, 11/78 to the second month, and so on. See *sum-of-the-years' digits depreciation.*

ruling (and balancing) an account. The process of summarizing a series of entries in an *account* by computing a new *balance* and drawing double lines to indicate the information above the double lines has been summarized in the new balance. The process is illustrated below. The steps are as follow. (1) Compute the sum of all *debit* entries including opening debit balance, if any—$1,464.16. (2) Compute the

sum of all credit entries including opening credit balance, if any—$413.57. (3) If the amount in (1) is larger than the amount in (2), then write the excess as a credit with a check mark—$1,464.16 − $413.57 = $1,050.59. (4) Add both debit and credit columns, which should both now sum to the same amount, and show that identical total at the foot of both columns. (5) Draw double lines under those numbers and write the excess of debits over credits as the new debit balance with a check mark. (6) If the amount in (2) is larger than the amount in (1), then write the excess as a debit with a check mark. (7) Do steps (4) and (5) except that the excess becomes the new credit balance. (8) If the amount in (1) is equal to the amount in (2), then the balance is zero and only the totals with the double lines beneath them need be shown. This process is illustrated in the accompanying figure.

S

SAB. Staff Accounting Bulletin of the *SEC.*

safe-harbor lease. The Congress has provided business with an incentive to invest in qualifying *plant and equipment* by granting an *investment credit,* which though it occurs as a reduction in *income taxes* otherwise payable, is effectively a reduction in the purchase price of the assets. Similarly, the Congress has granted an incentive to acqire such assets by allowing *accelerated cost recovery* (a form of unusually *accelerated depreciation*). Accelerating depreciation for tax purposes allows a reduction of taxes paid in early years of an asset's life which provides the firm with an increased *net present value* of *cash flows.* Both of these incentives are administered by the *IRS* through the income tax laws, rather than being granted as an outright cash payment by some other government agency. A business with no taxable income in many cases had been unable to reap the benefits of the investment credit or of accelerated depreciation because the Congress did not provide for tax refunds to those who acquire qualifying assets but who have no taxable income. In practice, one company, without taxable income, could lease from another, with taxable income, an asset that would have otherwise been purchased by the first company. The second company acquires the asset, gets the tax-reduction benefits from the acquisition, and leases it (presumably at a lower price reflecting its own costs lowered by the tax reductions) to the unprofitable company. Such leases were not widely allowed prior to the tax laws of 1981 which explicitly recognized that

---

An Open Account, Ruled and Balanced
(Steps indicated in parentheses correspond to steps described in "ruling an account.")

	Date 1982	Explanation	Ref.	Debit (1)		Date 1982	Explanation	Ref.	Credit (2)		
	Jan. 1	Balance	✔	100	00						
	Jan. 13		VR	121	37	Sept. 15		J		42	
	Mar. 20		VR	56	42	Nov. 12		J	413	15	
	June 5		J	1,138	09	Dec. 31	Balance	✔	1,050	59	(3)
	Aug. 18		J	1	21						
	Nov. 20		VR	38	43						
	Dec. 7		VR	8	64						
(4)	1983			1,464	16	1983			1,464	16	(4)
(5)	Jan. 1	Balance	✔	1,050	59						

tax credits and *deductions* to the profitable company in such leases shall be allowed. These leases have been called "safe-harbor leases." Because of the substantial tax savings arranged by large profitable companies "buying tax benefits" from unprofitable companies, the Congress in 1982 indicated that it might reduce the opportunity for such leases. The outcome is still uncertain as this book goes to press.

salary. Compensation earned by managers, administrators, professionals, not based on an hourly rate. Contrast with *wage*.

sale. A *revenue* transaction where *goods* or *services* are delivered to a customer in return for cash or a contractual obligation to pay.

sale and leaseback. Phrase used to describe a *financing* transaction where improved property is sold but is taken back for use on a long-term *lease*. Such transactions often have advantageous income tax effects, but usually have no effect on *financial statement income*.

sales allowance. A reduction in sales *invoice* price usually given because the goods received by the buyer are not exactly what was ordered. The amounts of such adjustments are often accumulated by the seller in a temporary *revenue contra account* having this, or a similar, title. See *sales discount*.

sales basis of revenue recognition. *Revenue* is recognized, not as goods are produced nor as orders are received, but only when the sale (delivery) has been consummated and cash or a legal receivable obtained. Most revenue is recognized on this basis. Compare with the *percentage of completion method* and the *installment method*. Identical with *completed contract method* but this latter term is ordinarily used only for *long-term* construction projects.

sales contra, estimated uncollectibles. A title for the *contra-revenue account* to recognize estimated reductions in income caused by accounts receivable that will not be collected. See *allowance for uncollectibles* and *allowance method*.

sales discount. Reduction in sales *invoice* price usually offered for prompt payment. See *terms of sale* and *2/10, n/30*.

sales return. The physical return of merchandise; the amounts of such returns are often accumulated by the seller in a temporary *revenue contra account*.

sales value method. *Relative sales value method*.

salvage value. Actual or estimated selling price, net of removal or disposal costs, of a used *plant asset* to be sold or otherwise retired. See *residual value*.

SAS. Statement on Auditing Standards of the *AICPA*.

SAV. *Supplemental actuarial value*.

schedule. Supporting set of calculations that show how figures in a statement or tax return are derived.

scientific method. *Effective interest method* of *amortizing* bond discount or premium.

scrap value. *Salvage value* assuming item is to be junked. A *net realizable value*. *Residual value*.

SEC. Securities and Exchange Commission, an agency authorized by the U.S. Congress to regulate, among other things, the financial reporting practices of most public corporations. The SEC has indicated that it will usually allow the

FASB to set accounting principles but it reserves the right to require more disclosure than required by the FASB. The SEC's accounting requirements are stated in its *Accounting Series Releases (ASR)* and *Regulation S-X*. See also *registration statement* and *10-K*.

secret reserve. *Hidden reserve*.

Securities and Exchange Commission. *SEC*.

security. Document that indicates ownership or indebtedness or potential ownership, such as an *option* or *warrant*.

segment (of a business). As defined by *APB Opinion No. 30*, "a component of an *entity* whose activities represent a separate major line of business or class of customer . . . [It may be] a *subsidiary*, a division, or a department. . . . provided that its *assets*, results of *operations*, and activities can be clearly distinguished, physically and operationally for financial reporting purposes, from the other assets, results of operations, and activities of the entity." In *SFAS No. 14* a segment is defined as "A component of an enterprise engaged in promoting a product or service or a group of related products and services primarily to unaffiliated customers . . . for a profit."

segment reporting. Reporting of *sales*, *income* and *assets* by *segments of a business*, usually classified by nature of products sold but sometimes by geographical area where goods are produced or sold or by type of customers. Sometimes called "line of business reporting." *Central corporate expenses* are not allocated to the segments.

self-balancing. A set of records with equal *debits* and *credits* such as the *ledger* (but not individual accounts), the *balance sheet*, and a *fund* in nonprofit accounting.

self-insurance. See *insurance*.

selling and administrative expenses. *Expenses* not specifically identifiable with, nor assigned to, production.

semifixed costs. *Costs* that increase with activity as a step function.

semivariable costs. *Costs* that increase strictly linearly with activity but that are positive at zero activity level. Royalty fees of 2 percent of sales are variable; royalty fees of $1,000 per year plus 2 percent of sales are semivariable.

senior securities. *Bonds* as opposed to *preferred stock*; *preferred stock* as opposed to *common stock*. The senior security has a claim against *earnings* or *assets* that must be met before the claim of less senior securities.

serial bonds. An *issue* of *bonds* that mature in part at one date, another part on another date, and so on; the various maturity dates usually are equally spaced; contrast them with *term bonds*.

service basis of depreciation. *Production method*.

service department. A department, such as the personnel or computer department, that provides services to other departments, rather than direct work on a salable product; contrast with *production department*. Costs of service departments whose services benefit manufacturing operations must be *allocated* to as *product costs* under *absorption costing*.

service life. Period of expected usefulness of an asset; may not coincide with *depreciable life* for income tax purposes.

service potential. The future benefits embodied in an item that cause the item to be classified as an *asset*. Without service potential, there are no future benefits and the item should not be classified as an asset: *SFAS No. 3* suggests that the primary characteristic of service potential is the ability to generate future net cash inflows.

services. Useful work done by a person, a machine, or an organization. See *goods and services*.

setup. The time or costs required to prepare production equipment for doing a job.

SFAC. Statement of Financial Accounting Concepts from the *FASB*.

SFAS. *Statement of Financial Accounting Standards* from the *FASB*.

share. A unit of *stock* representing ownership in a corporation.

shareholders' equity. *Proprietorship* or *owners' equity* of a corporation. Because *stock* means inventory in Australian, British, and Canadian usage, the term "shareholders' equity" is usually used by Australian, British, and Canadian writers.

short-term. Current; ordinarily, due within one year.

shrinkage. An excess of *inventory* shown on the *books* over actual physical quantities on hand. Can result from theft or shoplifting as well as from evaporation or general wear and tear.

sight draft. A demand for payment drawn by a person to whom money is owed. The *draft* is presented to the borrower's (the debtor's) bank in expectation that the borrower will authorize its bank to disburse the funds. Such drafts are often used when a seller sells goods to a new customer in a different city. The seller is not sure whether the buyer will pay the bill. The seller sends the *bill* of lading, or other evidence of ownership of the goods, along with a sight draft to the buyer's bank. Before the goods can be released to the buyer, the buyer must instruct its bank to honor the sight draft by withdrawing funds from the buyers' account. Once the sight draft is honored, the bill of lading or other document evidencing ownership is handed over to the buyer and the goods become the property of the buyer.

simple interest. *Interest* calculated on *principal* where interest earned during periods before maturity of the loan is neither added to the principal nor paid to the lender. *Interest = principal × interest rate × time*. Seldom used in economic calculations except for periods less than 1 year; contrast with *compound interest*.

single-entry accounting. Accounting that is neither *self-balancing* nor *articulated*; that is, it does not rely on equal *debits* and *credits*. *No journal entries* are made. *Plugging* is required to derive *owners' equity* for the *balance sheet*.

single proprietorship. *Sole proprietorship*.

single step. Said of an *income statement* where *ordinary revenue* and *gain* items are shown first and totaled. Then all ordinary *expenses* and *losses* are totaled. Their difference, plus the effect of *income from discontinued operations* and *extraordinary items*, is shown as *net income*; contrast with *multiple-step* and see *proprietorship theory*.

sinking fund. *Assets* and their earnings earmarked for the retirement of bonds or other long-term obligations. Earnings

of sinking fund investments are taxable income of the company.

sinking fund method of depreciation. The periodic charge is an amount so that when the charges are considered to be an *annuity*, the value of the annuity at the end of depreciable life is equal to the *acquisition cost* of the asset. In theory, the charge for a period ought also to include interest on the accumulated depreciation at the start of the period as well. A *fund* of cash is not necessarily, or even usually, accumulated. This method is rarely used.

skeleton account. *T-account*.

slide. The name of the error made by a bookkeeper in recording the digits of a number correctly with the decimal point misplaced; for example, recording $123.40 as $1,234.00 or as $12.34.

soak-up method. The *equity method*.

Social Security taxes. Taxes levied by the federal government on both employers and employees to provide *funds* to pay retired persons (or their survivors) who are entitled to receive such payments, either because they paid Social Security taxes themselves or because the Congress has declared them eligible. See *Old Age, Survivors, Disability*, and *(Hospital) Insurance*.

sole proprietorship. All *owners' equity* belongs to one person.

solvent. Able to meet debts when due.

SOP. *Statement of Position* (of AcSEC of the AICPA).

sound value. A phrase used mainly in appraisals of *fixed assets* to mean *fair market value* or *replacement cost* in present condition.

source of funds. Any *transaction* that increases *working capital*.

sources and uses statement. *Statement of changes in financial position*.

SOYD. *Sum-of-the-years'-digits depreciation*.

special assessment. A compulsory levy made by a governmental unit on property to pay the costs of a specific improvement, or service, presumed not to benefit the general public but only the owners of the property so assessed. Accounted for in a special assessment fund.

special journal. A *journal*, such as a sales journal or cash disbursements journal, to record *transactions* of a similar nature that occur frequently.

special revenue debt. Debt of a governmental unit backed only by revenues from specific sources such as tolls from a bridge.

specific identification method. Method for valuing *ending inventory* and *cost of goods sold* by identifying actual units sold and in inventory and summing the actual costs of those individual units. Usually used for items with large unit value, such as jewelry, automobiles, and fur coats.

specific price changes. Changes in the market prices of specific *goods and services*; contrast with *general price level changes*.

specific price index. A measure of the price of a specific good or service, or a small group of similar goods or services, at one time relative to the price during a base period; contrast with *general price index*. See *dollar-value LIFO method*.

spending variance. In *standard cost systems*, the *rate* or *price variance* for *overhead costs*.

split. *Stock split*. Sometimes called "splitup."

splitoff point. The point where all costs are no longer *joint costs* but can be identified with individual products or perhaps with a smaller number of *joint products*.

spoilage. See *abnormal spoilage* and *normal spoilage*.

spread sheet. A *work sheet* organized like a *matrix* that provides a two-way classification of accounting data. The rows and columns are both labeled with *account* titles. An entry in a row represents a *debit* whereas an entry in a column represents a *credit*. Thus, the number "100" in the "cash" row and the "accounts receivable" column records an entry debiting cash and crediting accounts receivable for $100. A given row total indicates all debit entries to the account represented by that row and a given column total indicates the sum of all credit entries to the account represented by the column.

squeeze. A term sometimes used for *plug*.

SSARS. See *Statement on Standards for Accounting and Review Services*.

stabilized accounting. *Constant dollar accounting*.

stable monetary unit assumption. In spite of *inflation* that appears to be a way of life, the assumption that underlies *historical-cost/nominal dollar accounting*—namely that current dollars and dollars of previous years can be meaningfully added together. No specific recognition is given to changing values of the dollar in the usual *financial statements*. See *constant dollar accounting*.

Staff Accounting Bulletin. An interpretation issued by the Staff of the Chief Accountant of the *SEC* "suggesting" how the various *Accounting Series Releases* should be applied in practice.

standard cost. Anticipated *cost* of producing a unit of output; a predetermined cost to be assigned to products produced. Standard cost implies a norm: what costs should be. Budgeted cost implies a forecast, something likely, but not necessarily a "should," as implied by a norm. Standard costs are used as the benchmark for gauging good and bad performance. While a budget may similarly be used, it need not. A budget may simply be a planning document, subject to changes whenever plans change, whereas standard costs are usually not changed until technology changes or costs of labor and materials change.

standard cost system. *Product costing* using *standard costs* rather than actual costs. May be based on either *absorption* or *direct costing* principles.

standard price (rate). Unit price established for materials or labor used in *standard cost systems*.

standard quantity allowed. The quantity of direct material or direct labor (inputs) that should have been used if the units of output had been produced in accordance with preset *standards*.

standby costs. A type of *capacity cost*, such as property taxes, incurred even if operations are shut down completely. Contrast with *enabling costs*.

stated capital. Amount of capital contributed by shareholders. Sometimes used to mean *legal capital*.

stated value. A term sometimes used for the *face amount of capital stock*, when no *par value* is indicated. Where there is stated value per share, it may be set by the directors (in which case, capital *contributed in excess of stated value* may come into being).

statement of affairs. A *balance sheet* showing immediate *liquidation* amounts, rather than *historical costs*, usually prepared when *insolvency* or *bankruptcy* is imminent. The *going concern assumption* is not used.

statement of changes in financial position. As defined by *APB Opinion* No. 19, a statement that explains the changes in *working capital* (or cash) balances during a period and shows the changes in the working capital (or cash) accounts themselves. Sometimes called the "funds statement." See *dual transactions assumption* and *all financial resources*.

Statement of Financial Accounting Standards. SFAS. See *FASB*.

Statement of Financial Accounting Concepts. SFAC. One of a series of *FASB* publications in its *conceptual framework* for *financial accounting* and reporting. Such statements set forth objectives and fundamentals to be the basis for specific financial accounting and reporting standards.

statement of financial position. *Balance sheet*.

Statement of Position. SOP. A recommendation on an emerging accounting problem issued by the *AcSEC* of the *AICPA*. The AICPA's Code of Professional Ethics specifically states that *CPAs* need not treat SOPs as they do rules from the FASB, but a CPA would be wary of departing from the recommendations of a SOP.

statement of retained earnings (income). A statement that reconciles the beginning-of-period and end-of-period balances in the *retained earnings* account. It shows the effects of *earnings*, *dividend declarations*, and *prior-period adjustments*.

Statement on Auditing Standards. SAS. No. 1 of this series (1973) codifies all statements on auditing standards previously promulgated by the AICPA. Later numbers deal with specific auditing standards and procedures.

Statement on Standards for Accounting and Review Services. SSARS. Pronouncements issued by the *AICPA* on *unaudited financial statements* and unaudited financial information of nonpublic entities.

static budget. *Fixed budget*.

statutory tax rate. The tax rate specified in the *income tax* law for each type of income (for example, *ordinary income*, *capital gain or loss*).

step cost. Semifixed cost.

step-down method. The method for *allocating service department* costs that starts by allocating one service department's costs to *production departments* and to all other service departments. Then a second service department's costs, including costs allocated from the first, are allocated to production departments and to all other service departments except the first one. In this fashion, the costs of all service departments, including previous allocations, are allocated to production departments and to those service departments whose costs have not yet been allocated.

sterilized allocation. Optimal decisions result from considering *incremental costs*, only. *Allocations* of *joint* or *common costs* are never required for optimal decisions. An allocation of these costs that causes the optimal decision choice not to differ from the one that occurs when joint or common costs are unallocated is "sterilized" with respect to that decision. The term was first used in this context by Arthur L. Thomas. Because *absorption costing* requires that all manufacturing costs be allocated to product, and because some allocations can lead to bad decisions, Thomas (and we) advocate that the allocation scheme chosen lead to sterilized allocations that do not alter the otherwise optimal decision. There is, however, no single allocation scheme that is always sterilized with respect to all decisions. Thus, Thomas (and we) advocate that decisions be made on the basis of incremental costs before any allocations.

stock. *Inventory. Capital stock.* A measure of the amount of something on hand at a specific time; in this sense, contrast with *flow.*

stock appreciation rights. The employer promises to pay to the employee an amount of *cash* on a certain future date. The amount of cash is the difference between the *market value* of a certain number of *shares* of *stock* in the employer's company on a given future date and some base price set on the date the rights are granted. This is a form of compensation used because both changes in tax laws in recent years and stock market performance have made *stock options* relatively less attractive. *GAAP* computes compensation based on the difference between market value of the shares and the base price set at the time of the grant. *Expense* is recognized as the holder of the rights performs the services required for the rights to be exercised.

stock dividend. A so-called *dividend* where additional *shares* of *capital stock* are distributed, without cash payments, to existing shareholders. It results in a *debit* to *retained earnings* in the amount of the market value of the shares issued and a *credit to capital stock* accounts. It is ordinarily used to indicate that earnings retained have been permanently reinvested in the business; contrast with a *stock split,* which requires no entry in the capital stock accounts other than a notation that the *par* or *stated value* per share has been changed.

stock option. The right to purchase a specified number of shares of *stock* for a specified price at specified times, usually granted to employees; contrast with *warrant.*

stock right. See *right.*

stock split. Increase in the number of common shares outstanding resulting from the issuance of additional shares to existing shareholders without additional capital contributions by them. Does not increase the total *par* (or *stated) value of common stock* outstanding because par (or stated) value per share is reduced in inverse proportion. A three-for-one stock split reduces par (or stated) value per share to one-third of its former amount. Stock splits are usually limited to distributions that increase the number of shares outstanding by 20 percent or more; compare with *stock dividend.*

stock subscriptions. See *subscription* and *subscribed stock.*

stock warrant. See *warrant.*

stockholders' equity. See *shareholders' equity.*

stores. *Raw materials,* parts, and supplies.

straight-debt value. An estimate of what the *market value* of a *convertible bond* would be if the bond did not contain a conversion privilege.

straight-line depreciation. If the *depreciable life* is n periods, then the periodic *depreciation* charge is 1/n of the *depreciable cost.* Results in equal periodic charges and is sometimes called "straight-time depreciation."

Subchapter S Corporation. A firm legally organized as a *corporation* but taxed as if it were a *partnership.*

subject to. Qualifications in an *auditor's report* usually caused by a *material* uncertainty in the valuation of an item, such as future promised payments from a foreign government or outcome of pending litigation.

subordinated. Said of *debt* whose claim on income or assets is junior to, or comes after, claims of other debt.

subscribed stock. A *shareholders' equity* account showing the capital that will be contributed as soon as the subscription price is collected. A subscription is a legal contract so that an entry is made debiting an owners' equity contra account and crediting subscribed stock as soon as the stock is subscribed.

subscription. Agreement to buy a *security,* or to purchase periodicals such as magazines.

subsequent events. *Post-statement events.*

subsidiary. Said of a company more than 50 percent of whose voting stock is owned by another.

subsidiary (ledger) accounts. The *accounts* in a *subsidiary ledger.*

subsidiary ledger. The *ledger* that contains the detailed accounts whose total is shown in a *controlling account* of the *general ledger.*

successful-efforts accounting. In petroleum accounting, the *capitalization* of the drilling costs of only those wells that contain oil. See *reserve recognition accounting* for an example.

summary of significant accounting principles. *APB Opinion* No. 22 requires that every *annual report* summarize the significant *accounting principles* used in compiling the annual report. This summary may be a separate exhibit or the first *note* to the financial statements.

sum-of-the-years'-digits depreciation. SYD. SOYD. An *accelerated depreciation* method for an asset with *depreciable life* of n years where the charge in period $i(i = 1, \ldots, n)$ is the fraction $(n + 1 - i)/[n(n + 1)/2]$ of the *depreciable cost.* If an asset has a depreciable cost of $15,000 and a 5-year depreciable life, for example, the depreciation charges would be $5,000 (= 5/15 \times $15,000) in the first year, $4,000 in the second, $3,000 in the third, $2,000 in the fourth, and $1,000 in the fifth.

sunk cost. *Costs* incurred in the past that are not affected by, and hence irrelevant for, current decisions, aside from *income tax* effects; contrast with *incremental costs* and *imputed costs.* For example, the *acquisition cost* of machinery is irrelevant to a decision of whether or not to scrap the machinery. The current *exit value* of the machine is the imputed cost of continuing to own it and the cost of, say, electricity to run the machine is an incremental cost of its operation. Sunk costs become relevant for decision making when *income taxes* (gain or loss on disposal of asset) are taken into account because the cash payment for income taxes depends on the tax basis of the asset.

supplemental actuarial value. Actuarial accrued liability.

59

supplementary statements (schedules). Statements (schedules) in addition to the four basic *financial statements* (including the retained earnings reconciliation as a basic statement).

surplus. A word once used but now considered poor terminology; prefaced by "earned" to mean *retained earnings* and prefaced by "capital" to mean *capital contributed in excess of par* (or *stated*) *value*.

surplus reserves. Of all the words in accounting, *reserve* is the most objectionable and *surplus* is the second most objectionable. This phrase, then, has nothing to recommend it. It means, simply, *appropriated retained earnings*.

suspense account. A *temporary account* used to record part of a transaction prior to final analysis of that transaction. For example, if a business regularly classifies all sales into a dozen or more different categories but wants to deposit the proceeds of cash sales every day, it may credit a sales suspense account pending detailed classification of all sales into sales, type 1; sales, type 2; and so on.

sustainable income. The part of *distributable income* (computed from *current cost* data) that the firm can be expected to earn in the next accounting period if operations are continued at the same levels as during the current period. *Income from discontinued operations*, for example, may be distributable but not sustainable.

S-X. See *Regulation S-X*.

SYD. *Sum-of-the-years'-digits depreciation. SOYD.*

T

T-account. Account form shaped like the letter T with the title above the horizontal line. *Debits* are shown to the left of the vertical line, *credits* to the right.

take-home pay. The amount of a paycheck; earned wages or *salary* reduced by deductions for *income taxes, Social Security taxes*, contributions to fringe benefit plans, union dues, and so on. Take-home pay might be as little as 60 percent of earned compensation.

take-or-pay contract. As defined by *SFAS* No. 47, an agreement between a purchaser and a seller that provides for the purchaser to pay specified amounts periodically in return for products or services. The purchaser must make specified minimum payments even if it does not take delivery of the contracted products or services.

taking a bath. To incur a large loss. See *big bath*.

tangible. Having physical form. Accounting has never satisfactorily defined the distinction between tangible and *intangible assets*. Typically, intangibles are defined by giving an exhaustive list and everything not on the list is defined as tangible.

target cost. *Standard cost.*

tax. A nonpenal, but compulsory, charge levied by a government on income, consumption, wealth, or other bases for the benefit of all those governed. The term does not include fines or specific charges for benefits accruing only to those paying the charges, such as licenses, permits, special assessments, admissions fees, and tolls.

tax allocation: interperiod. See *deferred income tax liability*.

tax allocation: intrastatement. The showing of income

tax effects on *extraordinary items, income from discontinued operations*, and *prior-period adjustments* along with these items, separately from income taxes on other income. See *net-of-tax reporting*.

tax avoidance. See *tax shelter*.

tax credit. A subtraction from taxes otherwise payable, contrast with *tax deduction*.

tax deduction. A subtraction from *revenues* and *gains* to arrive at taxable income. Tax deductions are technically different from tax *exemptions*, but the effect of both is to reduce gross income in computing taxable income. Both are different from *tax credits*, which are subtracted from the computed tax itself in determining taxes payable. If the tax rate is the fraction t of pretax income, then a *tax credit* of $1 is worth $1/t of *tax deductions*.

tax evasion. The fraudulent understatement of taxable revenues or overstatement of deductions and expenses or both; contrast with *tax shelter*.

tax exempts. See *municipal bonds*.

tax shelter. The legal avoidance of, or reduction in, *income taxes* resulting from a careful reading of the complex income tax regulations and the subsequent rearrangement of financial affairs to take advantage of the regulations. Often the term is used pejoratively, but the courts have long held that an individual or corporation has no obligation to pay taxes any larger than the legal minimum. If the public concludes that a given tax shelter is "unfair," then the laws and regulations can be changed. Sometimes used to refer to the investment that permits tax avoidance.

tax shield. The amount of an *expense* that reduces taxable income but does not require *working capital*, such as *depreciation*. Sometimes this term is expanded to include expenses that reduce taxable income and use working capital. A depreciation deduction (or *R&D expense* in the expanded sense) of $10,000 provides a tax shield of $4,600 when the marginal tax rate is 46 percent.

tax-transfer lease. *Safe harbor lease.*

Technical Bulletin. The *FASB* has authorized its staff to issue bulletins to provide guidance on financial accounting and reporting problems. Although the FASB does not formally approve the contents of the bulletins, their contents are presumed to be part of *GAAP*.

technology. The sum of a firm's technical *trade secrets* and *know-how*, as distinct from its *patents*.

temporary account. *Account* that does not appear on the *balance sheet*. *Revenue* and *expense* accounts, their *adjuncts* and *contras, production cost accounts, dividend distribution accounts*, and purchases-related accounts (which are closed to the various inventories). Sometimes called a "nominal account."

temporary difference. See *timing difference*.

temporary investments. Investments in *marketable securities* that the owner intends to sell within a short time, usually 1 year, and hence classified as *current assets*.

10-K. The name of the annual report required by the *SEC* of nearly all publicly held corporations.

term bonds. A *bond issue* whose component bonds all mature at the same time; contrast with *serial bonds*.

term loan. A loan with a *maturity* date, as opposed to a demand loan which is due whenever the lender requests payment. In practice bankers and auditors use this phrase only for loans for a year or more.

terms of sale. The conditions governing payment for a sale. For example, the terms *2/10, n(et)/30* mean that if payment is made within 10 days of the invoice date, a *discount* of 2 percent from *invoice* price can be taken; the invoice amount must be paid, in any event, within 30 days or it becomes overdue.

3-5-10 rule. For income tax purposes (since the income tax legislation of 1981), almost all *depreciable assets* are grouped into one of three classes: those to be depreciated for tax purposes over 3 years (such as automobiles), those to be depreciated for tax purposes over 5 years (such as most machinery and equipment), and those to be depreciated over 10 years (such as industrial and retail buildings leased by their owners). Some assets are to be depreciated over 15 years and others over 18 years. Because most assets have service lives for tax purposes of 3, 5, or 10 years, the rule has come to be known as the 3-5-10 rule. Officially it is designated as the Accelerated Cost Recovery System (ACRS). For financial reporting the depreciable life is chosen as the best estimate of its useful life. Income tax *timing differences* for *depreciation* are created when a shorter life is used for tax reporting than for financial reporting.

throughput contract. As defined by *SFAS* No. 47, an agreement between a shipper (processor) and the owner of a transportation facility (such as an oil or natural gas pipeline or a ship) or a manufacturing facility that provides for the shipper (processor) to pay specified amounts periodically in return for the transportation (processing) of a product. The shipper (processor) is obligated to make cash payments even if it does not ship (process) the contracted quantities.

ticker file. A collection of vouchers or other memoranda arranged chronologically to remind the person in charge of certain duties to make payments (or to do other tasks) as scheduled.

time-adjusted rate of return. *Internal rate of return.*

time cost. *Period cost.*

time deposit. Cash in bank earning interest; contrast with *demand deposit.*

time series analysis. See *cross section analysis* for definition and contrast.

times-interest earned. Ratio of pretax *income* plus *interest* charges to interest charges. See *ratio.*

timing difference. A difference between taxable income and pretax income reported to shareholders that will be reversed in a subsequent period and requires an entry in the *deferred income tax* account. For example, the use of *accelerated depreciation* for tax returns and *straight-line depreciation* for financial reporting.

total assets turnover. *Sales* divided by average total *assets.* Contrast with *permanent difference.*

trade acceptance. A *draft* drawn by a seller which is presented for signature (acceptance) to the buyer at the time goods are purchased and which then becomes the equivalent of a *note receivable* of the seller and the *note payable* of the buyer.

trade credit. One business allows another to buy from it in return for a promise to pay later. As contrasted with consumer credit, where a business extends the privilege of paying later to a retail customer.

trade discount. A *discount* from *list price* offered to all customers of a given type; contrast with a *discount* offered for prompt payment and *quantity discount.*

trade payables (receivables). *Payables (receivables)* arising in the ordinary course of business transactions. Most accounts payable (receivable) are of this kind.

trade secret. Technical or business information such as formulas, recipes, computer programs, and marketing data not generally known by competitors and maintained by the firm as a secret. A famous example is the secret formula for *Coca Cola* (a registered *trademark* of the company). Compare with *know-how.* Theoretically capable of having an infinite life, this intangible asset is capitalized only if purchased and then amortized over a period not to exceed 40 years. If it is developed internally, then no asset will be shown.

trade-in. Acquiring a new *asset* in exchange for a used one and perhaps additional cash. See *boot* and *trade-in transaction.*

trade-in transaction. The accounting for a trade-in depends whether or not the asset received is "similar" to the asset traded in and whether the accounting is for *financial statements* or for *income tax* returns. Assume that an old asset cost $5,000, has $3,000 of *accumulated depreciation* (after recording depreciation to the date of the trade-in), and hence has a *book value* of $2,000. The old asset appears to have a market value of $1,500, according to price quotations in used-asset markets. The old asset is traded-in on a new asset with a list price of $10,000. The old asset and $5,500 cash *(boot)* are given for the new asset. The generic entry for the trade-in transaction is:

New Asset	A		
Accumulated Depreciation (Old Asset) .	3,000		
Adjustment on Exchange of Asset	B	or	B
Old Asset		5,000	
Cash			5,500

(1) The *list price* method of accounting for trade-ins rests on the assumption that the list price of the new asset closely approximates its market value. The new asset is recorded at its list price (A = $10,000 in the example); B is a *plug* (= $2,500 credit in the example). If B requires a *debit* plug, the Adjustment on Exchange of Asset is a *loss*; if a *credit* plug is required (as in the example), the adjustment is a *gain.*

(2) Another theoretically sound method of accounting for trade-ins rests on the assumption that the price quotation from used-asset markets gives a more reliable measure of the market value of the old asset than is the list price a reliable measure of the market value of the new asset. This method uses the *fair market value* of the old asset, $1,500 in the example, to determine B (= $2,000 book value − 1,500 assumed proceeds on disposition $500 debit or loss). The exchange results in a loss if the book value of the old asset exceeds its market value and in a gain if the market value exceeds the book value. The new asset is recorded on the books by plugging for A ($7,000 in the example).

(3) For income tax reporting, no gain or loss may be recognized on the trade-in. Thus the new asset is recorded on the books by assuming B is zero and plugging for A (= $7,500 in the example). In practice, firms that wish to recognize the loss currently will sell the old asset directly, rather than trading it in, and acquire the new asset entirely for cash.

(4) *Generally accepted accounting principles (APB Opinion* No. 29) require a variant of these methods. The basic method is (1) or (2), depending upon whether the list price of the new asset (1) or the quotation of the old asset's market value (2) is the more reliable indication of market value. If, when applying the basic method, a debit entry, or loss, is required for the Adjustment on Exchange of Asset, then the trade-in is recorded as described in (1) or (2) and the full amount of the loss is recognized currently. If, however, a credit entry, or gain, is required for the Adjustment on Exchange of Asset, then the amount of gain recognized currently depends upon whether or not the old asset and the new asset are "similar". If the assets are not similar, then the entire gain is recognized currently. If the assets are similar and cash is not received by the party trading in, then no gain is recognized and the treatment is like that in (3); that is B = 0, plug for A. If the assets are similar and cash is received by the party trading in—a rare case—then a portion of the gain recognized currently. The portion of the gain recognized currently is the fraction *cash received/fair market value of total consideration received.* (When the list price method, (1), is used, the market value of the old asset is assumed to be the list price of the new asset plus the amount of cash received by the party trading in.)

The results of applying *GAAP* to the example can be summarized as follows:

More Reliable Information As To Fair Market Value	Old Asset Compared with New Asset	
	Similar	Not Similar
New Asset List Price	A = $7.500	A = $10.000
	B = 0	B = 2.500 gain
Old Asset Market Price	A = $7.000	A = $ 7.000
	B = 500 loss	B = 500 loss

trademark. A distinctive word or symbol affixed to a product, its package or dispenser, which uniquely identifies the firm's products and services. See *trademark right*.

trademark right. The right to exclude competitors in sales or advertising from using words or symbols that may be confusingly similar to the firm's *trademarks*. Trademark rights last as long as the firm continues to use the trademarks in question. In the United States, trademark rights arise from use and not from government registration. They therefore have a legal life independent of the life of a registration. Registrations last 20 years and are renewable as long as the trademark is being used. Thus, as an asset, purchased trademark rights might, like land, not be subject to amortization if management believes that the life of the trademark is indefinite. In practice, accountants amortize a trademark right over some estimate of its life, not to exceed 40 years. Under *SFAS No. 2*, internally developed trademark rights must be *expensed*.

trading on the equity. Said of a firm engaging in *debt financing*; frequently said of a firm doing so to a degree considered abnormal for a firm of its kind. *Leverage*.

transaction. A *transfer* between the accounting *entity* and another party, or parties.

transfer. *SFAC No. 3* distinguishes "reciprocal" and "nonreciprocal" transfers. In a reciprocal transfer, or "exchange," the entity both receives and sacrifices. In a nonreciprocal transfer the entity sacrifices but does not receive (examples include gifts, distributions to owners) or receives but does not sacrifice (investment by owner in entity). *SFAC No.*

3 suggests that the term "internal transfer" is self-contradictory and that the term "internal event" be used instead.

transfer agent. Usually a bank or trust company designated by a corporation to make legal transfers of *stock (bonds)* and, perhaps, to pay *dividends (coupons)*.

transfer price. A substitute for a *market,* or *arm's-length, price* used in *profit center*, or *responsibility, accounting* when one segment of the business "sells" to another segment. Incentives of profit center managers will not coincide with the best interests of the entire business unless transfer prices are properly set.

translation gain (or loss). *Foreign exchange gain (or loss).*

transportation-in. *Freight-in.*

transposition error. An error in record keeping resulting from reversing the order of digits in a number, such as recording "32" for "23." If an error of this sort has been made in a number added in a total, then the incorrect total will differ from the correct total by a number divisible by nine. Thus if *trial balance* sums differ by a number divisible by nine, one might search for a transposition error.

treasury bond. A bond issued by a corporation and then reaquired; such bonds are treated as retired when reacquired and an *extraordinary gain or loss* on reacquisition is recognized. Also, a *bond* issued by the U.S. Treasury Department.

treasury shares. *Capital stock* issued and then reacquired by the corporation. Such reacquisitions result in a reduction of *shareholders' equity*, and are usually shown on the balance sheet as *contra* to shareholders' equity. Neither *gain* nor loss is recognized on transactions involving treasury stock. Any difference between the amounts paid and received for treasury stock transactions is debited (if positive) or credited (if negative) to *additional paid-in capital*. See *cost method* and *par value method.*

treasury stock. *Treasury shares.*

trial balance. A listing of *account balances*; all accounts with *debit* balances are totaled separately from accounts with *credit* balances. The two totals should be equal. Trial balances are taken as a partial check of the arithmetic accuracy of the entries previously made. See *adjusted, preclosing, postclosing, unadjusted trial balance.*

troubled debt restructuring. As defined in *SFAS No. 15*, a concession (changing of the terms of a *debt*) granted by a *creditor* for economic or legal reasons related to the *debtor's* financial difficulty that the creditor would not otherwise consider.

turnover. The number of times that *assets*, such as *inventory* or *accounts receivable*, are replaced on average during the period. Accounts receivable turnover, for example, is total sales on account for a period divided by average accounts receivable balance for the period. See *ratio.*

turnover of plant and equipment. See *ratio.*

two-T-account method. A method for computing either (1) *foreign exchange gains and losses* or (2) monetary gains or *losses* for *constant dollar accounting statements*. The left-hand *T-account* shows actual net balances of *monetary items* and the right-hand T-account shows implied *(common) dollar* amounts.

2/10, n(et)/30. See *terms of sale.*

U

unadjusted trial balance. *Trial balance* before *adjusting* and closing entries are made at the end of the period.

unappropriated retained earnings. *Retained earnings* not appropriated and therefore against which *dividends* can be charged in the absence of retained earnings restrictions. See *restricted retained earnings*.

uncertainty. See *risk* for definition and contrast.

uncollectible account. An *account receivable* that will not be paid by the *debtor*. If the preferable *allowance method* is used, the entry on judging a specific account to be uncollectible is to *debit* the allowance for uncollectible accounts and to *credit* the specific account receivable. See *sales contra, estimated uncollectibles*.

unconsolidated subsidiary. A *subsidiary* not consolidated and, hence, accounted for on the *equity method*.

uncontrollable cost. The opposite of *controllable cost*.

underapplied (underabsorbed) overhead. An excess of actual *overhead costs* for a period over costs applied, or charged, to products produced during the period. A *debit balance* remaining in an overhead account after overhead is assigned to product.

underlying document. The record, memorandum, *voucher*, or other signal that is the authority for making an *entry* into a *journal*.

underwriter. One who agrees to purchase an entire *security issue* for a specified price, usually for resale to others.

unearned income (revenue). *Advances from customers*; strictly speaking, a contradiction in terms.

unemployment tax. See *FUTA*.

unencumbered appropriation. In governmental accounting, portion of an *appropriation* not yet spent or *encumbered*.

unexpired cost. An *asset*.

unfavorable variance. In *standard cost* accounting, an excess of actual cost over standard cost assigned to product.

unfunded. Not *funded*. An obligation or *liability*, usually for *pension costs*, exists but no *funds* have been set aside to discharge the obligation or liability.

Uniform Partnership Act. A model law, enacted by many states, to govern the relations between partners where the *partnership* agreement fails to specify the agreed-upon treatment.

unissued capital stock. *Stock* authorized but not yet issued.

units of production method. The *production method of depreciation*.

unlimited liability. The liability of *general partners* or the sole proprietor for all debts of the *partnership* or *sole proprietorship*.

unqualified opinion. See *auditor's report*.

unrealized appreciation. An *unrealized holding gain*; frequently used in the context of *marketable securities*.

unrealized gross margin (profit). A *contra* account to *installment accounts receivable* used with the *installment method* of revenue recognition. Shows the amount of profit that will eventually be realized when the receivable is collected. Some accountants show this account as a *liability*.

unrealized holding gain. See *inventory profit* for definiton and an example.

unrealized loss on marketable securities. An *income statement account* title for the amount of *loss* during the current period on the portfolio of *marketable securities* below the beginning-of-period *book value* of that portfolio. *SFAS No. 12* requires that losses caused by declines in price below market be *recognized* in the income statement, even though they have not been *realized*.

unrecovered cost. *Book value* of an *asset*.

usage variance. *Quantity variance*.

use of funds. Any transaction that reduces funds (however funds is defined).

useful life. *Service life*.

V

valuation account. A *contra account* or *adjunct account*. When *marketable securities* are reported at *lower-of-cost-or-market*, any declines in market value below cost will be credited to a valuation account. In this way, the acquisition cost and the amount of price declines below cost can both be shown. *SFAS No. 3* says a valuation account is "a separate item that reduces and increases the carrying amount" of an asset (or liability). The accounts are part of the related assets (or liabilities) and are neither assets (nor liabilities) in their own right.

value. Monetary worth; the term is usually so subjective that it ought not to be used without a modifying adjective unless most people would agree on the amount; not to be confused with *cost*. See *fair market value, entry value, exit value*.

value added. *Cost* of a product or *work in process*, minus the cost of the material purchased for the product or work in process.

value variance. *Price variance*.

variable annuity. An *annuity* whose periodic payments depend upon some uncertain outcome, such as stock market prices.

variable budget. *Flexible budget*.

variable costing. *Direct costing*.

variable costs. *Costs* that change as activity levels change. Strictly speaking, variable costs are zero when the activity level is zero. See *semivariable costs*. In accounting this term most often means the sum of *direct costs* and variable *overhead*.

variance. Difference between actual and *standard costs* or between *budgeted* and actual *expenditures* or, sometimes, *expenses*. The word has completely different meanings in accounting and statistics, where it is a measure of dispersion of a distribution.

variance analysis. The investigation of the causes of *variances* in a *standard cost system*. This term has a different meaning in statistics.

variation analysis. Analysis of the causes of changes in items of interest in financial statements such as net *income* or *gross margin*.

vendor. A seller. Sometimes spelled, "vender."

verifiable. A qualitative *objective* of financial reporting specifying that items in *financial statements* can be checked by tracing back to *underlying documents*—supporting *invoices*, canceled *checks*, and other physical pieces of evidence.

verification. The auditor's act of reviewing or checking items in *financial statements* by tracing back to *underlying documents*—supporting *invoices*, canceled *checks*, and other business documents—or sending out *confirmations* to be returned. Compare with *physical verification*.

vertical analysis. Analysis of the financial statements of a single firm or across several firms for a particular time, as opposed to *horizontal* or time series analysis where items are compared over time for a single firm or across firms.

vested. Said of an employee's *pension plan* benefits that are not contingent on the employee continuing to work for the employer.

volume variance. *Capacity variance.*

voucher. A document that signals recognition of a *liability* and authorizes the disbursement of cash. Sometimes used to refer to the written evidence documenting an *accounting entry*, as in the term *journal voucher*.

voucher system. A method for controlling *cash* that requires each *check* to be authorized with an approved *voucher*. No cash *disbursements* are made except from *petty cash funds*.

W

wage. Compensation of employees based on time worked or output of product for manual labor. But see *take-home pay*.

warrant. A certificate entitling the owner to buy a specified number of shares at a specified time(s) for a specified price. Differs from a *stock option* only in that options are granted to employees and warrants are issued to the public. See *right*.

warranty. A promise by a seller to correct deficiencies in products sold. When warranties are given, proper accounting practice recognizes an estimate of warranty *expense* and an *estimated liability* at the time of sale. See *guarantee* for contrast in proper usage.

wash sale. The sale and purchase of the same or similar *asset* within a short time period. For *income tax* purposes, *losses* on a sale of stock may not be recognized if equivalent stock is purchased within 30 days before or 30 days after the date of sale.

waste. Residue of material from manufacturing operations with no sale value. Frequently, it has negative value because additional costs must be incurred for disposal.

wasting asset. A *natural resource* having a limited *useful life* and, hence, subject to *amortization*, called *depletion*. Examples are timberland, oil and gas wells, and ore deposits.

watered stock. *Shares* issued for *assets* with *fair market value* less than *par* or *stated value*. The assets are put onto the books at the overstated values. In the law, for share to be considered watered, the *board of directors* must have acted in bad faith or fraudulently in issuing the shares under these circumstances. The term originated from a former practice of cattlemen who fed cattle ("stock") large quantities of salt to make them thirsty. The cattle then drank a lot of water before being taken to market. This was done to make the cattle appear heavier and more valuable than otherwise.

weighted average. An average computed by counting each occurrence of each value, not merely a single occurrence of each value. For example, if one unit is purchased for $1 and two units are purchased for $2 each, then the simple average of the purchase prices is $1.50 but the weighted average price per unit is $5/3 = $1.67. Contrast with *moving average*.

weighted-average inventory method. Valuing either *withdrawals* or *ending inventory* at the *weighted average* purchase price of all units on hand at the time of withdrawal or of computing ending inventory. The *inventory equation* is used to calculate the other quantity. If the *perpetual inventory* method is in use, often called the "moving-average method."

where-got, where-gone statement. A term used by W.M. Cole for a statement much like the *statement of changes in financial position*.

window dressing. The attempt to make financial statements show *operating* results, or *financial position*, more favorable than would be otherwise shown.

with recourse. See *note receivable discounted*.

withdrawals. *Assets* distributed to an owner. *Partner's drawings*. See *inventory equation* for another context.

withholding. Deductions from *salaries* or *wages*, usually for *income taxes*, to be remitted by the employer, in the employee's name, to the taxing authority.

without recourse. See *note receivable discounted*.

work in process. Partially completed product; an *asset* that is classified as *inventory*.

work sheet. A tabular schedule for convenient summary of *adjusting* and *closing entries*. The work sheet usually begins with an *unadjusted trial balance*. Adjusting entries are shown in the next two columns, one for *debts* and one for *credits*. The horizontal sum of each line is then carried to the right into either the *income statement* or *balance sheet* columns, as appropriate. The *plug* to equate the income statement column totals is the income, if a debit plug is required, or loss, if a credit plug is required, for the period. That income will be closed to retained earnings on the balance sheet. The income statement credit columns are the revenues for the period and the debit columns are the expenses (and revenue *contras*) to be shown on the income statement.

Work sheet is also used to refer to *schedules* for determining other items appearing on the *financial statements* that require adjustment or compilation.

working capital. *Current assets* minus *current liabilities*. The *statement of changes in financial position* usually explains the changes in working capital for a period.

working capital equation. The *balance sheet* states that Assets Equities. The information in comparative balance sheets from the start and end of a period can be restated as:

Change in Assets = Change in Equities

This equation can be further broken down to say that

Change in Current Assets Plus Change in Noncurrent Assets	=	Change in Current Liabilities Plus Change in Noncurrent Equities

which is equivalent to

Change in Current Assets Less Change in Current Liabilities	=	Change in Noncurrent Equities Less Change in Noncurrent Assets

The left-hand side of this equation is the change in *working capital* for the period. The items on the right-hand side cause the change in working capital during the period. The *statement of changes in financial position* typically shows the causes of the changes (right-hand side of the equation) at the top of the statement and the way working capital has changed (left-hand side of the equation) at the bottom of the statement.

working capital provided by operations. See *funds provided by operations.*

working papers. The schedules and analyses prepared by the *auditor* in carrying out investigations prior to issuing an *opinion* on *financial statements.*

worth. *Value.* See *net worth.*

worth-debt ratio. Reciprocal of the *debt-equity ratio.* See *ratio.*

write-down. *Write off,* except that not all the assets' cost is charged to expense or *loss.* Generally used for nonrecurring items.

write off. *Charge* an *asset* to *expense* or *loss;* that is, *debit* expense (or loss) and *credit* asset.

write-off method. A method for treating *uncollectible accounts* that charges *bad debt expense* and credits accounts receivable of specific customers as uncollectible amounts are identified. May not be used when uncollectible amounts are significant and can be estimated. See *sales contra, estimated uncollectibles* and the *allowance method* for contrast.

write up. To increase the recorded *cost* of an *asset* with no corresponding *disbursement* of *funds;* that is, *debit* asset and *credit revenue,* or perhaps, *owners' equity.* Seldom done because currently accepted accounting principles are based on actual transactions. When a portfolio of *marketable equity securities* increases in market value subsequent to a previously-recognized decrease, the *book value* of the portfolio is written-up—the debit is to the *contra account.*

Y

yield. *Internal rate of return* of a stream of cash flows. Cash yield is cash flow divided by book value. See also *dividend yield.*

yield to maturity. At a given time, the *internal rate of return* of a series of cash flows, usually said of a *bond.* Sometimes called the "effective rate."

Z

zero base(d) budgeting. ZBB. In preparing an ordinary *budget* for the next period, a manager starts with the budget for the current period and makes adjustments as seem necessary, because of changed conditions for the next period. Because most managers like to increase the scope of the activities managed and since most prices increase most of the time, amounts in budgets prepared in the ordinary, incremental way seem to increase period after period. The authority approving the budget assumes operations will be carried out in the same way as in the past and that next period's expenditures will have to be at least as large as the current period's. Thus, this authority tends to study only the increments to the current period's budget. In ZBB, the authority questions the process for carrying out a program and the entire budget for next period. Every dollar in the budget is studied, not just the dollars incremental to the previous period's amounts. The advocates of ZBB claim that in this way: (1) programs or divisions of marginal benefit to the business or governmental unit will more likely be deleted from the program, rather than being continued with costs at least as large as the present ones, and (2) alternative, more cost-effective, ways of carrying out programs are more likely to be discovered and implemented. ZBB implies questioning the existence of programs, and the fundamental nature of the way they are carried out, not merely the amounts used to fund them. Experts appear to be evenly divided as to whether the middle word should be "base" or "based."

zero salvage value. If the *salvage value* of a *depreciable asset* is estimated to be less than 10 percent of its *cost,* then the tax regulations permit an assumption of zero salvage value in computing *depreciation* for federal *income tax* purposes. This convention is often used in financial reporting as well, but seldom in textbooks.

GENERAL ⊛ ELECTRIC

1981 Annual Report

Authors' Introduction

This is an excerpt from GE's Annual Report. GE's annual reports are consistently among the best we see. The first 38 pages of the Annual Report give general information about the company, illustrations, and highlights of the year's operations. Here we comment on various aspects of the financial statements, which follow the general information, in numbered footnotes keyed to the GE annual report. The page numbers of the original are left intact and references, both in the report and our notes, use these numbers.

Our notes appear on a page facing (or near) the page of the annual report being commented on. Our notes begin at the bottom of this page. The circled numbers shown in the margins of the annual report do not, of course, appear in the original. All accounting terms used in our supplementary footnotes are explained in the Glossary.

We think there is no better way to learn financial accounting than to try to understand all that appears in GE's statements. (The GE corporate signature as it appears above is a trademark of General Electric Company. It is, perhaps, the single most valuable asset of the Company. In accord with generally accepted accounting principles, this asset does not appear anywhere in the financial statements.)

Authors' Notes to General Electric Annual Report

① This is the first of our commentary footnotes. The statement shown here is the income statement.

② Provision usually means "estimated expense" in this country; see the Glossary at *provision* for the contrast in this word's meanings in the U.S. and the U.K.

③ GE does not own all the shares in all of its consolidated subsidiaries. Some of the shares belong to outsiders, called the *minority interest*. The minority interest's share of the earnings of the subsidiary companies does not belong to GE's shareholders. Hence, in deriving income to GE's shareholders the minority interest's share in earnings is subtracted from the earnings of the consolidated group of companies. Note, however, that this reduction in income uses no cash or other funds, so that there is an adjustment on the Statement of Changes in Financial Position for this charge against income. See our comment 15.

④ This is primary earnings per share, as called for by APB *Opinion No. 15*. See GE's Note 6 for a discussion of fully diluted earnings per share. Fully diluted earnings per share is not separately shown here because the amount is within one percent of the primary earnings per share amount. (In general, fully diluted earnings per share need not be separately shown if it is within 3 percent of primary earnings per share.)

⑤ Generally accepted accounting principles call for a reconciliation of changes in all of the owners' equity accounts during the year. The only major changes in GE's retained earnings account are caused by the earning of income and the declaration of dividends. GE's Note 17 explains other changes in owners' equity.

① Statement of earnings

General Electric Company and consolidated affiliates

For the years ended December 31 (In millions)		1981	1980	1979
Sales	Sales of products and services to customers	$27,240	$24,959	$22,461
Operating costs	Cost of goods sold	18,945	17,751	15,991
	Selling, general and administrative expense	4,966	4,258	3,716
	Depreciation, depletion and amortization	882	707	624
	Operating costs (notes 1 and 2)	24,793	22,716	20,331
	Operating margin	2,447	2,243	2,130
	Other income (note 3)	614	564	519
	Interest and other financial charges (note 4)	(401)	(314)	(258)
Earnings	Earnings before income taxes and minority interest	2,660	2,493	2,391
	② Provision for income taxes (note 5)	(962)	(958)	(953)
	③ Minority interest in earnings of consolidated affiliates	(46)	(21)	(29)
	Net earnings applicable to common stock	$ 1,652	$ 1,514	$ 1,409
	④ Earnings per common share (in dollars) (note 6)	$7.26	$6.65	$6.20
	Dividends declared per common share (in dollars)	$3.15	$2.95	$2.75
	Operating margin as a percentage of sales	9.0%	9.0%	9.5%
	Net earnings as a percentage of sales	6.1%	6.1%	6.3%

⑤

Statement of retained earnings

General Electric Company and consolidated affiliates

For the years ended December 31 (In millions)		1981	1980	1979
Retained earnings	Balance January 1	$7,151	$6,307	$5,522
	Net earnings	1,652	1,514	1,409
	Dividends declared on common stock	(715)	(670)	(624)
	Balance December 31	$8,088	$7,151	$6,307

The information on pages 38 and 42-50 is an integral part of these statements.

Statement of financial position

General Electric Company and consolidated affiliates

At December 31 (In millions)	1981	1980
Assets		
Cash (note 7)	$ 2,219	$ 1,601
Marketable securities (note 7)	252	600
Current receivables (note 8)	4,872	4,339
Inventories (note 9)	3,461	3,343
Current assets	10,804	9,883
Property, plant and equipment – net (note 10)	6,844	5,780
Investments (note 11)	1,907	1,820
Other assets (note 12)	1,387	1,028
Total assets	$20,942	$18,511
Liabilities and equity		
Short-term borrowings (note 13)	$ 1,171	$ 1,093
Accounts payable (note 14)	2,012	1,671
⑥ Progress collections and price adjustments accrued	2,519	2,084
Dividends payable	182	170
Taxes accrued	753	628
Other costs and expenses accrued (note 15)	2,097	1,946
Current liabilities	8,734	7,592
Long-term borrowings (note 16)	1,059	1,000
Other liabilities	1,855	1,565
Total liabilities	11,648	10,157
⑦ Minority interest in equity of consolidated affiliates	166	154
Preferred stock ($1 par value; 2,000,000 shares authorized; none issued)	—	—
Common stock ($2.50 par value; 251,500,000 shares authorized; 231,463,949 shares issued 1981 and 1980)	579	579
Amounts received for stock in excess of par value	657	659
Retained earnings	8,088	7,151
	9,324	8,389
⑧ Deduct common stock held in treasury	(196)	(189)
Total share owners' equity (notes 17 and 18)	9,128	8,200
Total liabilities and equity	$20,942	$18,511
Commitments and contingent liabilities (note 19)		

The information on pages 38 and 42-50 is an integral part of this statement.

⑥ GE uses the completed contract method of recognizing revenue from long-term construction contracts; see GE's Summary of Significant Accounting Policies at "Sales." As GE incurs costs on these contracts it makes journal entries such as:

Work in Process Inventory for Long-term Contracts X	
Various Assets and Liabilities	X
To record cost of construction activity.	

Some of GE's long-term construction contracts provide that the customer shall make progress payments to GE as the work is done. GE does not recognize revenue until the work is completed, so the journal entry made at the time cash is received is one such as:

Cash . . . . Y	
Advances from Customers on Long-term Contracts	Y
To record cash received and to set up the corresponding liability.	

When the balance sheet is prepared, the amounts in the inventory accounts, X (debit balance), are netted against the amounts in the liability accounts, Y (credit balance). If there is a net credit balance, as here, with Y greater than X, then the difference, $Y - X$, is recorded as a liability. GE shows this liability under the title "Progress collections." On contracts where the amounts in the inventory account exceed the cash collections, then the difference, $X - Y$, is shown as an asset under a title such as "Costs Incurred on Long-term Contracts in Excess of Billings." This netting of costs incurred against cash collections and the separate showing of the excesses is required by ARB *No. 45*.

On many of GE's contracts the only cash collected before completion of construction is for engineering costs incurred in preparation to undertake construction. GE expenses these engineering costs, rather than accumulating them in Work-in-Process inventory accounts. Thus, there is no asset account to net against the liability. The "Progress collections" title is appropriate because it tends to represent gross "advances from customers," rather than a netting of work in process inventory against advances from customers.

⑦ (Refer to our comment 3 for a description of "minority interest" on the income statement.) This account represents the equity of the minority shareholders in the consolidated affilitates. From the point of view of GE's shareholders, this equity belonging to the minority is a liability. From the point of view of the consolidated entity, the minority shareholders' interest is part of total owners' equity. Thus whether one believes that minority interest is a liability or an item of owners' equity depends upon whether one views the financial statements as being prepared for the shareholders of GE (the proprietorship theory) or for all potential readers (the entity theory). Note that GE avoids the issue by not classifying "minority interest" either with liabilities or with owners' equity.

⑧ GE uses the cost method of accounting for treasury stock and shows the cost of its own shares acquired on the market as contra to all of owners' equity. Refer to our comment 76.

Statement of changes in financial position

General Electric Company and consolidated affiliates

For the years ended December 31 (In millions)		1981	1980	1979
Source of funds ⑨	From operations			
	Net earnings ⑩	$1,652	$1,514	$1,409
	⑪ Depreciation, depletion and amortization	882	707	624
	⑫ Investment tax credit deferred — net	46	56	45
	⑬ Income tax timing differences	33	63	(37)
	⑭ Earnings retained by nonconsolidated finance affiliates	(27)	(22)	(17)
	⑮ Minority interest in earnings of consolidated affiliates	46	21	29
		2,632	2,339	2,053
	⑯ Increase in long-term borrowings	160	122	50
	Disposition of treasury shares	169	136	148
	⑰ Increase in current liabilities other than short-term borrowings	1,064	498	786
	Other — net	(78)	143	101
	Total source of funds	3,947	3,238	3,138
Application of funds	Additions to property, plant and equipment	2,025	1,948	1,262
	Dividends declared on common stock	715	670	624
	Increase in investments	87	129	281
	⑯ Reduction in long-term borrowings	101	69	97
	Purchase of treasury shares	176	145	156
	⑱ Increase in current receivables	533	692	358
	⑲ Increase in inventories	118	182	158
	Total application of funds (note 12)	3,755	3,835	2,936
Net change	Net change in cash, marketable securities and short-term borrowings ⑳	$ 192	$ (597)	$ 202
Analysis of net change	Increase (decrease) in cash and marketable securities	$ 270	$ (375)	$ 113
	Decrease (increase) in short-term borrowings	(78)	(222)	89
	Increase (decrease) in net liquid assets ⑳	$ 192	$ (597)	$ 202

The information on pages 38 and 42-50 is an integral part of this statement.

㉑ Report of independent certified public accountants

To Share Owners and Board of Directors of
General Electric Company

We have examined the statement of financial position of General Electric Company and consolidated affiliates as of December 31, 1981 and 1980, and the related statements of earnings, retained earnings and changes in financial position for each of the three years in the period ended December 31, 1981. Our examinations were made in accordance with generally accepted auditing standards, and accordingly included such tests of the accounting records and such other auditing procedures as we considered necessary in the circumstances.

In our opinion, the aforementioned financial statements present fairly the financial position of General Electric Company and consolidated affiliates at December 31, 1981 and 1980, and the results of their operations and the changes in their financial position for each of the three years in the period ended December 31, 1981, in conformity with generally accepted accounting principles applied on a consistent basis.

Peat, Marwick, Mitchell & Co

Peat, Marwick, Mitchell & Co.
345 Park Avenue, New York, N.Y. 10154

February 26, 1982

41

⑨ Most companies define funds as working capital = current assets − current liabilities. GE uses a more restrictive definition of funds; for GE, funds = cash + marketable securities − short-term borrowings.

⑩ This statement, as is customary, starts with net income as shown in the income statement. The next few lines show subtractions for revenues and other credits to income that did not produce funds and additions for expenses and other charges against income that did not use funds. Total funds produced by operations appears after these adjustments to income. An acceptable alternative shows only those revenues that produce funds and subtracts only those expenses that use funds in deriving funds produced by operations.

⑪ Depreciation is *not* a source of funds. Rather, it is an expense that reduces net income without using any funds. The funds were used in the past when the depreciable assets were acquired.

⑫ See our comment 51. GE realizes investment credits in the year it puts new qualifying assets into operation. Because it uses the conservative deferral method for investment credits, it recognizes the effect on income over the lives of the assets acquired. More funds are provided by the investment credit than are recognized in income in the year of acquisition. On the other hand, income is increased somewhat because of the effect of amounts deferred in prior years that are used to reduce reported tax expense in the current year. The net difference is added to net income in deriving funds provided by operations. Accounting for the investment credit is described in our comment 51.

⑬ In 1981 and 1980, income tax expense for the year exceeded the amount of income taxes payable. See the discussion at GE's Note 5 and our comments 52–56. Because less cash was used for income taxes than was reported as income tax expense, there has to be an addition for the amount of expense not using funds in deriving funds from operations. The results for 1979 show that taxes payable exceeded tax expense.

⑭ Earnings of the GE Credit Corporation net of support payments ($129 million in 1981) are included in income under the equity method. See "Other income," GE's Note 3. Only $102 million of dividends were declared by the Credit Corporation; see the "Current and retained earnings statement" of the Credit Company in GE's Note 11. The difference, $27 (= $129 − $102) million, provided no funds to GE and must be subtracted from net income to derive GE's funds from operations. That is, the entire $129 million is included in the $1,652 million shown as net earnings by GE, but dividend declarations of the Credit Corporation provided funds of only $102 million.

⑮ See our comment 3. The charge on the income statement for the minority's interest in earnings (of $46 million in 1981) reduces the income reported to GE's shareholders, but does not reduce the amount of funds provided by operations of the consolidated entity. Thus, there is an addback to net income for $46 million in 1981 in deriving funds produced by operations.

⑯ As is preferable, GE shows separately funds provided by new borrowings and funds used to reduce old borrowings. Some companies show only the net effect either as a source or as an application of funds; they provide no information about the amount of actual borrowings and repayments during the period.

⑰ GE's definition of funds does not include current payables. Thus, an increase in current liabilities provides funds just as new long-term borrowing provides funds. Some might call this an operating source of funds.

⑱ GE's definition of funds does not include current receivables. An increase in current receivables uses funds just as any increase in investments uses funds. Some might call this an operating use of funds.

⑲ GE's definition of funds does not include inventories. Increases in inventories use funds. Some might call this an operating use of funds.

⑳ Notice the self-balancing nature of this statement. The actual increase in funds (= cash + marketable securities − short-term borrowings) of $192 million in 1981 is exactly explained in the top part of the statement with the various sources and applications of funds.

㉑ This is the auditors' report. This particular report is both nonqualified ("clean") and in standard format. The first paragraph of the auditors' report is the scope paragraph—telling the work done—and the last paragraph is the opinion. The auditors' report appears in the published annual report on page 38.

Summary of significant ㉒ accounting policies

Basis of consolidation ㉓

The financial statements consolidate the accounts of the parent General Electric Company and those of all majority-owned ㉔ and controlled companies ("affiliated companies"), except finance companies whose operations are not similar to those of the consolidated group. All significant transactions among the parent and affiliated companies are eliminated from the consolidated statements. ㉕

The nonconsolidated finance companies are included in the statement of financial position under investments and are valued at equity plus advances. In addition, companies in which GE and/or its consolidated affiliates own 20% to 50% of the voting stock ("associated companies") are included under investments, valued at the appropriate share of equity plus advances. After-tax earnings of nonconsolidated finance companies and associated companies are included in the statement of earnings under other income.

A nonconsolidated uranium mining company (see note 11) is also included under investments and is valued at lower of cost or equity, plus advances.

Sales ㉗

A sale is recorded only when title to products passes to the customer or when services are performed in accordance with contract terms.

Foreign currency translation ㉘

Foreign currencies are translated in accordance with Statement of Financial Accounting Standards No. 8. The Financial Accounting Standards Board has issued a new standard for foreign currency translation (SFAS No. 52) which, when implemented in the future by GE, is not expected to have a material effect on the Company's financial statements.

Pensions

Assets and liabilities of the General Electric Pension Trust, which funds the obligations of the General Electric Pension Plan, are not consolidated with those of the Company. Investments of the Trust are carried at amortized cost plus programmed appreciation in the common stock portfolio. Beginning in 1981, the funding program and Company cost ㉙ determination for the Pension Plan use 7½% as the estimated rate of future Trust income. Trust income includes recognition of appreciation in the common stock portfolio on a systematic basis which does not give undue weight to short-term market fluctuations. Programmed appreciation will not be recognized if average carrying value exceeds average market value, calculated on a moving basis over a multiyear period. Changes in prior service liabilities of the Plan are amortized over 20 years. Actuarial gains and losses are amortized over 15 years.

Costs of the General Electric Supplementary Pension Plan, a separate plan primarily affecting long-service professional and managerial employees, are not funded. Current service costs ㉚

and amortization of prior service liabilities over a period of 20 years are being charged to operating expenses currently.

Investment tax credit ㉛

The investment tax credit is deferred and amortized as a reduction of the provision for taxes over the lives of the facilities to which the credit applies, rather than being "flowed through" to income in the year the asset is acquired.

Inventories

Substantially all manufacturing inventories located in the U.S., as well as a number of those outside the U.S., are valued on a ㉜ last-in first-out, or LIFO, basis. The remaining manufacturing inventories outside the U.S. are generally valued on a first-in first-out, or FIFO, basis. Valuations are based on the cost of material, direct labor and manufacturing overhead, and do not �33 exceed net realizable values. Certain indirect manufacturing expenses are charged directly to operating costs during the period incurred, rather than being capitalized as inventory.

Mining inventories, which include principally mined ore and coal, metal concentrates and mining supplies, are stated at the lower of average cost or market. Mining inventories include both direct and indirect costs consisting of labor, purchased supplies and services, and depreciation, depletion and amortization of property, plant and equipment.

Property, plant and equipment

Manufacturing plant and equipment includes the original cost of land, buildings and equipment less depreciation, which is the estimated cost consumed by wear and obsolescence. An accelerated depreciation method, based principally on a sum-of-the-years digits formula, is used to record depreciation of the original cost of manufacturing plant and equipment in the U.S. Most manufacturing plant and equipment located outside the U.S. is depreciated on a straight-line basis. If manufacturing plant and equipment is subject to abnormal economic conditions or obsolescence, additional depreciation is provided. Expenditures for maintenance and repairs of manufacturing plant and equipment are charged to operating costs as incurred.

The cost of mining properties includes initial expenditures and cost of major rebuilding projects which substantially increase the useful lives of existing assets. The cost of mining properties is depreciated, depleted or amortized over the useful lives of the related assets by use of unit-of-production, straight-line or declining-balance methods.

Mining exploration costs are expensed until it is determined that development of a mineral deposit is likely to be economically feasible. After this determination, all costs related to further development are capitalized. Amortization begins upon commencement of production and is over the productive life of the property.

The full-cost accounting method is used for oil and gas �34 properties.

㉒   APB *Opinion No. 22* requires that all annual reports include a summary of significant accounting principles used so that the reader can know which accounting alternatives have been chosen by the company.

㉓   A parent, such as GE, usually consolidates a subsidiary when all three of the following criteria are met:
   (i) The parent owns more than 50 percent of the voting shares of the subsidiary.
   (ii) There are no important restrictions on the ability of the parent to exercise control of the subsidiary.
   (iii) The asset and equity structure of the subsidiary is not significantly different from that of the parent.

㉔   GE tells us here that it consolidates all "majority-owned" (greater than 50 percent) and "controlled" companies except the finance companies which are not similar to the others in the consolidated group. Instead, the finance affiliates are accounted for under the equity method. As can be seen from GE Credit Corporation's balance sheet in Note 11, most (90 percent at year-end 1981) of the Credit Corporation's assets are receivables and most (80 percent) of its sources of financing are debt, rather than owner's equity. In this sense, the operations of the finance affiliates "are not similar to those of the consolidated group." As our comment 70 points out, the nonconsolidation of the finance company makes GE's balance sheet differ substantially from its appearance if the finance affiliates were consolidated. Although there is no effect on reported net income, the components of income are affected.

㉕   Consolidated financial statements present information about a group of affiliated companies as if the group were one economic entity. Consequently, gains or losses on sales of assets between companies in the consolidated group must be eliminated from reported financial statements. The recognition of such gains or losses is postponed until the assets are sold by one company of the consolidated group to a buyer outside of the consolidated group.

㉖   GE tells us that it uses the equity method for the nonconsolidated finance affiliate. Under the equity method, GE's net earnings include its share of the earnings, not just the dividends, of these companies. See our comment 14.

㉗   GE uses the completed contract method of recognizing revenue on long-term construction projects. See our comment 6.

㉘   See our comment 37.

㉙   That is, in computing future values of pension fund investments and interest on unfunded obligations for prior service costs, a $7\frac{1}{2}$-percent rate is used. GE's Note 2 indicates that the rate earned in 1981 was 10.1 percent.

㉚   See our comment 73.

㉛   See our comment 51 for a discussion of the investment credit and the effect of GE's using the conservative deferral method.

㉜   Many foreign governments do not allow LIFO for tax purposes. Some companies, nevertheles, use LIFO for foreign inventories.

㉝   GE tells us it will not show an item of inventory on the balance sheet at an amount greater than net realizable value; we can deduce that it must be using a lower-of-cost-or-market valuation basis.

㉞   GE uses "full cost" accounting for its oil and gas operations. See the Glossary at *reserve recognition accounting* for discussion of the options. The U.S. Congress passed a law that required the SEC (and FASB) to set uniform accounting in the petroleum industry by the end of 1977. *FASB Statement No. 19* was issued in 1977 to comply. The statement required successful efforts accounting and forbade full cost accounting. In 1978, the SEC said it would allow either successful efforts or full cost accounting until it could write rules for "reserve recognition accounting." In 1981, the SEC indicated that it was delaying indefinitely use of reserve recognition accounting in the principal financial statements; either successful efforts or full cost can be used. GE's reported income is probably slightly larger because it uses full cost accounting rather than successful efforts accounting.

Notes to financial statements

1. Operating costs

(In millions)	1981	1980	1979
Employee compensation, including benefits	$10,208	$ 9,196	$ 8,286
Materials, supplies, services and other costs	13,475	12,696	11,320
Depreciation, depletion and amortization	882	707	624
Taxes, except Social Security and those on income	346	299	259
Increase in inventories during the year ㉟	(118)	(182)	(158)
Total operating costs	$24,793	$22,716	$20,331
Supplemental details:			
Maintenance and repairs	$897	$784	$775
Company-funded research and development ㊱	814	760	640
Social Security taxes	567	484	471
Advertising	331	315	282
Mineral royalties and export duties	105	80	82

Foreign currency translation gains after taxes and minority interest share, calculated in accordance with Statement of Financial Accounting Standards No. 8, were $78 million in 1981, $40 million in 1980 and $12 million in 1979. This SFAS No. 8 calculation excludes the effect of exchange rate changes on inventory-related amounts. The inventory-related effects in cost of sales have generally offset the GE translation gains calculated in accordance with SFAS No. 8 and, therefore, exchange rate changes have had virtually no effect on GE's net earnings. ㊲

2. Pensions

Total pension costs of General Electric and consolidated affiliates were $549 million in 1981, $478 million in 1980, and $413 million in 1979.

General Electric and its affiliates have a number of pension plans. The most significant of these plans is the General Electric Pension Plan (the "Plan"), in which substantially all employees in the U.S. are participating. Pension benefits under the Plan are funded through the General Electric Pension Trust (the "Trust"). The other principal pension plan is the General Electric Supplementary Pension Plan. These two plans account for over 90% of GE's pension benefits. Approximately 86,000 persons were receiving benefits at year-end 1981.

For funding and annual cost determination purposes, changes were made in 1981 in mortality assumptions and, recognizing the impact of inflation, in projections of pension benefits and by increasing from 6% to 7½% the estimated rate of future Trust income. The net effect of these changes on 1981 pension costs was not material.

Earnings of the Trust, including programmed recognition of common stock appreciation as a percentage of the carrying value of the portfolio, were 10.1% in 1981 and 8.4% in 1980 and 1979.

Condensed current-value information for the Trust appears below. Current-value information is presented in accordance with Statement of Financial Accounting Standards No. 36 requirements, which differ from the carrying value used by the Company for funding and cost determination purposes.

General Electric Pension Trust

Change in net assets at current value

For the year (In millions)	1981	1980	1979
Net assets at January 1	$6,418	$4,968	$4,202
Company contributions	443	404	341
Employee contributions	103	86	94
Investment income	601	435	383
Pensions paid	(300)	(254)	(225)
Unrecognized portion of change in current value ㊳	(686)	779	173
Net assets at December 31	$6,579	$6,418	$4,968

Net assets at current value ㊳

December 31 (In millions)	1981	1980	1979
U.S. government obligations and guarantees	$ 432	$ 44	$ 118
Corporate bonds and notes	813	727	496
Real estate and mortgages	871	825	713
Common stocks and other equity securities	3,751	4,181	3,193
	5,867	5,777	4,520
Cash and short-term investments	644	553	371
Other assets — net	68	88	77
Current value of net assets	$6,579	$6,418	$4,968
Carrying value of net assets	$6,440	$5,593	$4,922

The actuarial present value of accumulated plan benefits for the General Electric Pension Plan and the Supplementary Pension Plan, calculated in accordance with Statement of Financial Accounting Standards No. 36, is shown below. The table also sets forth the total of the current value of Pension Trust assets and relevant accruals in the Company's accounts.

General Electric Pension Plan and Supplementary Pension Plan ㊴

December 31 (In millions)	1981	1980	1979
Estimated actuarial present value of accumulated plan benefits:			
Vested benefits	$6,032	$6,027	$5,426
Nonvested benefits	511	415	382
Total benefits	$6,543	$6,442	$5,808
Current value of trust assets plus accruals	$6,801	$6,580	$5,075

The present values were calculated using a 7½% interest rate

㉟ All manufacturing costs incurred during the year are shown as components of operating costs. If inventories have increased (ending inventory > beginning inventory), then some of those costs have not expired and are not expenses. Hence, the increase in inventories is deducted from total operating costs to derive operating *expenses*. Cost of goods sold shown on GE's income statement already reflects this reduction.

㊱ *SFAS No. 2* requires the expensing of research and development costs, and the disclosure, such as GE's here, of the costs incurred during the year for R & D. *SFAS No. 2* allows the capitalizing of R & D costs that are incurred under contract and that are reimbursable. GE is making clear that these costs ($760 million in 1982) do not qualify for capitalization.

㊲ GE has the option to use *SFAS No. 8* for 1981, rather than *SFAS No. 52*, which must be used after 1981. Many companies chose to use *SFAS No. 52* in 1981.

㊳ Note that pension assets are carried at current value, not at historical cost, as required by SFAS No. 35. The "unrecognized portion of changes in current value" is analogous to unrealized holding gains. There was a substantial holding loss in 1981.

㊴ *SFAS No. 36* requires that the assets and liabilities of the pension plan be disclosed in notes to the employer's financial statements. *SFAS No. 36* requires that the same actuarial cost method be used by all companies in their disclosures about their pension plans. In the paragraph following the schedule GE discloses the combined effects of applying the more conservative actuarial cost method and interest rate assumptions it formerly used.

㊵ GE uses the equity method of accounting for its 100-percent ownership of the GE Credit Corporation. Hence it shows 100 percent of the earnings of the Credit Corporation as "Other income." See our comments 14 and 70.

㊶ GECC borrows money from various lenders, agreeing to repay some time in the future. To protect their principal over the term of the loan, the lenders insert provisions in the loan agreements to restrict certain actions of the borrower, such as paying out too much cash to owners. GECC agreed in borrowing to maintain the fixed charge coverage ratio at 1.15 or more. See our comment 68 for computation of the coverage ratio. Because the coverage ratio would otherwise have fallen below the critical amount in 1981, GE paid cash to GECC to bolster the ratio. Had GE not done so, GECC would probably have violated its loan agreement and might have been required to repay some of its loans before their scheduled maturity dates or renegotiate the interest rates on these loans. The income support payment is included in the earnings of GECC (see Note 11). Because the support payment is an intercompany revenue of GECC and expense of GE, it must be eliminated in applying the equity method. Hence, the subtraction here.

㊷ "Customer financing" is interest on receivables held by GE arising from some of its sales.

㊸ See our comment 68.

㊹ *SFAS No. 34* requires separate disclosure of amounts of interest capitalized into plant under construction.

㊺ This first schedule shows the details of income tax expense, called a "provision." The bottom line is the total expense reported on the statement of earnings. It is the sum of U.S. federal, foreign, and other income tax expenses. The U.S. federal and foreign income tax expense amounts are derived in essentially two steps: first is shown the amount of taxes payable; then there is an adjustment for timing differences; GE also shows the effect of the investment credit, which is discussed below in our comment 51.

㊻ In 1981 income tax expense exceeded income taxes payable because of timing differences. The details of the U.S. federal timing differences are shown in the schedule in the right-hand column of page 44.

㊼ GE uses to deferral method of accounting for the investment credit; see our comment 51.

㊽ The Internal Revenue Service has not completed its audit of GE's tax returns for years after 1972.

assumption as of December 31, 1981, and 6% as of the end of 1980 and 1979. If the 1981 changes in the actuarial interest rate and mortality assumptions had not been made, the present value of total benefits at the end of 1981 in the preceding table would have been $855 million greater.

3. Other income

(In millions)	1981	1980	1979
Net earnings of GE Credit Corporation ㊵	$142	$115	$ 90
Income support payment (net) from GE ㊷	(13)	—	—
GE earnings from GECC	129	115	90
Income from:			
Marketable securities and bank deposits	230	229	229
Customer financing ㊷	80	72	70
Royalty and technical agreements	59	52	50
Associated companies and non-consolidated uranium mining affiliate	37	22	11
Other investments: Interest	18	21	20
Dividends	9	13	11
Other sundry items	52	40	38
	$614	$564	$519

GECC's reported 1981 net earnings ($142 million) include an income support payment ($13 million after taxes) made by GE to maintain GECC's fixed charge coverage ratio at 1.15. ㊸

4. Interest and other financial charges

Interest capitalized on major property, plant and equipment projects was $23 million and $21 million in 1981 and 1980, respectively. ㊹

5. Provision for income taxes ㊺

(In millions)	1981	1980	1979
U.S. federal income taxes:			
Estimated amount payable	$529	$574	$599
Effect of timing differences ㊻	31	14	(31)
Investment credit deferred — net ㊼	46	56	45
	606	644	613
Foreign income taxes:			
Estimated amount payable	317	238	323
Effect of timing differences	(15)	39	(6)
	302	277	317
Other (principally state and local income taxes)	54	37	23
	$962	$958	$953

All General Electric consolidated U.S. federal income tax returns have been closed through 1972. ㊽

GECC, a nonconsolidated finance affiliate, is included in General Electric's U.S. federal income tax return. Primarily because of tax credits and timing differences related to its leasing activities, GECC records provisions for taxes recoverable, which represent the effect of GECC's operations on the aggregate taxes payable. GECC's provisions, which offset corresponding amounts included in the estimated amounts payable by the consolidated companies shown in the preceding table, were $633 million for 1981, $244 million for 1980 and $164 million for 1979. For 1981, the net GE-GECC recoverable ㊾ amount will be realized by carryback against previous years' taxes.

Provision has been made for federal income taxes to be paid on that portion of the undistributed earnings of affiliates and ㊿ associated companies expected to be remitted to the parent company. Undistributed earnings intended to be reinvested indefinitely in affiliates and associated companies totaled $1,265 million at the end of 1981, $1,111 million at the end of 1980, and $944 million at the end of 1979.

Changes in estimated foreign income taxes payable and in the effect of timing differences result principally from fluctuations in foreign earnings and tax rates, and from recognizing in the current year for tax payment purposes the results of transactions in Australia recorded for financial reporting purposes in other years.

Investment credit amounted to $95 million in 1981, compared with $92 million in 1980 and $76 million in 1979. In (51) 1981, $49 million were included in net earnings, compared with $36 million in 1980 and $31 million in 1979. At the end of 1981, the amount still deferred and to be included in net earnings in future years was $306 million.

Effect of timing differences on U.S. federal income taxes

Increase (decrease) in provision for income taxes (In millions)		1981	1980	1979
Tax over book depreciation �53		$ 67	$ 48	$ 23
Undistributed earnings of affiliates and associated companies ㋼		7	29	(2)
Margin on installment sales ㋕		8	1	(10)
Provision for warranties ㋖		23	(46)	(36)
Other — net		(74)	(18)	(6)
	㋗	$ 31	$ 14	$(31)

㊽ See the Glossary at *safe-harbor lease*. It appears from GECC's balance sheet that GECC engaged in over $1 billion of new financing leases during 1981; see the increase in financing leases on the balance sheet in Note 11 on page 46. These transactions were generally with companies (such as Ford Motor Company and Pan American World Airways) so unprofitable that they were unable to take advantrage of the incentives in the Economic Recovery Tax Act of 1981 for the purchase of new depreciable assets. GECC acquires the asset and leases it to, say, Ford. Because GECC gets to keep the investment credit, it can pay a portion of that amount to Ford—either directly in cash or via smaller lease payments than otherwise. In return GECC gets a reduction in its tax bill. The reduction for 1981 is, apparently, $633 million, an amount larger than the entire taxes payable by GE (see GE's Note 5, where the amount payable is shown to be $529 million). Part of the reduction in GE's taxes is brought about by a refund of taxes paid in earlier years through the process of *carrybacks*; see the Glossary.

㊿ APB *Opinion No. 11* says that income of affilitates that is expected to be indefinitely reinvested in the affiliate need not be subject to income tax provisions by the parent. If the parent expects to receive dividends from the affiliate in the foreseeable future, then the parent must make an income tax provision.

�51 GE uses the deferral method of accounting for the investment credit, rather than the less conservative flow-through method. (Most U.S. corporations use the flow-through method.) GE realized $95 million of investment credits during 1981. A portion (which cannot be computed from the published data) of this $95 million reduced reported tax expense in 1981; the remainder is shown as a deferred investment credit on the balance sheet (probably under "Other liabilities"). A portion of previous years' investment credits, which had been deferred, also served to reduce 1981 reported tax expense. The total of these two reductions of reported tax expense in 1981 was $49 million. If GE had used the flow-through method, income tax expense would have been reduced by an additional $46 (= $95 − $49) million and 1981 net income would have been $46 million larger. Under the flow-through method, retained earnings at the end of 1981 would have been $306 million larger.

㊿52 This schedule shows the components of the timing differences on U.S. federal income taxes.

㊿53 Depreciation on the tax return exceeded the amount included in cost of goods sold and other expenses on the financial statements. For most companies, tax depreciation exceeds book depreciation because the Accelerated Cost Recovery System is used for taxes and the straight-line method over normal service lives, is used for financial reporting. GE, however, uses an accelerated method (based on the sum-of-the-years' digits) in its financial statements for plant and equipment located in the U.S.; see the Summary of Significant Accounting Policies and the Glossary at *Accelerated Cost Recovery System*. We can compute the excess of tax depreciation deductions over the book depreciation expense reported in the financial statements by using the $67 million timing difference shown here for 1981. If income tax expense exceeds income taxes payable by $67 million because of depreciation timing differences and if the marginal income tax rate is 46 percent of pretax income, then depreciation on the tax return must have exceeded depreciation on the financial statements by x where

$$.46x = \$67 \text{ million or}$$
$$x = \$67 \text{ million}/.46, \text{ or}$$
$$x = \$140 \text{ million.}$$

㊿54 Revenues from subsidiaries ("affiliates") shown on the financial statements under the equity method exceeded taxable revenue from these subsidiaries.

㊿55 GE makes sales on credit, with cash payments from the customer to GE spread over time. Such sales are called "installment sales." APB *Opinion No. 10* requires that revenue from most such sales be recognized in the financial statements for the period of sale. For tax purposes, GE recognizes revenue on such sales when the cash payments are collected. Thus a timing difference is created. The amount shown here for GE is relatively small because GE tends not to have large percentages of its sales on the installment method.

**Reconciliation from statutory to effective ⑤⑧
income tax rates**

	1981	1980	1979
U.S. federal statutory rate	46.0%	46.0%	46.0%
Reduction in taxes resulting from:			
Varying tax rates of consolidated			
affiliates (including DISC)	(5.2)	(4.7)	(3.3)
Inclusion of earnings of the			
Credit Corporation in before-tax			
income on an after-tax basis	(2.2)	(2.1)	(1.7)
Investment credit	(1.8)	(1.5)	(1.3)
Income tax at capital gains rate	(0.2)	(0.1)	—
Other — net	(0.4)	0.8	0.2
Effective tax rate	36.2%	38.4%	39.9%

Based on the location of the component furnishing goods or services, domestic income before taxes was $2,014 million in
⑤⑨ 1981 ($1,854 million in 1980 and $1,706 million in 1979). The corresponding amounts for foreign-based operations were $646 million, $639 million and $685 million in each of the last three years, respectively. Provision for income taxes is determined on the basis of the jurisdiction imposing the tax liability. Therefore, U.S. and foreign taxes shown at the left do not compare directly with these segregations.

⑥⓪ **6. Earnings per common share**

Earnings per share are based on the average number of shares outstanding. Any dilution which would result from the potential exercise or conversion of such items as stock options or convertible debt outstanding is insignificant (less than 1% in 1981, 1980 and 1979).

7. Cash and marketable securities

Deposits restricted as to usage and withdrawal or used as par-
⑥① tial compensation for short-term borrowing arrangements were not material.

Marketable securities (none of which are equity securities)
⑥② are carried at the lower of amortized cost or market value. Carrying value was substantially the same as market value at year-end 1981 and 1980.

8. Current receivables

December 31 (In millions)	1981	1980
Customers' accounts and notes	$3,989	$3,816
Associated companies	49	25
Nonconsolidated affiliates	21	17
Other	927	584
	4,986	4,442
Less allowance for losses	(114)	(103)
	$4,872	$4,339

The increase in other current receivables resulted primarily
⑥③ from tax refunds and carrybacks attributable to increased leasing activity as discussed in note 5.

9. Inventories

December 31 (In millions)	1981	1980
Raw materials and work in process	$2,089	$2,082
Finished goods	1,099	961
Unbilled shipments	273	300
	$3,461	$3,343

About 82% of total inventories are valued using the LIFO method of inventory accounting.

If the FIFO method of inventory accounting had been used ⑥④
to value all inventories, they would have been $2,465 million higher than reported at December 31, 1981 ($2,240 million higher at year-end 1980).

10. Property, plant and equipment

(In millions)	1981	1980
Major classes at December 31:		
Manufacturing plant and equipment		
Land and improvements	$ 164	$ 139
Buildings, structures and		
related equipment	2,581	2,329
Machinery and equipment	7,121	6,197
Leasehold costs and manufac-		
turing plant under construction	576	453
Mineral property, plant and		
equipment	2,263	1,917
	$12,705	$11,035
Cost at January 1	$11,035	$ 9,365
Additions	2,025	1,948
Dispositions	(355)	(278)
Cost at December 31	$12,705	$11,035
Accumulated depreciation, depletion and amortization		
Balance at January 1 ⑥⑤	$ 5,255	$ 4,752
Current-year provision	882	707
Dispositions	(267)	(214)
Other changes	(9)	10
Balance at December 31 ⑥⑤	$ 5,861	$ 5,255
Property, plant and equipment less depreciation, depletion and amortization at December 31	$ 6,844	$ 5,780

㊻ Estimated warranty expense recognized by the "allowance method" does not qualify as a tax deduction. GE uses the "allowance method" of recognizing warranty expense for financial reporting. As products carrying warranties are sold, GE makes the following entry recognizing the estimated liability for future repairs and replacements:

Estimated Warranty Expense (Provision) X
   Estimated Warranty Liability... X
Entry made in the period of sale for expected warranty costs.

Later, when repairs are made, and warranty costs are incurred, the entry is:

Estimated Warranty Liability... Y
   Assets Used and Liabilities Incurred .... Y
To recognize cost of actual repairs and replacements.

The repair and, therefore, the second entry often occur in a year subsequent to the year of sale. The cost of providing the warranty services does not become a tax deduction until the repair is actually made. Thus timing differences are created: an expense is subtracted on the financial statements in one year but is deducted on the tax return in a later year. In 1981, the amounts spent for warranty repairs, Y above, exceeded the estimated warranty expense, X above. The amount is approximately $23/.46 = $50 million. We can make the following statements about 1979 and 1980: The provision for warranties (the estimated expense) results in income taxes payable being larger than income tax expense. Therefore, it must be true that the estimated expense of rendering warranty service in future years for sales made in the current year is greater than the actual costs of warranty repairs made in the current year, most of which related to sales of earlier years.

㊼ Primarily because of the accounting (explained just above) for warranties, GE's cumulative income tax payments have exceeded cumulative income tax expense reported in the financial statements although this cumulative excess was reduced in 1981. This has resulted in a small "deferred tax debit" whereas most companies have the reverse situation and a "deferred tax credit" which (as is made clear in the 1980 annual report) GE reports on the "Other" line of the schedule in Note 12.

㊽ Most readers of financial statements are aware that the U.S. federal tax rate on most corporate income is 46 percent of pretax income. The SEC requires that companies report in its notes why the reported income tax expense rate differs from 46 percent. The $129 million of income in 1981 from GE Credit reported in GE's Note 3 is after taxes. Yet it appears in GE's income statement before the income tax calculation. GE need pay no further taxes on the income from GE Credit; this accounts for part of the difference between GE's effective tax rate on "pretax income," 36.2 percent in 1981, and the statutory rate, 46 percent. The investment credit reduces taxes otherwise payable and this accounts for another part of the difference.

㊾ The SEC requires disclosure of the disaggregation of pretax income into domestic and foreign sources.

㊿ GE reports only primary earnings per share. Because it has so few dilutive securities outstanding, fully diluted earnings per share would be less than one percent below the primary earnings per share. A dual presentation of earnings per share is required only when fully diluted earnings per share is 97 percent or less of primary earnings per share.

㉖ See *compensating balance* in the Glossary. Compensating balances increase the stated cost of borrowing; accordingly, the SEC requires disclosure of such amounts, if they are significant. GE states that its compensating balances are not significant.

㉗ *ARB No. 43* requires disclosure of aggregate cost and aggregate market value of these nonequity, marketable securities.

㊿ See our comment 49.

㉔ GE provides information that allows us to calculate what the operating income would have been if a FIFO cost flow assumption had been used. The IRS does not allow companies using LIFO for tax purposes to disclose directly on the income statement what income would have been under FIFO. The SEC requires the disclosure of beginning and ending inventories as they would have been under FIFO, if these amounts are significantly different from the LIFO amounts. The SEC's required disclosure of inventory differences allows the reader to compute the income difference. As of December 31, 1981, cumulative pretax income is $2,465 million less than it would have been under FIFO. As of January 1, 1981, cumulative pretax income is $2,240 million less than it would have been under FIFO. This difference increased by $225 (= $2,465 − $2,240) million during the year 1981. Hence 1981 pretax income would have been $225 million, or about 10 percent, larger if FIFO had been used.

   This calculation may be seen more clearly in the accompanying exhibit.

Inventory Data from Financial Statements and Footnotes

(For Authors' Comment 64. Amounts shown in **boldface** *are given in General Electric Company's financial statements. Other amounts are computed as indicated.)*

	(Dollar Amounts in Millions)				
	LIFO Cost-Flow Assumption (Actually Used)	+	Excess of FIFO over LIFO Amount	=	FIFO Cost-Flow Assumption (Hypothetical)
Beginning Inventory..............	**$ 3,343**		**$ 2,240**		$ 5,583
Purchases	19,063[a]		0		19,063
Cost of Goods Available for Sale....	$22,406		**$ 2,240**		$24,646
Less Ending Inventory	**3,461**		2,465		5,926
Cost of Goods Sold..............	**$18,945**		($ 225)		$18,720
Sales..........................	**$27,240**		0		**$27,240**
Less Cost of Goods Sold..........	**18,945**		($ 225)		18,720
Gross Margin on Sales............	$ 8,295		$ 225		$ 8,520

[a]Computation of Purchases not presented in GP's financial statements:

Purchases = Cost of Goods Sold + Ending Inventory − Beginning Inventory
$19,063   =   **$18,945**   +   **$3,461**   −   **$3,343**

⑥⑤ If an asset costing $1,000 is being depreciated on a straight-line basis in the amount of $100 per year and has accumulated depreciation of $400 at year-end, then the asset must be four (= $400/$100) years old. If GE used straight-line depreciation for financial reporting, then the analogous computation indicates the dollars used by GE to acquire Property, plant, and equipment were spent, on average, 6.7 (= $5,861/$882) years before the end of 1981. GE uses accelerated depreciation for some of its depreciable assets, see page 42 of the Annual Report; thus, accumulated depreciation builds up at a faster rate than under straight-line depreciation and we can conclude that the dollars for plant were spent on average less than 6.7 years before the end of 1981. GE has a relatively young plant compared to some; U.S. Steel for example spent its dollar for plant, on average, more than 14 years before the end of 1981.

⑥⑥ The disclosure of both historical cost and current market values follows from the requirement of *SFAS No. 12*. The net realizable value of these securities at year-end 1981 is $240 million; the cost (see GE's Note 11) was $290 million. Thus GE has an unrealized holding loss on these securities of $50 (= $240 value − $290 cost) million at year-end 1981. At year-end 1980, the unrealized holding loss was $36 (= $287 value − $323 cost) million. Thus, the unrealized holding loss increased during the year by $14 million, from $36 million to $50 million. Therefore, on these securities GE had unrealized holding losses during 1981 of $14 million which are not included in net income under the cost method.

⑥⑦ The aggregate market value of these securities at year-end 1981 is $365 million; the cost is $43 million. Thus, the unrealized holding gain at the end of 1981 is $322 (= $365 − $43) million. At year-end 1980, the unrealized holding gain was $198 (= $242 value − $44 cost) million. Thus, the unrealized holding gain increased by $124 (= $322 − $198) million during the year 1981. GE had an increase in wealth of $124 million which is not reported in the conventional income statement.

⑥⑧ See the text under the schedule in GE's Note 3 and our comment 41. We cannot be certain exactly which items enter the calculation but note that if the fixed charge coverage ratio is (Interest and discount + Operating income)/Interest and discount, then the calculation ($1,045 + $149)/$1,045 = 1.14. Loan agreements require this umber to be at least 1.15.

⑥⑨ Note that the two events both occurred during 1981:
   (i) GE required GECC to declare dividends (payable to GE) in the amount of $102 million, and
   (ii) GE invested an additional $103 (= $761 − $658) million in GECC through the purchase of "Capital stock."
One might wonder why the parent bothers to have the subsidiary declare dividends and then turn right around and re-invest that cash in the same subsidiary. We have been told that the executive compensation for the top managers of GE provides bonuses tying total pay to the reported income of the parent company as computed with a special formula. In that formula, the income from the Credit Company is based on accounting using the *cost method*, not the equity method.

   If the compensation agreement specifies that the cost method, not the equity method, will be used in computing a firm's income for the purpose of computing salary bonuses, then a manager who prefers more salary to less will arrange for cost method income to be higher than otherwise. In the equity method, share of earnings are recorded by the investor, independent of actual dividends. In the cost method, however, if there are no dividends then the investor has no reported income. The dividend declarations enable management of GE to be compensated for the performance of the Credit Corporation. (One might wonder why the dividends are not equal to, or even greater than, the Credit Corporation's full earnings.)

11. Investments

December 31 (In millions)		1981	1980
Nonconsolidated finance affiliates		$1,082	$ 938
Nonconsolidated uranium mining affiliate		168	188
Miscellaneous investments (at cost):			
Government and government-guaranteed securities		186	187
Other		104	136
	⑥⑥	290	323
Marketable equity securities		43	44
Associated companies	⑥⑦	345	342
Less allowance for losses		(21)	(15)
		$1,907	$1,820

Condensed consolidated financial statements for the principal nonconsolidated finance affiliate, General Electric Credit Corporation (GECC), follow. During the normal course of business, GECC has transactions with the parent General Electric Compa 1y and certain of its consolidated affiliates, and GECC results are included in General Electric's consolidated U.S. federal income tax return. Virtually all products financed by GECC are manufactured by companies other than General Electric.

GECC's net earnings as shown in its earnings statement ($142 million) have been reduced by the after-tax effect ($13 million) of the income support payment to arrive at the $129 million presented in note 3.   ⑥⑧

General Electric Credit Corporation
Current and retained earnings

For the year (In millions)		1981	1980	1979
Earned income		$1,782	$1,389	$1,102
Expenses:				
Interest and discount		1,045	719	528
Operating and administrative		490	451	396
Provision for losses				
— receivables		101	75	69
— other assets		(3)	3	(2)
		1,633	1,248	991
Operating income		149	141	111
Income support payment ⑥⑧ from GE		25	—	—
Earnings before income taxes		174	141	111
Provision for income taxes		32	26	21
Net earnings		142	115	90
Less dividends		(102)	(93)	(72)
Retained earnings at ⑥⑨ January 1		261	239	221
Retained earnings at December 31		$ 301	$ 261	$ 239

General Electric Credit Corporation
Financial position   ⑦⓪

December 31 (In millions)		1981	1980
Cash and marketable securities		$ 463	$ 531
Receivables:			
Time sales and loans		9,157	8,159
Deferred income		(1,642)	(1,380)
		7,515	6,779
Investment in financing leases		2,732	1,643
Sundry receivables		571	197
Total receivables		10,818	8,619
Allowance for losses		(294)	(249)
Receivables — net		10,524	8,370
Equipment on operating leases — net		433	288
Other assets		392	155
Total assets		$11,812	$9,344
Notes payable:			
Due within one year		$ 5,800	$4,425
Long-term — senior		2,321	1,984
— subordinated		480	400
Other liabilities		903	707
Total liabilities		9,504	7,516
Deferred income taxes		1,202	876
Deferred investment tax credits		32	21
Capital stock ⑥⑨		761	658
Additional paid-in capital		12	12
Retained earnings		301	261
Equity		1,074	931
Total liabilities, deferred tax items and equity		$11,812	$9,344

More information is available in GECC's 1981 Annual Report, which may be obtained by writing to: General Electric Credit Corporation, P.O. Box 8300, Stamford, Conn. 06904.

Investment in the nonconsolidated uranium mining affiliate consists of investment in a wholly owned affiliate, all common stock of which is in a voting trust controlled by independent voting trustees. In February 1982, the GE Board of Directors approved a transaction involving the sale of 80% of this affiliate's common stock at approximately book value. This transaction is not expected to have a material impact on GE's consolidated financial statements.

The estimated realizable value of miscellaneous investments was $240 million at December 31, 1981 ($287 million at December 31, 1980).   ⑥⑥

Marketable equity securities are valued at the lower of cost or market. Aggregate market value of marketable equity securities was $365 million and $242 million at year-end 1981 and 1980, respectively.   ⑥⑦

Investments in nonconsolidated affiliates and associated companies included advances of $72 million at December 31, 1981 ($180 million at December 31, 1980).

⑦⓪   If the Credit Corporation were consolidated, rather than accounted for on the equity method, all these assets, liabilities, and deferred credits would be shown on GE's balance sheet. GE's consolidated retained earnings would be no different, however, because the equity method records income of unconsolidated subsidiaries as earned. The $1,074 (= $11,812 − $9,504 − $1,202 − $32) million of net assets added to GE's balance sheet would be offset with the elimination of $1,074 of the $1,082 shown on the balance sheet and detailed in GE's Note 11.

If GE were to consolidate GE Credit Corporation, the results would be as shown in the accompanying exhibit. We also show two key financial ratios, as they would be calculated from year-end account balances. The consolidation policy with respect to GE Credit Corporation affects the appearance of the financial statements, particularly the debt-equity ratio. For an even larger effect, refer to the financial statements of General Motors Corporation and go through the exercise of consolidating GMAC (General Motors Acceptance Corporation), which GM accounts for by the equity method.

General Electric and GE Credit Corporation, 1981
(For Authors' Comment 70)

Income Statement	Equity Method (as Reported)	Adjustment Debit	Adjustment Credit	Consolidated
Revenues (other than from Credit Corporation)[a]	$27,725	$	$1,782 (1)	$29,507
Equity Method Revenues from Credit Corporation	129	129 (1)		
Total Revenues[b]	$27,854			
Total Expenses[c]	26,202	1,653 (1)		27,855
Net Income	$1,652			$1,652
Balance Sheet				
All Assets Except Investment in Credit Corporation	$19,868	11,812 (2)		$31,680
Investment in Credit Corporation	1,074		1,074 (2)	
Total Assets	$20,942			$31,680
Liabilities (including Minority Interest)	$11,814		10,738[d] (2)	$22,552
Owner's Equity	9,128			9,128
Total Equities	$20,942	$11,812	$11,812	$31,680

All Capital Earnings Rate:

$$\frac{\$1,652 + \$46^e + (.54 \times \$401^f)}{\$20,942}$$

$$= \frac{\$1,915}{\$20,942} = 9.1\%$$

$$\frac{\$1,652 + \$46^e + .54 \times (\$401^f + \$1,045^g)}{\$31,680}$$

$$= \frac{\$2,479}{\$31,680} = 7.8\%$$

Debt-Equity Ratio:

$$\frac{\$11,814}{\$20,942} = 56\%$$

$$\frac{\$22,552}{\$31,680} = 71\%$$

a $27,240 + $614 − $129; a plug. See b for derivation of $27,854.

b $27,240 shown as Sales on the income statement plus $614 of Other income = $27,854.

c $24,793 (operating expenses) + $401 (interest) + 962 (income taxes) + $46 (minority interest).

d GE Credit's "liabilities" ($9,504) plus "deferred income taxes" ($1,202) plus "deferred investment credit" ($32).

e Minority interest in net income from income statement.

f GE's interest expense. Multiply by .54 to state on aftertax basis.

g GE Credit's interest expense. Multiply by .54 to state on aftertax basis.

Adjusting entry (1) adds the revenues and expenses of the Credit Corporation to the consolidated totals, while removing the equity method revenue reported by GE.

Adjusting entry (2) adds the assets and liabilities of the Credit Corporation to the consolidated totals, while removing GE's net investment from the asset account for Investments. Refer to GE's Note 14 and observe $411 million accounts payable to nonconsolidated affiliates. Presumably, some of this is payable by GE to GECC and should be eliminated in this entry to avoid double counting. We omit this adjustment because we cannot be sure of its amount.

12. Other assets

December 31 (In millions)	1981	1980
Long-term receivables	$ 385	$ 340
Deferred charges	206	198
Licenses and other intangibles (71)	189	49
Real estate development projects	148	132
Recoverable engineering costs on government contracts	145	113
Goodwill	141	26
Customer financing	118	103
Other	55	67
	$1,387	$1,028

During 1981, a number of companies were acquired to augment General Electric's plans for future growth. Consideration for these acquisitions included $381 million in cash and 486,000 shares of GE common stock from the treasury. In certain cases, there may be future cash consideration contingent upon attaining specified performance goals.

The acquisitions were accounted for as purchases. The difference between total acquisition costs of $409 million and the value of net tangible and identifiable intangible assets acquired was recorded as goodwill to be amortized over periods no (72) greater than 20 years. Net assets and operating results of the acquired companies are not material to consolidated 1981 financial results.

13. Short-term borrowings

December 31 (In millions)	1981 Amount	1981 Average rate at Dec. 31	1980 Amount	1980 Average rate at Dec. 31
Parent notes with trust departments	$ 371	12.6%	$ 353	15.1%
Consolidated affiliate bank borrowings	449	28.5	539	30.8
Other, including current portion of long-term borrowings	351		201	
	$1,171		$1,093	

The average balance of short-term borrowings, excluding the current portion of long-term borrowings, was $991 million during 1981 (calculated by averaging all month-end balances for the year), compared with an average balance of $822 million in 1980. The maximum balance included in these calculations was $1,205 million and $962 million at the end of April 1981 and October 1980, respectively. The average effective interest rate for the year 1981 was 21.8% and for 1980 was 18.9%. These average rates represent total short-term interest incurred, divided by the average balance outstanding.

Other borrowings included amounts from nonconsolidated affiliates of $141 million in 1981 ($95 million in 1980).

Although the total unused credit available to the Company through banks and commercial credit markets is not readily quantifiable, confirmed credit lines in excess of $1 billion had been extended by about 80 banks at year-end 1981. Of these lines, approximately $500 million are also available for use by General Electric Credit Corporation.

14. Accounts payable

December 31 (In millions)	1981	1980
Trade accounts	$1,371	$1,402
Collected for the account of others	230	203
Nonconsolidated affiliates	411	66
	$2,012	$1,671

15. Other costs and expenses accrued

The balances at year-end 1981 and 1980 included compensation and benefit costs accrued of $735 million and $703 million, respectively. (73)

16. Long-term borrowings

Outstanding December 31 (In millions)	1981	1980	Due date	Sinking fund/ prepayment period
General Electric Company:				
5¾% Notes	$ 56	$ 62	1991	1972-90
5.30% Debentures	62	70	1992	1973-91
7½% Debentures	133	135	1996	1977-95
8½% Debentures	284	288	2004	1985-03
Utah International Inc.:				
Notes with banks	71	37	1993	1982-93
8% Guaranteed Sinking Fund Debentures	13	15	1987	1977-87
7.6% Notes	24	28	1988	1974-88
Other	28	32		
General Electric Overseas Capital Corporation:				
4¼% Bonds	23	23	1985	1976-84
4¼% Debentures	50	50	1987	None
5½% Sterling/Dollar Guaranteed Loan Stock	7	9	1993	None
Other	33	34		
All other	275	217		
	$1,059	$1,000		

The amounts shown above are after deduction of the face value of securities held in treasury, of which the more significant amounts are shown below.

Face value of long-term borrowings in treasury

December 31 (In millions)	1981	1980
General Electric Company:		
5.30% Debentures	$48	$50
7½% Debentures	31	35
8½% Debentures	16	12

⑦① Licenses and other intangibles acquired before October 1970 need not be amortized. APB *Opinion, No. 17* requires that licenses and intangibles acquired after October 1970 be amortized over a period of not more than 40 years.

⑦② Such goodwill might, under *APB Opinion No. 17*, be amortized over periods as long as 40 years. GE uses a shorter period.

⑦③ Refer to the GE annual report near our reference to note 30. GE states that the costs of this pension plan are not funded. For its primary pension plan referred to in the context of the GE Pension Trust, GE funds pension liabilities as they are recognized. Thus the ordinary pension related entries are, first, to debit pension expense and to credit pension liability:

Pension Expense X	
Pension Liability	X

and then to fund the liability with a debit to Pension Liability and a credit to Cash:

Pension Liability X	
Cash	X

The actual funding need not be, but usually is, exactly equal to the amount of pension expense recognized in the entry just preceding.

For this supplementary pension plan, the first entry is being made (with prior service costs being amortized over 20 years; see page 42), but the liability is not being funded. Therefore an explicit pension liability is included in GE's balance sheet on page 40. The amount is included here.

⑦④ GE's Note 13 gives the details of its short-term borrowings. GE's Note 16 gives the details of its long-term borrowings. This paragraph helps the analyst to understand GE's intermediate-term borrowings. From these data, the analyst can estimate cash requirements for debt retirement over the next several years.

⑦⑤ APB *Opinion No. 12* (1966) requires the disclosure of all changes in owners' equity accounts. GE shows the sources of the changes in the retained earnings account below the income statement, on page 39 of the annual report. The schedule in Note 17 shows the sources of the changes in the other owners' equity accounts.

⑦⑥ Neither gain nor loss can be recognized on transactions by a company in its own shares (called *treasury shares*). GE's accounting is correct, but the use of the terms *gain* and *loss* may be misleading. When GE reissues previouly-acquired treasury shares, the adjustment to achieve equal debits and credits is not to a gain or loss account (to appear on the income statement), but to the account "Amounts received for stock in excess of par value." If treasury shares are acquired for an outlay of $1,000 and then are reissued for

Utah International Inc. notes with banks were subject to average interest rates at year-end 1981 and 1980 of 10.4% and 11.3%, respectively.

Borrowings of General Electric Overseas Capital Corporation are unconditionally guaranteed by General Electric as to payment of principal, premium if any, and interest. This Corporation primarily assists in financing capital requirements of foreign companies in which General Electric has an equity interest, as well as financing certain customer purchases. Borrowings include 4¼% Guaranteed Debentures due in 1987, which are convertible into General Electric common stock at $80.75 a share, and 5½% Sterling/Dollar Guaranteed Loan Stock due in 1993 in the amount of £3.6 million ($7 million), convertible into GE common stock at $73.50 a share.

All other long-term borrowings were largely by foreign and real estate development affiliates with various interest rates and maturities, and included amounts due to nonconsolidated affiliates of $7 million in 1981 and 1980.

(74) Long-term borrowing maturities during the next five years, including the portion classified as current, are $104 million in 1982, $139 million in 1983, $75 million in 1984, $83 million in 1985 and $61 million in 1986. These amounts are after deducting reacquired debentures held in treasury for sinking fund requirements.

(75) 17. Common stock

(In millions)	1981	1980	1979
Common stock issued			
Balance January 1 and December 31	$579	$579	$579
Amounts received for stock in excess of par value			
Balance January 1	$659	$656	$658
Gain/(loss) on disposition of treasury stock (76)	(2)	3	(2)
Balance December 31	$657	$659	$656
Common stock held in treasury			
Balance January 1	$189	$180	$172
Purchases	176	145	156
Dispositions:			
Employee savings plans	(113)	(99)	(124)
Employee stock ownership plan	(24)	(16)	(11)
Incentive compensation plans	(5)	(7)	(8)
Stock options and appreciation rights	(14)	(14)	(5)
Business acquisitions	(13)	—	—
Balance December 31	$196	$189	$180

At December 31, 1981, 1980 and 1979, respectively, 227,761,000 and 227,765,000 and 227,839,000 common shares were outstanding after deducting common stock held in treasury as summarized at upper right.

Shares of treasury stock

December 31 (In thousands)	1981	1980	1979
Deferred incentive compensation	2,037	1,922	1,785
Other corporate purposes	1,666	1,777	1,840
	3,703	3,699	3,625

Shares held for deferred compensation provisions of incentive compensation plans are carried at market value at the time of allotment, which was $105 million, $96 million and $88 million at December 31, 1981, 1980 and 1979, respectively. The liability is recorded in other liabilities. Remaining common stock in treasury is carried at cost. The maximum number of shares required for conversion of General Electric Overseas Capital Corporation convertible debt was 734,000 at December 31, 1981. Requirements of shares for conversions and benefit plans may be met either from unissued shares or from shares in treasury.

18. Stock option information (77)

(Shares in thousands)	Shares subject to option	Option price	Market price
Balance at January 1, 1980	4,759	$50.67	$50.63
Options granted	98	61.50	61.50
Options exercised	(273)	44.13	56.16
Options surrendered on exercise of appreciation rights	(124)	41.93	54.92
Options terminated	(157)	51.02	—
Balance at December 31, 1980	4,303	51.56	61.25
Options granted	921	56.20	56.20
Options exercised	(254)	48.99	63.74
Options surrendered on exercise of appreciation rights	(130)	48.00	63.29
Options terminated	(200)	55.65	—
Balance at December 31, 1981 (78)	4,640	52.55	57.48

Stock option plans, appreciation rights and performance units are described in the Company's current Proxy Statement. The number of shares available for granting additional options at the end of 1981 was 1,044,373 (1,862,756 at the end of 1980).

19. Commitments and contingent liabilities (79)

Lease commitments and contingent liabilities, consisting of guarantees, pending litigation, taxes and other claims, in the opinion of management, are not considered to be material in relation to the Company's financial position.

$1,200, then the entries would be:

Common Stock Held in Treasury	1,000	
Cash		1,000
To record acquisition of treasury shares.		
Cash	1,200	
Common Stock Held in Treasury		1,000
Amounts Received for Stock in Excess of Par Value		
(not Gain on Disposition of Treasury Shares)		200
To record reissue of treasury shares for an amount greater than outlay to acquire them.		

If proceeds of reissue are $800, not $1,200, then in the second entry the $200 is debited, not credited, to the account "Amount Received for Stock in Excess of Par Value."

(77) *Accounting Research Bulletin No. 43* (1953) requires the disclosure of the details of stock option plans and of the currently outstanding options.

(78) At the end of 1981, the market price of a share of GE common stock was $57.48. The average price of the 4,640,000 options exercisable at the end of 1982 was $52.55. Thus, if all the options were exercised, the present owners' equity would be diluted approximately $23 million [= ($57.48 − $52.55) × 4,640,000 shares] in comparison to the issue of new shares at the current market price.

(79) Both the SEC and the FASB (*Statement No. 13*) require disclosure of material commitments under long-term noncancelable leases. GE has no such material commitments. In general, the disclosures must include the effects on both the income statement and the balance sheet of capitalizing such leases.

(80) *FASB Statement No. 14* requires disclosure of segment data. Segments are required to be defined both by kind of operation (consumer products, industrial power, etc.) and by location (United States, Far East, etc.).

(81) Earnings of the individual segments sum to an amount larger than net income for 1981 of $1,652 by $19 million, the amount of unallocated central corporate expenses. Assets of the individual segments sum to an amount smaller than total assets by $2,381 million, the amount of unallocated central corporate assets. Hence rates of return computed for individual segments will overstate true rate of return. If a "true" rate of return for the company as a whole is defined to be net income over total assets, then GE's rate of return is 7.9 percent (= $1,652/$20,942). The incomes of the individual segments total $1,633 (= $1,652 − $19) million and the sum of the segments assets is $18,561 (= $20,942 − $2,381) million. If one were computing rates of return to individual segments, then, the aggregate rate of return might be computed as 8.8 percent (= $1,633/$18,561). For GE, the resulting overstatement of the combined segment rates of return is not as dramatic as it is for some other companies. Some who criticize segment reporting have in mind the misleading inferences the unwary analyst (or politician or government regulator) might draw from computing rates of return for individual segments where the sum of segment income overstates corporate income and the sum of segment assets understates corporate assets.

(82) *SFAS No. 14* requires disclosure of this information about customers whose purchases represent 10 percent or more of a firm's revenues.

(83) The major difficulty in constructing meaningful and useful segment reports is the allocation of these "corporate items" to the major categories. They are truly common or joint costs of running the entire corporation but must be allocated to the various segments in order to present subtotals for segment earnings that add up to the total earnings, $1,652 million for 1981.

(84) The next page of the GE annual report, page 51, has been moved in this book to the next chapter where it is discussed along with all of GE's "changing prices" disclosures.

Industry segment information ⑧⓪

(In millions)

Revenues
For the years ended December 31

	Total revenues			Intersegment sales			External sales and other income		
	1981	1980	1979	1981	1980	1979	1981	1980	1979
Services and materials	$ 2,464	$ 2,115	$ 1,901	$ 91	$ 84	$ 73	$ 2,373	$ 2,031	$ 1,828
Earnings of GE Credit Corp.	129*	115	90	—	—	—	129*	115	90
Total services and materials	2,593	2,230	1,991	91	84	73	2,502	2,146	1,918
Consumer products	6,643	6,342	5,990	128	111	126	6,515	6,231	5,864
Industrial products	4,871	4,690	4,375	363	352	350	4,508	4,338	4,025
Natural resources	1,722	1,374	1,260	—	—	—	1,722	1,374	1,260
Power systems	5,982	5,815	5,124	223	272	201	5,759	5,543	4,923
Technical systems	3,979	3,252	2,761	195	206	170	3,784	3,046	2,591
Aircraft engine	2,950	2,660	2,190	55	36	13	2,895	2,624	2,177
Corporate items and eliminations	(886)	(840)	(711)	(1,055)	(1,061)	(933)	169	221	222
Total	$27,854	$25,523	$22,980	$ —	$ —	$ —	$27,854	$25,523	$22,980

Operating profit ⑧①
For the years ended December 31

Net earnings
For the years ended December 31

	Operating profit			Net earnings		
	1981	1980	1979	1981	1980	1979
Services and materials	$ 477	$ 403	$ 385	$ 253	$ 206	$ 212
Earnings of GE Credit Corp.	129*	115	90	129*	115	90
Total services and materials	606	518	475	382	321	302
Consumer products	549	615	617	292	312	338
Industrial products	495	438	335	242	225	171
Natural resources	493	404	431	284	224	208
Power systems	446	366	349	224	201	183
Technical systems	249	230	215	98	105	113
Aircraft engine	322	275	185	149	141	97
Total segment operating profit	3,160	2,846	2,607			
Interest and other financial charges	(401)	(314)	(258)			
Corporate items and eliminations	(99)	(39)	42	(19)	(15)	(3)
Total	$ 2,660	$ 2,493	$ 2,391	$ 1,652	$ 1,514	$ 1,409

⑧① Assets
At December 31

Property, plant and equipment
For the years ended December 31

	Assets			Additions			Depreciation, depletion and amortization		
	1981	1980	1979	1981	1980	1979	1981	1980	1979
Services and materials	$ 2,150	$ 1,835	$ 1,461	$ 340	$ 352	$ 252	$ 126	$ 94	$ 80
Investment in GE Credit Corp.	1,074	931	817	—	—	—	—	—	—
Total services and materials	3,224	2,766	2,278	340	352	252	126	94	80
Consumer products	2,926	2,656	2,500	309	267	221	162	145	127
Industrial products	2,074	2,031	1,916	187	170	126	93	83	82
Natural resources	2,359	2,109	1,679	325	446	201	111	94	83
Power systems	3,718	3,702	3,381	285	250	202	181	150	139
Technical systems	2,309	1,713	1,328	327	167	113	104	76	65
Aircraft engine	1,951	1,703	1,225	187	239	123	86	50	37
Corporate items and eliminations	2,381	1,831	2,337	65	57	24	19	15	11
Total	$20,942	$18,511	$16,644	$ 2,025	$ 1,948	$ 1,262	$ 882	$ 707	$ 624

*Excluding income support payment by GE.

The grouping of products and services for industry segment reporting purposes was revised in 1981. The new grouping closely parallels the organization of the Company into Sectors for internal management purposes but is on a worldwide basis. This means that products and services of multi-industry foreign affiliates are classified by appropriate industry segments. The types of products and services within each segment, as well as additional commentary relevant to segment operations, are on pages 22 through 28 of this Report. Because the several segment groupings are substantially different from those presented previously, all years shown have been restated to a comparable basis.

⑧② Approximately one-eighth of external sales were to agencies of the U.S. government, which is the Company's largest single customer. Most of these sales were aerospace products and services, which are included in the Technical Systems industry segment, and aircraft engines and related products and services.

⑧③
Net earnings for industry segments include allocation of corporate interest income, expense and other financial charges to parent company components based on change in individual component average nonfixed investment. Interest and other financial charges of a number of affiliated companies recognize

that such companies service their own debt. In 1981, responsibility for the financing programs of certain affiliates was transferred to the Corporate Treasury Operation. Appropriate reclassifications of operating results and total assets for this change are reflected in the years shown.

General corporate expenses are allocated principally on the basis of cost of operations, with certain exceptions and reductions which recognize the varying degrees to which affiliated companies maintain their own corporate structures.

In addition, provision for income taxes ($962 million in 1981, $958 million in 1980, and $953 million in 1979) is allocated based on the total corporate effective tax rate, except for GECC and Natural Resources, whose income taxes are calculated separately.

Minority interest ($46 million in 1981, $21 million in 1980 and $29 million in 1979) is allocated to operating components having responsibility for investments in consolidated affiliates.

In general, it is GE policy to price internal sales as nearly as practicable to equivalent commercial selling prices.

Geographic segment information

(In millions)	Revenues For the years ended December 31								
	Total revenues			Intersegment sales			External sales and other income		
	1981	1980	1979	1981	1980	1979	1981	1980	1979
United States	$22,697	$20,750	$18,859	$ 667	$ 484	$ 467	$22,030	$20,266	$18,392
Far East including Australia	1,624	1,277	1,183	397	355	280	1,227	922	903
Other areas of the world	4,798	4,459	3,814	201	124	129	4,597	4,335	3,685
Elimination of intracompany transactions	(1,265)	(963)	(876)	(1,265)	(963)	(876)	—	—	—
Total	$27,854	$25,523	$22,980	$ —	$ —	$ —	$27,854	$25,523	$22,980

	Net Earnings For the years ended December 31			Assets At December 31		
	1981	1980	1979	1981	1980	1979
United States	$ 1,373	$ 1,175	$ 1,120	$16,004	$13,732	$12,693
Far East including Australia	228	169	174	1,187	1,090	842
Other areas of the world	68	181	120	3,902	3,808	3,207
Elimination of intracompany transactions	(17)	(11)	(5)	(151)	(119)	(98)
Total	$ 1,652	$ 1,514	$ 1,409	$20,942	$18,511	$16,644

Geographic segment information (including allocation of income taxes and minority interest in earnings of consolidated affiliates) is based on the location of the operation furnishing goods or services. Included in United States revenues were export sales to unaffiliated customers of $3,681 million in 1981, $3,781 million in 1980, and $2,772 million in 1979. Of such sales, $2,024 million in 1981 ($2,089 million in 1980 and $1,581 million in 1979) were to customers in Europe, Africa and the Middle East; and $776 million in 1981 ($926 million in 1980 and $741 million in 1979) were to customers in the Far East including Australia. U.S. revenues also include royalty

and licensing income from unaffiliated foreign sources.

Revenues, net earnings and assets associated with foreign operations are shown in the tabulations above. At December 31, 1981, foreign operation liabilities, minority interest in equity and GE interest in equity were $2,789 million, $154 million and $2,146 million, respectively. On a comparable basis, the amounts were $2,562 million, $141 million and $2,195 million, respectively, at December 31, 1980; and $2,101 million, $139 million and $1,809 million, respectively, at December 31, 1979. ⑧④

Ten-year summary (a) ⑧⑤

Selected financial data

(Dollar amounts in millions; per-share amounts in dollars)	1981	1980	1979
Summary of operations			
Sales of products and services to customers	$27,240	$24,959	$22,461
Cost of goods sold	18,945	17,751	15,991
Selling, general and administrative expense	4,966	4,258	3,716
Depreciation, depletion and amortization	882	707	624
Operating costs	24,793	22,716	20,331
Operating margin	2,447	2,243	2,130
Other income	614	564	519
Interest and other financial charges	(401)	(314)	(258)
Earnings before income taxes and minority interest	2,660	2,493	2,391
Provision for income taxes	(962)	(958)	(953)
Minority interest	(46)	(21)	(29)
Net earnings	$ 1,652	$ 1,514	$ 1,409
Earnings per common share	$ 7.26	$ 6.65	$ 6.20
Dividends declared per common share (b)	$ 3.15	$ 2.95	$ 2.75
Earnings as a percent to sales	6.1%	6.1%	6.3%
Earned on average share owners' equity	19.1%	19.5%	20.2%
Dividends declared	$ 715	$ 670	$ 624
Shares outstanding–average (in thousands)	227,528	227,541	227,173
Share owner accounts–average	514,000	524,000	540,000
Market price range per share (b)	69⅞-51⅛	63-44	55⅜-45
Price/earnings ratio range (b)	10-7	9-7	9-7
Current assets	$10,804	$ 9,883	$ 9,384
Current liabilities	8,734	7,592	6,872
Working capital	$ 2,070	$ 2,291	$ 2,512
Short-term borrowings	$ 1,171	$ 1,093	$ 871
Long-term borrowings	1,059	1,000	947
Minority interest in equity of consolidated affiliates	166	154	152
Share owners' equity	9,128	8,200	7,362
Total capital invested	$11,524	$10,447	$ 9,332
Earned on average total capital invested	17.4%	17.3%	17.6%
Share owners' equity per common share–year end	$ 40.08	$ 36.00	$ 32.31
Total assets	$20,942	$18,511	$16,644
Property, plant and equipment additions	$ 2,025	$ 1,948	$ 1,262
Worldwide employment–average	404,000	402,000	405,000

(a) Data for years prior to 1976 have been adjusted as appropriate to reflect the December 1976 acquisition of Utah International Inc., which was accounted ⑧⑥ for as a pooling of interests.
(b) For General Electric common stock as reported in the years shown.

52

⑧⑤   The detail shown here by GE goes beyond the five years required by the SEC in its 1980 *ASR 279–ASR 281*. GE shows ten years of data so that one can construct time series analysis for at least nine years in all cases. Note that if only five columns are shown, then growth rates for items like sales can be computed for only four years.

1978	1977	1976	1975	1974	1973	1972
$19,654	$17,519	$15,697	$14,105	$13,918	$11,945	$10,474
13,915	12,288	11,048	10,210	10,092	8,445	7,381
3,205	3,011	2,635	2,238	2,240	2,058	1,872
576	522	486	470	415	372	344
17,696	15,821	14,169	12,918	12,747	10,875	9,597
1,958	1,698	1,528	1,187	1,171	1,070	877
419	390	274	174	207	203	207
(224)	(199)	(175)	(187)	(197)	(143)	(121)
2,153	1,889	1,627	1,174	1,181	1,130	963
(894)	(773)	(668)	(460)	(458)	(457)	(385)
(29)	(28)	(28)	(26)	(18)	(12)	(5)
$ 1,230	$ 1,088	$ 931	$ 688	$ 705	$ 661	$ 573
$ 5.39	$ 4.79	$ 4.12	$ 3.07	$ 3.16	$ 2.97	$ 2.57
$ 2.50	$ 2.10	$ 1.70	$ 1.60	$ 1.60	$ 1.50	$ 1.40
6.3%	6.2%	5.9%	4.9%	5.1%	5.5%	5.5%
19.6%	19.4%	18.9%	15.7%	17.8%	18.4%	17.5%
$ 570	$ 477	$ 361	$ 326	$ 315	$ 287	$ 268
227,985	227,154	225,791	224,262	222,921	222,631	222,503
552,000	553,000	566,000	582,000	566,000	543,000	542,000
$57\frac{5}{8}$-$43\frac{5}{8}$	$57\frac{1}{4}$-$47\frac{3}{8}$	$59\frac{1}{4}$-46	$52\frac{7}{8}$-$32\frac{3}{8}$	65-30	$75\frac{7}{8}$-55	73-$58\frac{1}{4}$
11-8	12-10	14-11	17-10	19-9	24-17	25-20
$ 8,755	$ 7,865	$ 6,685	$ 5,750	$ 5,334	$ 4,597	$ 4,057
6,175	5,417	4,605	4,163	4,032	3,588	2,921
$ 2,580	$ 2,448	$ 2,080	$ 1,587	$ 1,302	$ 1,009	$ 1,136
$ 960	$ 772	$ 611	$ 667	$ 656	$ 676	$ 453
994	1,284	1,322	1,239	1,403	1,166	1,191
151	132	119	105	86	63	54
6,587	5,943	5,253	4,617	4,172	3,774	3,420
$ 8,692	$ 8,131	$ 7,305	$ 6,628	$ 6,317	$ 5,679	$ 5,118
16.3%	15.8%	15.1%	12.5%	13.4%	13.7%	12.7%
$ 28.88	$ 26.05	$ 23.18	$ 20.49	$ 18.65	$ 16.94	$ 15.35
$15,036	$13,697	$12,050	$10,741	$10,220	$ 9,089	$ 8,051
$ 1,055	$ 823	$ 740	$ 588	$ 813	$ 735	$ 501
401,000	384,000	380,000	380,000	409,000	392,000	373,000

53

86 You can test your understanding of the accounting for mergers and acquisitions by computing the amount of the goodwill shown in the schedule in GE's Note 12 that arises from the aquisition in 1976 of Utah International. The answer is given in the next paragraph.

Because the merger with Utah was a pooling of interests, rather than a purchase, none of the $141 million of goodwill arose from this merger. Goodwill can arise only in a purchase.

Accounting for the Effects of Changing Prices:

Constant Dollar Accounting and Current Cost Accounting

The conventional financial accounting statements assume that a *common* or *uniform measuring unit* is used in recording the results of transactions and events in the accounting records. That is, the measuringunit (the dollar) applied in recording the acquisition of a machine costing $10,000 five years ago is treated as if it is the same as the measuring unit applied in recording the purchase of merchandise inventory one week ago for $10,000. Because the purchasing power of the dollar changes over time, this asumption may be unwarranted.

The conventional accounting statements assume that the *attribute measured* in accounting is historical cost. (See the discussion in the Glossary at *attribute measured*.) Just as one might measure different attributes of a person, such as age, height, or color of eyes, so one might measure different attributes of an asset such as its historical cost, location, size, or *current cost*. Because the conventional accounting model measures the attribute historical cost, it assumes a *realization convention*: increases in the market prices of individual assets are generally not recognized as gains in reporting net income until the assets are sold (or otherwise retired) and higher values are realized in arm's length transactions. Only at the time of sale is the calculation of the amount of the gain considered to be sufficiently objective to warrant recognition in the accounts. In the conventional statements, asets are generally carried in the accounting records at *historical or acquisition* cost, less amortization if appropriate.[1]

During earlier periods of relative price stability, assuming a common measuring unit presented no special problems. Since 1945, however, the general level of prices in the United States has increased at an average rate of approximately 4 percent per year. In recent years, the rate of inflation has been more than double that. Even during periods when prices in general have remained relatively stable, the prices of some goods and services have increased or decreased significantly. Changing prices, either in general or for specific goods and services, raise serious questions about the appropriateness of the common monetary measuring unit assumption and the historical cost measurement as the attribute to be measured. The accounting problems associated with changing prices should be separated into those related to *changes in the general price level* and those associated with *changes in prices of specific goods and services*.

The FASB requires that certain large firms provide supplementary disclosures of the effects of changing prices. The proposal requires two types of disclosure. One is based on constant dollar accounting (where the measuring unit is changed) while the other is based on current cost accounting (where the attribute measured is changed). The following sections illustrate both.

---

[1] Exceptions occur where the current cost of marketable securities or inventories is less than acquisition cost. In those cases these assets are written down to the lower current cost (market) under a lower-of-cost-or-market rule.

Constant Dollar Financial Statements

The objective of constant dollar financial statements is to state all amounts in dollars of uniform general purchasing power, thereby obtaining a common, or uniform, measuring unit. The purchasing power of the dollar on the date of the most recent balance sheet is usually recommended as the unit of measurement when balance sheet data is presented. When only income statement data are presented, the average purchasing power for the period is the usual base for the constant dollar presentation. The Consumer Price Index (CPI), a general price level index prepared by the Bureau of Labor Statistics, is used to measure the general purchasing power of the dollar on various dates. The general approach is to convert the number of dollars received or expended at various price levels to an equivalent number of dollars in terms of the price level on the date of the current financial statements. The justification for use of the CPI is that shares of stock of corporations are largely owned by consumers, so the report should be in units of measurement relevant for consumers.

To illustrate this procedure, assume that two parcels of land are held on December 31, Year 10, when an index of the general price level is 155. Tract A was acquired during Year 2 for $100,000, when the general price index was 100. Tract B was acquired during Year 4 for $100,000, when the general price index was 106. The acquisition cost of these parcels of land would be restated from Year 2 and Year 4 dollars to an equivalent number of Year 10 dollars as shown in Exhibit 1.

EXHIBIT 1
Illustration of General Price Level Restatement Procedure for Land

Item	Conventionally Reported Acquisition Cost	Conversion Factor as of December 30 Year 10	General Price Level Restated Acquisition Cost as of December 31 Year 10
Tract A.............	$100,000	155/100	$155,000
Tract B.............	$100,000	155/106	$146,226

The sacrifice in general purchasing power made during Year 2 when Tract A was acquired for $100,000 is equivalent to sacrificing $155,000 (= 155/100 × $100,000) in general purchasing power on December 31, Year 10. Likewise, the sacrifice in general purchasing power made during Year 4 when Tract B was acquired for $100,000 is equivalent to sacrificing $146,226 (= 155/106 × $100,000) in general purchasing power on December 31, Year 10. The restated amounts in Exhibit 1 use a measuring unit of uniform general purchasing power.

Two important aspects of the constant dollar restatement procedure should be noted. First, the procedure does *not* represent a departure from the use of acquisition cost as the principal valuation basis in preparing financial statements. Second, the amounts shown for general price level restated acquisition cost do *not* attempt to reflect the current market values of these two parcels of land. The market values of the land could have changed in an entirely different direction and pattern from that of the general price level changes. The constant dollar procedure restates the acquisition cost data in comparable units but does *not* reflect current values of individual assets and equities.

Four aspects of dollar adjusted income statements deserve mention. These four are illustrated with disclosures from page 37 of the 1981 General Electric Company Annual Report and are reproduced in Exhibit 2. In the top panel of Exhibit 2, the first column summarizes the conventional financial income statement, the second shows part of constant dollar income statement, and the third shows part of the current cost income statement.

① **Revenue and expenses occurring fairly evenly throughout the year.** Sales and expenses, other than cost of goods sold and depreciation, usually occur fairly evenly through the year. Thus, the nominal dollar amounts are equal to constant dollar amounts of year-average general purchasing power.

Exhibit 2

From 1981 Annual Report of the General Electric Company

Supplementary information Effect of changing prices		For the year ended December 31, 1981	
		Adjusted for[a]	
(In millions, except per-share amounts)	As reported	general inflation	current costs
Sales of products and services to customers ....①..	$27,240	$27,240	$27,240
Costs of goods sold ....②..	18,945	19,065	19,034
Selling, general and administrative expense ....①..	4,966	4,966	4,966
Depreciation, depletion and amortization ....③..	882	1,297	1,294
Operating costs	24,793	25,328	25,294
Operating margin...................................	2,447	1,912	1,946
Other income....................................①..	614	614	614
Interest and other financial charges ....①..	(401)	(401)	(401)
Earnings before income taxes........................	2,660	2,125	2,159
Provision for income taxes........................①..	(962)	(962)	(962)
Minority interest.................................	(46)	(33)	(33)
Net earnings	$ 1,652	$ 1,130	$ 1,164
Earnings per share	$ 7.26	$ 4.97	$ 5.12
Share owners' equity at December 31	$ 9,128	$14,076	$14,090

a In dollars of average 1981 purchasing power.

Selected financial data adjusted for the effect of changing prices ⑥
in dollars of average 1981 purchasing power

(Dollar amounts in millions, except per-share amounts)	1981	1980	1979	1978	1977
Sales..	$27,240	$27,555	$28,144	$27,400	$26,294
Current cost information					
Net earnings....................................	1,164	1,105	1,235	1,206	1,105
Net earnings per share	5.12	4.86	5.44	5.29	4.86
Share owners' equity at December 31	14,090	14,256	13,976	13,809	13,353
Excess of increase in general price level over increases in specific GE price levels[a] ....⑤....	703	216	412		
General price level only					
Net earnings....................................	1,130	1,136	1,334		
Net earnings per share	4.97	4.99	5.86		
Share owners' equity at December 31	14,076	13,664	13,077		
Other					
Purchasing power loss[b] ....④....	84	219	262	160	76
Dividends per share	3.15	3.26	3.44	3.49	3.16
Market price per share at December 31	56	65	60	63	73
Average Consumer Price Index (CPI-U; 1967 = 100)	272.4	246.8	217.4	195.4	181.5

a At December 31, 1981, in end-of-year dollars, the current cost of inventory was $6,018 million, and property, plant and equipment was $9,768 million. In dollars of average 1981 purchasing power, the increase that might have been expected from general inflation was more than the increase in specific GE current costs by the amount shown. A similar pattern is shown in the other years.
b On net monetary items.

The above data as well as the data on page 37 have been prepared in accordance with Financial Accounting Standards Board requirements. GE Annual Reports for 1979 and 1980 included technical information about the methodology used by GE in preparing these data. Copies of those earlier Reports my be obtained by writing to Investor Relations at the address shown on page 54.

Note: Circled numbers indicate parts of the text where the disclosure is discussed.

FIGURE 1
Mid-Point of Purchase Cycle
for FIFO and LIFO
Cost-Flow Assumptions

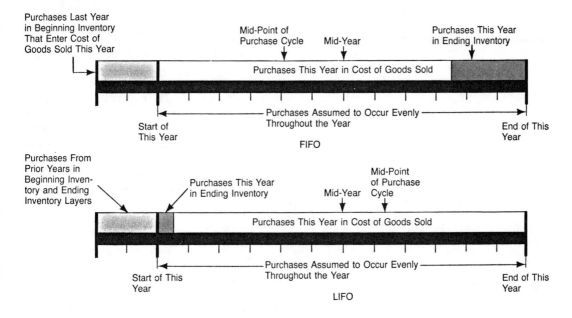

② **Cost of goods sold.** Whether the constant dollar or the nominal dollar amount for cost of goods sold is the larger number depends on inventory turnover, the cost flow assumption, the constant dollar date, and the direction of general price change. Assume for this discussion that general prices are rising (inflation rather than deflation) and that constant dollars represent mid-year purchasing power (not year-end). Then, a FIFO cost flow assumption usually implies a larger constant dollar than nominal dollar cost of goods sold and a LIFO cost flow assumption usually implies a larger nominal dollar than constant dollar cost of goods sold. Figure 1 illustrates why. Note that the mid-point of the FIFO purchase cycle occurs before mid-year, so that an increase is required to restate nominal dollars to mid-year purchasing power. The mid-point of the LIFO purchase cycle occurs after mid-year, so that a downward adjustment is required to restate nominal dollars to mid-year purchasing power. Because GE uses LIFO for most, but not all, of its investors and FIFO for the remainder, the direction of change caused by the restatement to dollars of mid-year purchasing power cannot be predicted from first principles. It is fortuitous that GE shows a slightly larger constant dollar cost of goods sold ($19,065 million) than nominal dollar amount ($18,945 million); the restatement to constant dollars might just as well have caused a reduction in the amount.

③ **Depreciation.** Constant dollar depreciation is almost always much larger than nominal dollar depreciation conventionally reported. Most firms' depreciable assets are acquired years before the period being reported on and general prices have increased since acquisition. Constant dollar depreciation adjustment reflects a portion (equal to the depreciation rate) of the cumulative change in prices since the depreciable assets were acquired. For example, if the depreciation rate for an asset is 10 percent and the general price level has increased by 60 percent since that asset was acquired, then depreciation will be increased by 6 percent (= .10 × .60) of the asset's acquisition cost.

④ **Purchasing power gain or loss on monetary items.** Constant dollar income statements explicitly show the gain for the period in purchasing power captured by a debtor (or the loss suffered by a creditor) during a period of rising general price levels. Because most industrial companies are typically net debtors, they will uually shown purchasing power gains from this debt. There is a gain because the liabilities will be paid off, or discharged, with dollars of smaller general purchasing power than was originally borrowed. The difference between the purchasing power borrowed and that repaid is the gain on a monetary liability during the term of the loan. The gain in purchasing power from being in a net monetary liability position does not produce an inflow of cash. (GE is a net lender; see the purchasing power losses shown in the bottom panel of Exhibit 2.)

The inflation gain or loss from holding monetary items is in many ways the most meaningful of the general price level adjustments. The interest expense reported in the conventional income statements is the nominal dollar cost of borrowing. It depends upon the interest rate negotiated at the time of the loan. That interest rate, in turn, depends in part on the lender's and borrower's anticipations about the rate of inflation during the term of the loan. (Interest rates are increased when the borrower expects to be repaid "cheaper" dollars.) Thus, the borrower's conventional income statement shows an interest expense that reflects the inflation expected by both the borrower and the lender. The gain from being in a net monetary liability position in a time of rising prices is, conceptually, an offset to reported interest expense. The loss from being in a net monetary asset position is, analogously, an offset to nominal dollar interest revenue. The gain from being a debtor or loss from being a creditor during the period of inflation reflects what both parties to the loan expected. After the fact, who benefited, the borrower or the lender, depends on whether the actual rate of price increase during the term of the loan differed from the rate anticipated by both parties to the loan at the time the loan was made. If the actual rate of price increase turns out to be less than the anticipated rate, then the lender benefits. If the actual rate turns out to be greater than the anticipated rate, then the borrower benefits.

The middle column of the top panel in Exhibit 2 presents the income statement data for General Electric for 1981 on a constant dollar basis in the form recommended by the FASB. The gain or loss on monetary items appears in a separate schedule, shown in the bottom panel of Exhibit 2.

Current Cost Accounting

Several approaches to accounting for specific price changes have been suggested, all of which involve changing the attribute measured to current cost. Among these alternative approaches are proposals for using current replacement cost (entry value) or net realizable value (exit value) as the valuation basis.

Current Replacement Cost Valuation Basis

When current replacement cost is used as the valuation basis, assets are stated on the balance sheet at the cost of replacing the productive capacity of assets in their current condition. Changes in the replacement cost of assets held during the period and not sold by the end of the period are reported as *unrealized holding gains* and *losses*. Expenses are stated at the cost of replacing the assets and services which are consumed during the period.

In computing the replacement cost of various financial statement items, several sources of price data might be used. For merchandise inventory, suppliers' catalogs could be consulted. For manufacturing firms with work in process and finished goods inventories, it is necessary to identify the various inputs into production (for example, raw material used, direct labor services consumed, depreciation recorded on factory equipment) and measure the replacement cost of each. There is likely to be greater difficulty establishing the replacement costs of manufacturing overhead components than of direct material and direct labor because of the numerous dissimilar indirect cost elements involved.

In cases where established second-hand markets exist for assets, such as automobiles, furniture, and standardized equipment, replacement cost data can be computed from information available from dealers in those markets. In some cases, the federal government prepares specific price indices for certain types of assets. These indices provide information concerning the change in the price indices for certain types of assets but the data track the the change in the price of these assets in a *new* condition. Some adjustment is necessary to reflect the used condition of the assets on hand. The current replacement cost of special designed equipment and buildings is perhaps the most difficult to estimate. A combination of suppliers' catalogs, specific price indices, and real estate appraisals is sometimes required.

Perhaps the major criticism of using current replacement cost in financial accounting reports is the subjectivity involved in estimating replacement cost. Several persons attempting to estimate the replacement cost of a specific asset could arrive at different amounts. These valuations could be difficult to audit.

Current Cost Disclosure

Concepts of Income

When current cost data are used, several measures of income are possible, each with different meanings. Exhibit 2 shows the information required to construct these income measures.

Consider a retailer who buys one toaster for $30 and later sells it for $50 at a time when the replacement cost of a toaster is $38. Then, current cost income from continuing operations is $12 (= $50 − 38). A retailer who paid out more than $12 in taxes and dividends under these circumstances would not retain sufficient funds to buy the next toaster and could not remain in business at current levels. For this reason, this income figure is relevant for those who wish to maintain the physical productive capacity of the business intact before paying dividends. The FASB calls this amount "current cost income from continuing operations."

Changes in the amount of current cost income from continuing operations over time probably measure the growth capability of a firm better than the changes in any other income figure. This is the income number that financial analysts may study in assessing growth prospects for the company and, hence, in assessing potential for price appreciation of the firm's shares in stock markets. For example, if dividend payments are regularly larger than this income, then the firm will likely have to contract operations in the long run or raise new capital just to maintain the current activity levels. GE's current cost income from continuing operations of $1,164 appears in the third column of the top panel in Exhibit 2.

Realized Holding Gains

Current cost income from continuing operations charges against revenues current costs measured at the time of sale rather than historical costs measured at the time of acquisition. The difference between current cost at the time of sale and historical cost ($8 = $38 − $30) in the toaster example above), is called a *realized holding gain*. It is a "holding gain" because owner's wealth increases when items purchased at one price are held during a period of rising prices. The gain is "realized" because the item has been sold. Holding gains are not generally expected to be repeated in subsequent periods unless the firm both (a) buys more items and (b) holds them while prices continue to increase. The amount of future holding gains depends on both the timing of future purchases and the amount of price increases during the holding period between purchase and sale. The realized holding gains for GE during 1981 on inventory sold is $89 (= $19,034 − $18,945) million and the gain realized through depreciation of plant is $412 (= $1,294 − $882) million.

Unrealized Holding Gains and Losses

When the current cost of ending inventory (or plant) exceeds its historical cost, there is an *unrealized holding gain*. The increase in the unrealized holding gain during the year is part of the increase in owners' wealth for the year. We believe that whether the gain has been realized or not is irrelevant and that holding gains are part of income (or not) independent of realization. Exhibit 3 shows the calculation of the unrealized holding gains on inventory and holding losses on plant during 1981 for GE. The current cost of assets at the beginning of the year, required for the calculation, is taken from the 1980 annual report.

Inflation Component of Holding Gains

Part of the increase in value that occurs while an asset occurs can be thought of as keeping up with the rise in general prices. For example, if an asset is purchased for $100, is held during a period of 12-percent inflation, and is worth $125 at the end of the period, then the holding gains in dollars is $25 (= $125 − $100). The inflation component of that gain is $12 (= .12 × $100). The holding gain net of inflation is $13 (= $25 − $12). The FASB requires that companies report data enabling the separation of holding gains into real and nominal components. For GE, that information appears in the bottom panel of Exhibit 2 at our circled number 5.

The data reported in the bottom panel of Exhibit 2 and the analysis from Exhibit 3 can be combined as follows:

Excess of Increase in General Price Level Over Specific GE Prices (from Exhibit 2, bottom panel)	$ 703
Nominal Dollar Realized and Unrealized Holding Gains from Exhibit 3...	597
Effect of Increase in General Price Level	$1,300

The total effect of increase in the general price level of $1,300 can be interpreted as follows. Had the specific assets held by GE during the year or until time of sale increased in value at the same rate as the general price level, then there would have been a nominal dollar total holding gain, realized and unrealized, of $1,300. But GE's specific asset prices increased in value by only $597 million. Thus, GE tells us in Exhibit 2 that specific asset value increases fell short by $703 million of keeping up with general inflation. The typical reader is probably unable to decipher this message from the style of presentation chosen here by GE.

Multi-Year Summary ⑥

The FASB requires a 5-year summary of changing prices data useful for following the trend of items over time. *SPAS No. 33* permits the use in this summary of either current dollars of dollars of some base period, such as

Exhibit 3
**General Electric Company
Summary of Data on Realized
and Unrealized Holding Gains
for 1981 in Nominal Dollars**

	Inventory and Cost of Goods Sold	Property, Plant Equipment and Depreciation
Asset Balances:		
December 31, 1981		
Current Cost[a]	$ 6,018	$ 9,768
Historical Cost[b]	(3,461)	(6,844)
Unrealized Holding Gain, End of Year .... ..(1)	$ 2,557	$ 2,924
December 31, 1980		
Current Cost[a]	$ 5,701	$ 8,797
Historical Cost[b]	(3,343)	(5,780)
Unrealized Holding Gain, Start of Year .... (2)	2,358	3,017
Unrealized Holding Gain (Loss)		
During 1981 = (2) − (1)	$ 199	($ 93)
Expense Totals:		
Based on		
Current Cost[c]	$19,034	$ 1,294
Historical Costs[c]	(18,945)	(882)
Realized Holding Gains..........................	89	402
Total Holding Gains of $597 (= $288 + $309)	$ 288	$ 309

a See GE notes reproduced in Exhibit 2; data for 1980 came from 1980 annual report not reproduced here.
b From GE's Statement of Financial Position.
c See GE data in Exhibit 2.
d From GE's Statement of Income and Retained Earnings.

1967, which is the base period for the CPI-U. Using current dollars expresses the data in units that reflect current experience, but it requires the data of the earlier years in the summary to be restated each year to reflect the change in the measuring unit. When the summary is stated in base-period dollars, there is no need for annual revision of those data.

Excerpts from the constant-dollar summary and from the nominal dollar ten-year summary on pages 52 and 53 of the GE report reproduced on pages 90-91 of this book are instructive. Observe, for example, that the market price of a share of GE common stock is shown as C$73 for 1977, where "C$" indicates a constant dollar amount. Its actual market price at the end of 1977 was $48 5/8 (The amount shown is derived from C$73 = $48.625 × 272.4/181.5.) Whereas the nominal dollar amount of a share has increased over 15 percent (from $48 5/8 to $56) over the 4-year period from the end of 1977 to the end of 1981, the general purchasing power represented by an investment in that share has declined by about 23 percent, from C$73 to C$56. Similarly, although nominal dollar sales have increased over the years shown at about 12 percent per year, from $17.5 billion to $27.2 billion, sales measured in constant dollars have risen by less than 1 percent per year, from C$26.3 to C$27.2 billion.

GE reports purchasing power losses on net monetary items for each of the years 1977 through 1981. From this we can infer that GE's average balance of monetary assets exceeded the average balance of monetary liabilities in each of the years 1977 through 1981.

Purchasing Power Gains on Debt Not Equivalent to Holding Gains on Debt

The FASB does not require that firms show the holding gains (or losses) caused by changes in the market value of outstanding liabilities. This holding gain or loss differs from the purchasing power gain on monetary liabilities. The following series of examples illustrates the difference. Assume the following events occur in four successive years.

Year 1. A firm borrows $1,000 in perpetuity by agreeing to pay $40 per year forever. (Assume a 50-year coupon bond if you prefer not to think about a perpetuity.) Neither the borrower nor the lender expects any general inflation over the life of the loan. The interest rate for the firm on long-term borrowings is 4 percent. Interest expense for the year is $40 and there is neither constant dollar inflation gain (or loss) nor current cost holding gain (or loss).

Year 2. The market place expects there will be inflation in the future of about 6 percent per year. Interest rates on perpetuities issued by companies of this credit risk rise to 10 percent per year. The market price of the perpetuity falls from $1,000 to $400 (= $40/.10). There is a current cost holding gain to the borrower, and a holding loss to the lender, of $600 (= $1,000 − $400). There is no inflation during this period however, and no constant dollar inflation gain or loss.

Year 3. The market place continues to expect the inflation rate to be about 6 percent per year so there is no change in interest rates. The inflation rate for the year is exactly 6 percent. The market price of the perpetuity remains at $400. There is a constant dollar, historical cost inflation gain of $60 (= .06 inflation rate × $1,000 historical cost of debt) to the borrower and a $60 inflation loss to the lender.

Year 4. The market continues to expect about 6 percent annual inflation, 6 percent annual inflation occurs for the year, but the borrowing company's creditworthiness improves and the interest rate it must pay for long-term
• borrowing decreases from 10 percent during Year 3 to 8 percent in Year 4. The market value of the perpetuity increases from $400 to $500 (= $40/.08). The borrowing firm has a current cost holding loss of $100 (= $400 − $500), while the lender has a $100 gain. Meanwhile, because inflation has continued at the rate of 6 percent per year, the borrower has an inflation gain of $60 (= $.06 × $1,000) and the lender an inflation loss of $60 for the same reasons as in Year 3.

Current cost holding gains or losses differ from constant dollar inflation gains and losses. Current cost holding gins or losses occur whenever the interest rate appropriate for discounting a monetary item changes. Constant dollar inflation gains to borrowers (losses to lenders) occur whenever there is general gains (constant dollars) while experiencing either holding gains (increasing interest rates) or holding losses (decreasing interest rates).

Because current cost holding gains and losses on actual borrowings have been large in recent years we would have preferred that the FASB included these in the current cost disclosures.

Accounting Magic

Generally accepted accounting principles permit alternative treatments for certain accounting events. The treatment a company chooses affects the financial statements that the company issues. In this section, we shown how alternative accounting treatments of identical events can lead to reported income figures that are perhaps surprisingly different from each other.[1]

The Scenario

On January 1, two companies started in business. The two companies are alike except for their accounting treatment of several events. Conservative Company chooses the accounting alternatives that will minimize its reported income while High Flyer Company chooses the alternatives that will maximize its reported income. Both companies choose, where permitted, accounting methods that will minimize income taxes. The following events occur during the year.

1. Both companies issue common stock to raise funds necessary to commence a merchandising business.
2. Both companies purchase $7,000,000 of equipment that is assumed to have zero salvage value and estimated useful life of 10 years.
3. Both companies make the following purchases of merchandise inventory:

Date	Units Purchased		Unit Price		Cost of Purchase
January 1	85,000	@	$60	=	$ 5,100,000
May 1	95,000	@	$63	=	5,985,000
September 1	100,000	@	$68	=	6,800,000
Total	280,000				$17,885,000

4. During the year, both companies sell 210,000 units at an average price of $100 each so that each realizes sales revenues of $21,000,000.
5. During the year, both companies have selling, general and administrative expenses, excluding officers' salaries, of $3,350,000.
6. At the end of the year, both companies "pay" bonuses of $120,000 to officers for jobs well done in addition to the $350,000 paid to them during the year in salaries. Conservative Company pays cash bonuses of $120,000 while High Flyer Company awards options for purchasing shares of common stock to its officers. Comparable options have market value of $120,000.

---

[1] The idea and title for this example come from an article by Leonard Spacek, "Business Success Requires an Understanding of Unsolved Problems of Accounting and Financial Reporting," Arthur Andersen Pamphlet (September 25, 1959), pp. 19–28. Since the time Spacek prepared his illustration, there have been changes in generally accepted accounting principles, but several of the alternatives we illustrate were illustrated by him, too.

Accounting Alternatives

At the end of the year both companies prepare financial statements. Both must decide how to report the various events that occurred during the year. The following decisions made by each company are all generally acceptable.

Inventory Cost Flow Assumption. Because not all goods purchased during the year were sold, each company must make an assumption about the cost of goods sold to be shown on the income statement and, simultaneously, about the cost of ending inventory to be shown on the balance sheet. Conservative Company makes a last-in, first-out (LIFO) cost flow assumption while High Flyer Company makes a first-in, first-out (FIFO) assumption. Because the beginning inventory is zero, the cost of goods available for sale by each company is equal to the purchases of $17,885,000 during the year. Both companies have 70,000 units in ending inventory. Conservative Company, using LIFO, reports a cost of goods sold of $13,685,00 (= $17,885,000 − 70,000 × $60) while High Flyer Company reports a cost of goods sold of $13,125,000 (= $17,885,000 − 70,000 × $68). Income tax regulations have required a company to use LIFO in its financial statements if it uses LIFO for its tax return. (But see *LIFO conformity rule* in the Glossary.) High Flyer desires not to use LIFO in its financial statements and therefore foregoes the savings in taxes from using LIFO on its tax returns.

Depreciation. Conservative Company depreciates its equipment using the double-declining-balance method on its financial statements while High Flyer Company uses the straight-line method. Conservative Company takes a full year of depreciation in the year equipment is acquired, while High Flyer Company uses a half-year convention under which it takes only one-half year of depreciation in the first year. (The accelerated cost recovery system used by both companies for income tax reporting effectively requires that both take one-half year of depreciation on their tax returns.) Conservative Company therefore reports depreciation expense of $1,400,000 (= 2 × 1/10 × $7,000,000) while High Flyer Company reports depreciation expense of $350,000 (= 1/10 × $7,000,000 × 1/2).

Officers' Bonuses. Conservative Company reports expense of $120,000 for the cash bonuses it pays while High Flyer Company reports no expense for the stock options granted. Under generally accepted accounting principles, the fair market value of qualified stock options granted to employees is not shown as an expense. (When the options are exercised, there will be an accounting transaction but the entry will record merely the cash received at the time of exercise.)

Investment Tax Credit

Because both companies purchased long-term assets costing $7,000,000, each is entitled to a reduction, or "tax credit," of $700,000 (= .10 × $7,000,000) in its tax bill for the year.[2] On its financial statements to shareholders, Conservative Company chooses to repor the benefits of that tax reduction over the ten-year life of the equipment that gave rise to the tax reduction (*deferral method*, explained in the Glossary). On its financial statement to shareholders, High Flyer reports the entire benefit of the tax reduction in the first year (*flow-through method*, explained in the Glossary).

Published Income Statements

Income Tax Calculation. We assume an income tax rate of 40 percent. Both companies show deductions for ACRS depreciation of equipment on the income tax return different from the amounts reported to shareholders. These are *timing differences*. That is, in subsequent years, the companies may report on their tax return amounts different in opposite directions from the amounts reported to shareholders. Consequently, each company reports deferred income taxes on its income statement and will show deferred taxes on its balance sheet. High Flyer Company reports smaller depreciation on the income statement than the amount of depreciation claimed on the

---

[2] As this book goes to press, the percentage for the investment tax credit is 10 percent, but it changes from time to time. A larger rate will increase the difference between reported earnings of the two companies; a smaller rate will reduce the difference.

tax return and will have deferred tax credits on its balance sheet. (This is the situation usually observed in most published annual reports.) Conservative Company reports larger depreciation on the income statement than the amount claimed on the tax return and will have deferred tax debits on its balance sheet. (This case is rarely observed. The phenomenon arises here because there is only one item of equipment being depreciated and the first-year conventions for tax reporting and financial reporting differ.) The following equation holds for both companies:

Income Tax Expense		Income Tax Payable		Deferred Investment Credits		Deferred Tax Credits		Deferred Tax Debits
Conservative Company:								
$768	=	$278	+	$630	+	$0	–	$140
High Flyer Company:								
$830	=	$550	+	$0	+	$280	–	$0

The income statements for both companies appear on page 103. As a result of its conservative treatment of accounting alternatives, Conservative Company reports net income and earnings per share less than half of High Flyer Company's. Both companies used generally accepted accounting principles and each would receive a "clean" opinion from its auditor.

Comparisons of Fund Flows

Until the time when the two companies paid their respective executive bonuses and income taxes, they were exactly alike in all economically significant respects. Because of the difference in executives' bonuses—Conservative Company paid cash, while High Flyer granted stock options with the same value—Conservative Company paid out $120,000 more cash than did High Flyer for this item. High Flyer Company, in order to report higher net income, had to pay income taxes $272,000 (= $550,000 − $278,000) larger than did Conservative Company. Thus, after tax payments, Conservative Company, in a real sense, is considerably better off than is High Flyer. Overall, then, Conservative Company ends the year with $152,000 (= $272,000 − $120,000) more cash, or other liquid net assets, than does High Flyer.

You might find it instructive to construct statements of changes in financial position for each of the two companies. If you use cash as the definition of funds, you will find that Conservative Company generates $152,000 more cash than does High Flyer. If you use working capital (= current assets − current liabilities) as the definition of funds, you will find that High Flyer generates $408,000 more funds than does Conservative Company. The $560,000 spread between these two amounts arises from the different cost flow assumptions for inventory. High Flyer uses FIFO; its ending inventory is valued at $68 per unit. Conservative Company uses LIFO; its ending inventory is valued at $60 per unit. The difference in inventory valuation is $8 per unit. Because there are 70,000 more units in ending inventory than in beginning inventory, the difference in the increase in working capital over the increase in cash is $560,000 (= $8 × 70,000). The choice of inventory flow assumption in times of changing prices has a major impact on published financial statements.

Managing Reported Earnings

The simple illustration for Conservative Company and High Flyer Company by no means exhausts the set of choices available to a firm to "manage" its earnings. Managing earnings refers to a process of taking deliberate steps within the constraints of generally accepted accounting principles to bring about a desired level of reported earnings. This section describes some of the techniques for managing earnings and offers arguments for and against an earnings management policy.

**Accounting Magic Comparative Income Statements
For the Year Ending December 31
(Amounts in Thousands Except Per Share Amounts)**

	Conservative Company		High Flyer Company	
	Financial Statement	Tax Return	Financial Statement	Tax Return
Sales Revenues	$21,000	$21,000	$21,000	$21,000
Expenses				
Cost of Goods Sold	$13,685	$13,685	$13,125	$13,125
Depreciation on Equipment	1,400	1,050[b]	350	1,050[b]
Officers' Compensation:				
Salaries	350	350	350	350
Cash Bonuses	120	120	—	—
Stock Options	—	—	0	0
Other Selling, General and Administrative Expenses	3,350	3,350	3,350	3,350
Expenses Before Income Taxes	$18,905	$18,555	$17,175	$17,875
Income Before Taxes	$ 2,095	$ 2,445	$ 3,825	$ 3,125
Income Tax Expense[a]	768		830	
Net Income	$ 1,327		$ 2,995	
Earnings Per Share in Dollars (500,000 Shares Outstanding)	$ 2.65		$ 5.99	

[a]Computation of Income Tax Expense:				
Income Before Taxes	$ 2,095	$ 2,445	$ 3,825	$ 3,125
Income Tax on Current Income (at 40 percent)	$ 838	$ 978	$ 1,530	$ 1,250
Less: Tax Credit for Investment in Equipment	70	700	700	700
Income Tax Expense	$ 768		$ 830	
Income Tax Currently Payable		$ 278		$ 550
Deferred Investment Tax Credit ($700 – $70)	$ 630			

[b]Amounts based on ACRS.

Income taxes Deferred by Timing Difference for Depreciation:

Dr. = .40 × ($1,050 – $1,400)	$ (140)			
Cr. = .40 × ($1,050 – $350)			$ 280	

Techniques for managing earnings might be classified into three categories: (1) selection of accounting principles, (2) application of accounting principles, and (3) timing of asset acquisitions and dispositions. Some examples of actions in each of these three categories are given next.

Selection of Accounting Principles.

1. Revenue recognition—percentage of completion, completed contract, time of sale, installment.
2. Inventory cost-flow assumption—FIFO, LIFO, weighted average.
3. Depreciation method—straight-line, declining-balance, sum-of-the-years'-digits.
4. Investment credit—flow-through, deferral.
5. Corporate acquisitions—purchase, pooling of interests.
6. Mineral resource activities—successful-efforts costing, full costing.
7. Leases—operating, capital.

Application of Accounting Principles.

1. Estimates of degree of completion of contracts on which the percentage-of-completion method is used.
2. Estimates of service lives and salvage values of depreciable assets.
3. Estimates of uncollectible rate on accounts receivable.
4. Estimate of cost of warranty plans.
5. Treatment of indirect costs as product costs versus period expenses.
6. Classification of common stock investments as Marketable Securities. a current asset. or as Investment in Securities, a noncurrent asset.
7. Selection of actuarial cost basis for pension plan.
8. Selection of interest rates for capitalized leases and in pension accounting.

Timing of Asset Acquisitions and Dispositions.

1. Timing of discretionary expenditures for research and development. advertising. and maintenance costs, which are recognized as expenses in the period when the costs are incurred.
2. Timing of the sale of property, plant, and equipment to accelerate or delay the recognition of a gain or loss.
3. Accelerating or delaying shipments of merchandise to customers at the end of a period.

These lists are not intended to be exhaustive. They do indicate the wide variety of avenues available to management to manage earnings.

Arguments For and Against Managing Earnings

The arguments for and against managing earnings vary both as to their underlying logic and to the evidence that is brought to bear in support of the position. We present the arguments here in as unbiased a manner as possible so that readers can make up their own mind.

Capital Market Efficiency.   The major argument against managing earnings is that capital markets are efficient, in the sense that market prices adjust quickly and *in an unbiased manner* to publicly available information, and that earnings management is therefore a waste of valuable managerial time. An expanding number of theoretical and empirical studies have provided support for the efficiency of capital markets.[3] For example, several studies have examined the effects of changes in accounting methods on stock prices. Changes in accounting methods that have no real or economic effects (that is, those that do not affect cash flows) have been shown to have little effect on stock prices.[4] Using information from the financial statements and notes, the stock market at the aggregate level is able to distinguish changes with real effects from those that are merely "paper" changes and react accordingly.

Proponents of earnings management acknowledge this recent work but counter with three observations. First, all of the empirical work on market efficiency has looked at the aggregate market (for example, all stocks traded on the New York Stock Exchange). There are numerous examples of cases where the market has not been

---

[3] See Eugene F. Fama, "Efficient Capital Markets: A Review of Theory and Empirical Work," *Journal of Finance* (May 1970): 383–417.

Nicholas J. Gonedes and Nicholas Dopuch, "Capital Market Equilibrium, Information-Production and Selecting Accounting Techniques: Theoretical Framework and Review of Empirical Work," *Studies on Financial Accounting Objectives: 1974,* Supplement to Vol. 12, *Journal of Accounting Research:* 48–129; and Robert S. Kaplan, "Information Content of Financial Accounting Numbers: A Survey of Empirical Evidence," in: *Symposium of Impact of Accounting Research in Financial Accounting and Disclosure on Accounting Practice,* ed. by T. Keller and R. Abdel-khalik (Durham: Duke University Press, 1978).

[4] See, for example, Ray Ball, "Changes in Accounting Techniques and Stock Prices," *Empirical Research in Accounting: Selected Studies, 1972,* Supplement to Vol. 10, *Journal of Accounting Research* (Autumn 1968): 1–38; Robert S. Kaplan and Richard Roll, "Investor Evaluation of Accounting Information: Some Empirical Evidence," *Journal of Business* (April 1972): 225–257; Shyam Sunder, "Relationships Between Accounting Changes and Stock Prices: Problems of Measurement and Some Empirical Evidence," *Empirical Research in Accounting: Selected Studies, 1973,* Supplement to Vol. 11, *Journal of Accounting Research:* 1–45.

efficient at the individual-firm level (that is, in the pricing of securities for particular firms at a particular point in time). Proponents of this view point to examples where the market prices of particular firms' shares decreased dramatically after the effects of using specific accounting procedures were carefully analyzed and reported in the financial press.[5]

Second, the empirical work on market efficiency has focused for the most part on publicly-available information. There is little or no evidence to suggest that the market is able to access "inside" or non-public information. Information about the effects of changes in accounting methods is available in the financial statements and notes and has been studied empirically. However, information about management's efforts to manage earnings by way of the judicious application of accounting principles or the timing of asset acquisitions or dispositions is usually not disclosed separately and consequently has not been adequately studied.

Third, proponents of earnings management note that most of the empirical work on capital market efficiency has focused on equity securities traded on the New York Stock Exchange. The efficiency of other capital markets (for example, the over-the-counter-market) as well as short-term credit and long-term debt markets has not been adequately tested.

Proponents of earnings management would conclude that capital markets are not necessarily perfectly efficient in all cases. If, by managing earnings, the firm is able to take advantage of these inefficiencies and obtain capital at a lower cost than if earnings management were not practiced, then the shareholders of the firm are better off.

Opponents of earnings management might be willing to accept the notion that some degree of inefficiency exists in capital marekts. They would then argue, though, that capital resources might get allocated in a less than socially-optimal way if, because of earnings management, certain firms are able to receive more resources than would otherwise be the case.

Management Incentives and Survival.   Because, over long enough time periods, net income is equal to cash-in minus cash-out, some corporate managers acknowledge that earnings management is not particularly beneficial in the long run. They point out, however, that the long run is made up of a series of short-run periods in which shareholders' decisions to retain management are made. (See *agency theory* in the Glossary). Shareholders, they would argue, do not want to see wide, unexpected fluctuations in earnings from year to year. Earnings management is necessary to smooth out these fluctuations and create the impression that management has operations "under control." Corporate managers also observe that all firms practice earnings management and that management's survival dictates that they do so as well to maintain the firm's position relative to other firms for management survival. They further point out that sufficient and convincing evidence for not managing earnings has not yet been provided. The other viewpoint has been explored principally by academic researchers who point to an expanding number of studies that call into question the perceived benefits of earnings management. Whether the two viewpoints can ultimately be reconciled depends on the results of continuing research on the relationship between accounting numbers and stock prices.

---

[5] For several examples, see Abraham J. Briloff, *More Debits Than Credits* (New York: Harper & Row, 1976). For an analysis of these examples see George Foster, "Briloff and the Capital Market," *Journal of Accounting Research* (Spring 1979): 262–274.

Balance Sheet for a Company Approaching Bankruptcy

On June 21, 1970, the Penn Central Company filed a bankruptcy petition for its major subsidiary, the Penn Central Transportation Company. On March 12, 1970, only three months before, the 1969 financial statements of the Penn Central Transportation Company had been issued. The balance sheet from those statements appears here. It indicates one important point; analysis of the shareholders' equity section of a balance sheet need not give any indication of impending insolvency or bankruptcy.

Notice that at the end of 1969, Penn Central Transportation Company had retained earnings of almost half a billion dollars which was a part of shareholders' equity of over $1.8 billion. Much of this equity, however, was invested in track and roadbed, assets for which there is no ready market. Penn Central could not dispose of these assets to raise funds. You can compute that at the end of 1968 and 1969, the Transportation Company had negative working capital; that is, current liabilities (as shown, plus debt due within one year) exceeded current assets. Working capital increased by about $18 million during 1969, but net quick assets—cash and receivables less current liabilities—decreased. The Company was in a less liquid position at the end of the year than at the start.

At the end of 1969, the Transportation Company had over $100 million of debt to repay in the following year. Although the Transporation Company had sufficient "net worth" to show almost half a billion dollars of retained earnings and almost two billion dollars of shareholders' equity, it did not have the funds to meed "only" a few hundred million dollars in current obligations. The company was approaching insolvency by the end of 1969, as can be discerned from these statements.

Like Penn Central Transportation Company, many bankrupt firms have positive net assets, or shareholders' equity, on the books at the time of bankruptcy.

Balance Sheet

Assets	December 31	1969	1968
Current Assets	Cash and temporary cash investments	$ 80,331,000	$ 46,915,000
	Accounts receivable and unbilled revenue ..	293,181,000	240,211,000
	Material and supplies, etc., at cost	104,303,000	88,692,000
	Total Current Assets	477,815,000	375,818,000
Noncurrent Assets	Investments and advances, at cost or less (notes 2 and 7).....................	1,139,038,000	1,217,796,000
	New Haven—net assets acquired, at cost (note 1)..........................	—	127,544,000
	Properties (notes 3, 6, 7 and 12)		
	Road, structures, etc................	2,066,769,000	1,904,536,000
	Revenue equipment (rolling stock)......	1,662,759,000	1,745,448,000
	Other	96,051,000	90,541,000
		3,825,579,000	3,740,525,000
	Less accumulated depreciation and losses upon merger	902,731,000	992,036,000
	Total Properties—Net	2,922,848,000	2,748,489,000
	Deferred charges and sundry assets	56,939,000	43,703,000
	Total Assets	$4,596,640,000	$4,513,350,000

Liabilities and Shareholder's Equity

		1969	1968
Current Liabilities*	Notes payable (none to subsidiaries in 1969; $19,420,000 in 1968)	$ 102,048,000	$ 87,420,000
	Accounts payable and accrued expenses	396,407,000	356,519,000
	Total Current Liabilities (excluding debt due within one year)*	498,455,000	443,939,000
Long-Term Debt	Due within one year..................	106,058,000	76,716,000
	Due after one year	1,585,585,000	1,407,610,000
	Total Long-Term Debt (note 7)	1,691,643,000	1,484,326,000
Other	Estimated liabilities incurred upon merger (note 6)........................	101,935,000	119,346,000
	Casualty and other claims..............	90,667,000	81,803,000
	Amounts payable to subsidiary companies ..	167,711,000	122,582,000
	Other	240,857,000	231,015,000
	Total Other	601,170,000	554,746,000
Shareholder's Equity	Capital stock—$10 par value. Authorized 27,000,000 shares; issued 24,113,703 shares (1968—24,085,329) (note 8)	241,137,000	240,853,000
	Additional paid-in capital (note 8)........	1,068,730,000	1,068,257,000
	Retained earnings (note 13)	495,505,000	721,229,000
	Total Shareholder's Equity	1,805,372,000	2,030,339,000
	Total Liabilities and Shareholder's Equity	$4,596,640,000	$4,513,350,000

Accounting Pronouncements

The following list of accounting pronouncements comprises most of the generally accepted accounting principles.

Committee on Accounting Procedure (1953–1959)

Accounting Research Bulletins (ARBs)

ARB No.

Accounting Terminology Bulletins (ATBs)

ATB No.

Accounting Principles Board (APB) (1959–1973)

APB Opinions

APB No.

APB Statements

APB No.

Financial Accounting Standards Board (FASB) (1973 to present)

Statements of Financial Accounting Standards

SFAS No.